To Rick—
Hope this
helps with all your ~~~~ ~~~~~ ~~~!

Lone Pine Publishing

D1046413

Tree & Shrub

Gardening

Bill Aldrich

for

Illinois

3/18/07

William Aldrich
Don Williamson

Distributed by Lone Pine Publishing
1808 – B Street NW, Suite 140
Auburn, WA, USA 98001

Website: www.lonepinepublishing.com

National Library of Canada Cataloguing in Publication

Aldrich, William, 1948–
  Tree and shrub gardening for Illinois / William Aldrich and Don Williamson.

  Includes bibliographical references and index.
  ISBN 1-55105-404-3

  1. Ornamental trees—Illinois. 2. Ornamental shrubs—Illinois.
I. Williamson, Don, 1962– II. Title.

SB435.52.I3A43 2004   635.9'77'09773   C2004-900116-7

Editorial Director: Nancy Foulds
Editorial: Dawn Loewen, Shelagh Kubish, Lee Craig
Illustrations Coordinator: Carol Woo
Photo Editor: Don Williamson
Production Manager: Gene Longson
Book Design: Heather Markham
Layout & Production: Curtis Pillipow, Heather Markham
Cover Design: Gerry Dotto
Illustrations: Ian Sheldon
Scanning & Digital Film: Elite Lithographers Co.

Photography: all interior and front cover photos by **Tim Matheson** or **Tamara Eder**, except **Alison Beck** 80b, 328a; **Chicagoland Grows Inc.** 13b, 29b, 63, 126b, 127b, 148a, 149a&b, 238b, 240b, 243a, 313a; **Don Doucette** 81b, 140a, 189a, 209a, 212a, 272, 273b, 318; **Derek Fell** 14, 85a, 98, 99a&b, 101b, 114b, 147a, 186a&b, 189b, 194a, 195b, 217a, 242b, 250a, 252, 253a&b, 257a, 270, 277a&b, 293a, 323a&b; **Erika Flatt** 23b, 231a&b; **Anne Gordon** 147b, 216, 217b, 325b; **Lynne Harrison** 96b, 161b, 165b; **Saxon Holt** 138b, 141a; **Linda Kershaw** 137a; **Dawn Loewen** 166, 169b, 235b; **Janet Loughrey** 329b; **Morton Arboretum** 10&11, 15a, 24, 74; **Steve Nikkila** 160a, 179b, 197b, 230a, 258a&b, 259b, 280a&b, 281a; **Kim O'Leary** 56a&c, 239c; **Allison Penko** 20b, 41, 42b, 118, 121b&c, 124, 151a, 222, 226b, 239b, 242a, 268, 284, 287c, 298a, 306, 307a, 308, 312b, 320b; **Robert Ritchie** 18a, 22a, 67b, 70a, 72, 76, 77a&b, 79b, 96a, 97a, 116, 117b, 159a, 161a, 163b, 169a, 173a, 176, 177a&b, 197a, 240a, 249b, 250b, 251a, 267a, 271a, 297b, 299b, 329a, 332a, 333a; **Royal Botanical Gardens (Hamilton)/Chris Graham** 211b, 213a; **Mark Turner** 84, 86, 100, 115a, 148b, 229a&b, 237b, 251c, 269a, 276; **Tim Wood** 22b, 23a, 25a&b, 28b, 49b, 58a, 79a, 81a, 87a, 101a, 104a, 105b&c, 107a&b, 108a, 112, 113a, 115b, 117a, 119b, 121a, 123a&b, 129a, 130b, 131c, 133a, 135a&b, 139a, 140b&c, 141c, 144a&b, 145a, 152b, 153b, 155b, 157b, 167a&b, 168a&b, 171a, 173b, 183b, 185a&b, 187b, 194b, 199b, 203b&c, 204a, 205c, 206b, 210a, 219a&b, 223a, 224a&b, 225a, 233a, 234, 235a, 247a, 255b, 259a, 261b, 263a, 271b&c, 274a, 279a, 281b, 285a&b, 287a&b, 295a, 301a&b, 304, 305a&b, 309a&b, 310b, 314a&b, 315a&b, 319b&c, 321a&b, 322, 324a, 325a, 327b, 331c, 333b&c

Back cover author photos: William Aldrich by Roger Mattingly, Don Williamson by Alan Bibby

Map: based on USDA plant hardiness zone map (1990)

We acknowledge the financial support of the Government of Canada through the Book Publishing Industry Development Program (BPIDP) for our publishing activities.

PC: *P1*

CONTENTS

ACKNOWLEDGMENTS

THROUGHOUT MY JOURNALISTIC CAREER, I have benefited from the knowledge and generosity of the Morton Arboretum. For this project, guidance has come from Kris Bachtell—scientist, world traveler and hands-on tree expert. Bachtell, director of collections and grounds at the arboretum, provided counsel and questioning oversight that improved the manuscript greatly.

Another important resource in Illinois is the Chicago Botanic Garden. Many trees and shrubs recommended in this book are highlighted in their 'Best Plants for Illinois' collection, accessible online (see Resources, p. 342). Evaluating what does well in the state has led to a remarkable alliance between the Morton, the Garden and the Ornamental Growers Association of Northern Illinois to form Chicagoland Grows. These tree and shrub evaluations have led to superior plants entering the garden center and landscaping trade.

As always, one must credit the University of Illinois Extension. Available in every county in the state, the Extension helps gardeners identify problems and make informed decisions about their woody plants. Thanks to Jim Schuster for his countless attempts to make me understand how trees and shrubs function.

Finally, the great constant in the tree and shrub universe is Michael Dirr, the professor who started in Champaign before moving to Georgia. Dirr's books are the unparalleled reference source for almost any question regarding woody plants. My copy of *Manual of Woody Landscape Plants* was given to me by Roy Klehm, who has also profoundly influenced my career. You'll see many of Roy's plant introductions in this volume. —*William Aldrich*

I WOULD LIKE TO EXPRESS MY APPRECIATION to all the wonderful people involved in this project. Special thanks are extended to the many photographers who contributed all the superb pictures you see. I also acknowledge the many sources of information and inspiration that filled this book with great information. Finally, I thank The Creator. —*Don Williamson*

THE TREES & SHRUBS AT A GLANCE

A Pictorial Guide in Alphabetical Order, by Common Name

American Yellowwood
p. 76

Arborvitae
p. 78

Ash
p. 82

Bald-Cypress
p. 84

Barberry
p. 86

Bearberry
p. 88

Beech
p. 90

Birch
p. 94

Black Locust
p. 98

Cherry
p. 110

Black Tupelo
p. 100

Boxwood
p. 102

Butterfly Bush
p. 106

Chokeberry
p. 116

Cotoneaster
p. 118

Crabapple
p. 122

Dawn Redwood
p. 132

Deutzia
p. 134

Dogwood
p. 136

Daphne
p. 128

Elderberry
p. 142

Elm
p. 146

Euonymus
p. 150

False Cypress
p. 154

Filbert
p. 158

Fir
p. 162

Forsythia
p. 166

Fothergilla
p. 170

Ginkgo
p. 174

Golden Rain Tree
p. 176

Fringe Tree
p. 172

Hawthorn
p. 178

Hemlock
p. 182

Honeylocust
p. 190

Honeysuckle
p. 192

Holly
p. 184

Hornbeam
p. 196

Horsechestnut
p. 198

Hydrangea
p. 202

Juniper
p. 208

Larch
p. 220

Katsura-Tree
p. 214

Kentucky Coffee Tree
p. 216

Kerria
p. 218

Lilac
p. 222

Linden
p. 228

Magnolia
p. 232

Maple
p. 236

Mountain-Ash
p. 244

Ninebark
p. 246

Oak
p. 248

Potentilla
p. 260

Privet
p. 264

Pear
p. 252

Pine
p. 254

Redbud
p. 266

Rhododendron
p. 268

Sassafras
p. 276

Rose-of-Sharon
p. 272

Smokebush
p. 282

Serviceberry
p. 278

Spruce
p. 288

Stewartia
p. 292

St. Johnswort
p. 294

Spirea
p. 284

Sumac
p. 296

Summersweet Clethra
p. 300

Viburnum
p. 308

Sweetgum
p. 302

Sweetspire
p. 304

Tulip Tree
p. 306

Virginia Creeper
p. 316

Weigela
p. 318

Willow
p. 322

Witchhazel
p. 326

Yew
p. 330

INTRODUCTION

O ur first experiences with trees and shrubs in childhood often provide us with lasting memories. Many of us remember the pleasure of collecting, on autumn walks to school, the shiny, smooth, two-toned nuts littering the ground. We may or may not have known that the source of these treasures was buckeye or horsechestnut trees. And we may have equally vivid memories of these trees in late spring, when the splendiferous flower spikes point skyward.

Trees and shrubs are woody perennials. They maintain a permanent live structure above ground all year, and they live for three or more years. In cold climates, a few shrubs die back to the ground each winter. The root system, protected by the soil over winter, sends up new shoots in spring, and if the shrub forms flowers on new wood it will bloom that same year. Such plants act like herbaceous perennials, but because they are woody in their native climates they are still classified as shrubs. Butterfly bush falls into this category of perennial-like shrubs.

A tree is generally defined as a woody plant having a single trunk and growing greater than 15' tall. A shrub is multi-stemmed and no taller than 15'. These definitions are not absolute because some tall trees are multi-stemmed, and some short shrubs have single trunks. Even the height definitions are open to interpretation. For example, some of the Japanese maple cultivars may be multi-stemmed and grow only about 10' tall, but they are still usually referred to as trees. Furthermore, a given species may grow as a tree in favorable conditions but be reduced to a shrub in harsher sites. It is always best to simply look at the expected mature size of a tree or shrub and judge its suitability for your garden accordingly.

Some vines are also included in this guide. Like trees and shrubs, these plants maintain living woody stems above ground over winter. They generally require a supporting structure to climb upon, but many can also be grown as trailing groundcovers. Again, the definition is not absolute. Some vines can be trained to form free-standing shrubs with proper pruning, and conversely, some shrubs can be trained to grow up and over walls and other structures.

Butterfly bush, a perennial-like shrub
Japanese maple, a multi-stemmed tree

Woody plants are characterized by leaf type, whether deciduous or evergreen, and needled or broad-leaved. *Deciduous* plants lose all their leaves each fall or winter. They can have needles, like dawn redwood and larch, or broad leaves, like maple and dogwood. *Evergreen* trees and shrubs do not lose their leaves in winter. Evergreens can also be needled or broad-leaved, like pine and rhododendron, respectively. *Semi-evergreen* plants are generally evergreens that in cold climates lose some or all of their leaves. Some types of daphne fall into the semi-evergreen category.

For all the complaining about the weather that Illinoisans tend to do, our climate is generally conducive to growing a wide variety of trees and shrubs. Cold winters bring the dormancy that woody plants need to renew their growth cycle. The summers are warm enough to stimulate strong growth—a woody plant's primary defense against disease and insect attack.

The zone map on p. 15 shows how cold Canadian air tends to blow across the state from the northwest corner. The area around Rockford and to its north and west is rated as Zone 4, meaning the lowest winter temperature will be lower there than in other parts of the state. Those arctic winds present a problem when they come suddenly in mid-autumn. Woody plants prefer gradual cooling to send them into dormancy. They can be hurt when the state has one of its famous 'Indian summers,' with warm conditions that change within hours to far-below-freezing temperatures.

Once winter arrives, woody plants can be stressed, and young plants even killed, if there is a lack of snow and the freeze line extends too far into the rootzone. Winter winds can also test the mettle of woody plants. Some plants are even susceptible to too much sun in winter; one side of the plant may be warmed enough to start the sap flowing, only to have nighttime temperatures freeze it again. Bark cracks can then develop and injure the plant.

The availability of moisture is another challenge for Illinois gardens. Although the state receives enough natural moisture to allow many woody plants to survive, the timing of that moisture can be questionable. Supplemental watering may be needed for younger woody plants and for all evergreens if autumn rainfall is below average. Evergreens continue to transpire throughout winter, losing moisture to the atmosphere at a time when their frozen roots are unable to replace it.

Hardy trees thrive in the colder areas of Illinois, while many woody plants native to the southern states are perfectly at home in Zone 6 areas. Hardiness zones listed for a plant are useful in helping decide what to put in the garden as well as where to put it. Don't, however, be put off because a catalog or book says a plant is hardy only to a certain zone. Local topography in the garden creates microclimates, small areas that may be more or less favorable for growing different plants. Buildings, hills, low spots, drainage patterns and prevailing winds all influence your garden and the microclimates that occur in it (see Getting Started, p. 24, for more information on assessing the

Pine has evergreen needles.

Maple has deciduous broad leaves.

Rain may not provide all the water a tree needs.

conditions in your garden and growing out-of-zone plants). Pick the right spot in your garden for that tender shrub, and you just may be surprised at how well it does.

Illinois soils are influenced by many factors, some dating back to the glacial eras. Many soil types can be found in a small geographical area, so you will need to become familiar with your garden's particular soil profile. One very influential factor is how recently your home was built and whether it has a basement. Often when contractors dig the foundation, they unearth dense yellow clay subsoil that becomes the top layer of your garden soil. This nearly impermeable layer creates an inhospitable environment for many trees and shrubs. You will notice how often in this book the ideal soil for a plant is described as loose, deep, well drained and slightly acidic.

But no matter what challenges you face in your garden, you will find a tree, shrub or vine that can thrive in your space. You'll find a trip to a nearby park, arboretum or botanical garden, where trees are labeled and unusual specimens grown, invaluable for showing you species that thrive in Illinois. Also, keep your eyes open when walking through your neighborhood. You may see a species that you hadn't noticed before or that you were told wouldn't grow in your area. What is actually growing is the best guide.

Many enthusiastic and creative people garden in Illinois. From one end of the state to the other, individuals, growers, societies, schools and publications provide information, encouragement and fruitful debate for the novice or experienced gardener. Illinois gardeners are passionate about their plants and will gladly share their knowledge and opinions about what is best for any little patch of ground.

Outstanding garden shows, public gardens, arboretums and display gardens in our state attract gardeners and growers from all over the world. Seek them out as sources of inspiration and information. Open yourself to the possibilities, and you'll be surprised by the diversity of woody plants that thrive in our state. Initially, you may want to plant mostly tried and true, dependable varieties, but don't be afraid to try something different or new. Gardening with trees and shrubs is fun and can be a great adventure if you're willing to take up the challenge.

Plant enthusiasts at the Morton Arboretum in Lisle

HARDINESS ZONES MAP

ILLINOIS
AVERAGE ANNUAL MINIMUM TEMPERATURE

ZONE	TEMP (°F)
4b	−20 to −25
5a	−15 to −20
5b	−10 to −15
6a	−5 to −10
6b	−0 to −5

Woody Plants in the Garden

Trees and shrubs create a framework around which gardens can be designed. These long-lasting features anchor the landscape, and in a well-designed garden they create interest all year. In spring and summer, woody plants provide shade and beauty with foliage and flowers. In fall, the leaves of many tree and shrub species change color, and brightly colored fruit attracts attention and birds. In winter, the true backbone of the garden is revealed; the branches of deciduous trees and shrubs are laid bare, perhaps dusted with snow or frost, and evergreens take precedence in keeping the garden colorful.

Carefully selected and placed, woody plants are a vital and vibrant element of any landscape, from the smallest city lot to the largest country acreage. They provide privacy and can keep unattractive views hidden from sight. Conversely, they can frame an attractive view and draw attention to particular features or areas of the garden. Trees and shrubs soften the hard lines in the landscape created by such structures as buildings, fences, walls and driveways. Well-positioned woody plants create an attractive background against which other plants will shine. Trees and shrubs can be used in groups for spectacular flower or fall color shows, and a truly exceptional species, with year-round appeal, can stand alone as a specimen plant in a prime location.

Woody plants also help moderate the climate in your home and garden. As a windbreak, trees provide shelter from the winter cold, reducing heating costs and protecting tender garden plants. A well-placed

deciduous tree keeps the house cool and shaded in summer but allows the sun through in winter, when the warmth and light are appreciated. Woody plants also prevent soil erosion, retain soil moisture, reduce noise and filter the air.

Attracting wildlife is an often overlooked advantage of gardening. As cities expand, our living space encroaches on more and more wildlife habitat. By choosing plants, particularly native plants, that are beneficial to local wildlife, we provide food and shelter to birds and other animals, thereby helping fulfill our obligation as stewards of the environment. We can bring nature closer to home. The only difficulty is that the local wildlife may so enjoy a garden that they consume it. It is possible, though, to find a balance and attract wildlife while protecting the garden from ruin.

When the time comes to select woody plants, think carefully about the various physical constraints of your garden and the purposes you wish the plants to serve. First and foremost, consider the size of your garden in relation to the mature size of the plants in question. Very large plants are always a bad idea in a small garden. Remember, too, that

Nicely contrasting mixed conifers

Birds and squirrels are frequent garden visitors.

Oaks make good shade trees.

Climbing hydrangea (center), prostrate cotoneaster on boulder (below)

trees and shrubs not only grow up, they also grow out. Within a few years what started as a small plant may become a large, spreading tree. Spruces are often sold as very small trees, but many eventually grow too large for a small garden.

Another consideration that relates to size is placement. Don't plant trees and shrubs too close to houses, walkways, entryways or driveways. A tree planted right next to a house may hit the overhang of the roof, and trying to fix the problem by pruning will often spoil the natural appearance of the tree. Plants placed too close to paths, doors and driveways may eventually block access completely and will give the property an unkempt appearance.

Consider, too, the various features of tree and shrub species. A feature is an outstanding element, such as flowers, bark or shape, that attracts you to the plant. Decide which of the features that follow are most important to you and which will best enhance your garden.

Many plants have more than one feature, providing interest over a longer period. A carefully selected group of woody plants can add beauty to the garden all year. Whether you are looking for showy flowers, fall color, fast growth, unique bark or a beautiful fragrance, you can find trees or shrubs with features to suit your design. Consult the individual plant entries and the Quick Reference Chart at the back of the book.

Form is the general shape and growth habit of the plant. From tall and columnar to wide and gracefully weeping, trees come in a great variety of shapes. Similarly, shrubs may be rounded and bushy or low and ground hugging. Form can also vary as the year progresses and leaves are developed and lost. Often a unique winter habit makes a tree or shrub truly outstanding.

You should be familiar with some growth form terminology before considering a plant purchase. A *shade tree* commonly refers to a sizable deciduous tree but can be any tree that provides shade. An *upright, fastigiate* or *columnar* plant has the main branches and stems pointing upward and is often quite narrow. *Dwarf* properly refers to any variety, cultivar or hybrid that is smaller than the species, but the term is sometimes mistakenly used to mean a small, slow-growing plant. The crucial statistic is the expected size at maturity. If a species grows to 100', then a 30–50' variety would be a dwarf but might still be much too big for your garden. *Prostrate* and *procumbent* plants are low growing, with branches and stems that spread horizontally across the ground.

Dwarf cultivar of white spruce

Japanese maple with interesting form

Colorful 'Tricolor' beech foliage
Finely divided Japanese maple foliage

'Candicans' fir needles (below)

These forms are sometimes grafted onto upright stems to create lovely, weeping plant forms.

Foliage is one of the most enduring and important features of a plant. Leaves come in a variety of colors, shapes, sizes, textures and arrangements. You can find shades of green, blue, red, purple, yellow, white or silver. *Variegated* types have two or more colors combined on a single leaf. The variety of shapes is even more astounding, from short, sharply pointed needles to broad, rounded leaves the size of dinner plates. Leaf margins can be smooth, like those of many rhododendrons, or so finely divided the foliage appears lacy or fern-like, as with some Japanese maple cultivars. Foliage can often vary seasonally, progressing from tiny, pale green spring buds to the vibrant colors of fall. Evergreen trees provide welcome greenery even when winter is at its snowiest and coldest.

Growing plants with different leaf sizes, textures and colors creates contrast and makes your garden more interesting and appealing. An entire garden can be designed based on varied foliage. Whether it forms a neutral backdrop or stands out in sharp contrast with the plants around it, foliage is a vital consideration in any garden.

Flowers are such an influential feature that their beauty may be enough reason to grow a tree or shrub, such as forsythia, that is dull or even unattractive the rest of the year. Flowering generally takes place over a few weeks or occasionally a month; only a few woody plants flower for the entire summer. Keep this limitation in mind when selecting your plants. If you choose species with staggered flowering periods, you will always have something in bloom. You can achieve different but equally striking effects by grouping plants that flower at the same time, or by spreading them out around the garden. An easy, effective way to create a garden with a season-long progression of blooms is to visit your garden center on a regular basis. Because many people shop for plants only in spring, their gardens tend to be dominated by spring bloomers.

Goldflame honeysuckle blossoms

Tasty Nanking cherry fruit

Fruit comes in many forms, including winged maple samaras, dangling birch catkins, spiny horsechestnut capsules and the more obviously 'fruity' serviceberries and crabapple pomes. This feature can often be a double-edged sword. It can be very attractive and provides interest in the garden in late summer and fall, when most plants are past their prime. When the fruit drops, however, it can create quite a mess and even odor if allowed to rot on the ground. Choose the location of your fruiting tree carefully. If you know the fruit can be messy, don't plant near a patio or a sidewalk. Most fruit isn't terribly troublesome, but keep in mind that there may be some cleanup required during fruiting season.

Exfoliating layers of ninebark bark (below)

Bark is one of the most overlooked features of trees and shrubs. Species with interesting bark will greatly enhance your landscape, particularly in winter. Bark can be furrowed, smooth, ridged, papery, scaly, exfoliating or colorful. A few species valued for their bark are

Twisted branches of corkscrew hazelnut
'Cardinal' dogwood

birch, ninebark, cherry, paperbark maple, beech and hornbeam.

Fragrance, though usually associated with flowers, is also a potential feature of the leaves, fruit and even wood of trees and shrubs. Summersweet clethra, witchhazel, arborvitae, viburnum and lilac are examples of plants with appealing scents. Site fragrant plants near your home, where the scent can waft into an open window.

Branches as a feature combine elements of form and bark, and, like those two features, they can become an important winter attribute for the garden. Branches may have an unusual gnarled or twisted shape, like those of corkscrew hazelnut; they may bear protective spines or thorns, like those of barberry and hawthorn; or they may be brightly colored, like those of red-osier dogwood and kerria.

Growth rate and **life span,** though not really aesthetic features of woody plants, are nonetheless important aspects to consider.

A fast-growing tree or shrub that grows 24" or more a year will mature quickly and can be used to fill in space in a new garden. A slow-growing species that grows less than 12" a year may be more suitable in a space-limited garden.

A short-lived plant appeals to some people because they enjoy changing their garden design or aren't sure exactly what they want in their garden. Short-lived plants usually mature quickly and therefore reach flowering age quickly.

A long-lived tree, on the other hand, is an investment in time.

Some trees can take a human lifetime to reach their mature size, and some may not flower for 10 years after you plant them. You can enjoy a long-lived tree as it develops, and you will also leave a legacy for future generations—your tree may very well outlive you.

Fast-Growing Trees & Shrubs
  Ash
  Birch
  Black locust
  Butterfly bush
  Elderberry
  Forsythia
  Honeylocust
  Hydrangea (except *H. quercifolia*)
  Lilac
  Linden
  Privet
  Red-twig dogwood
  Silver maple
  Staghorn sumac
  Virginia creeper

Slow-Growing Trees & Shrubs
  Bearberry
  Beech
  Boxwood
  Chokeberry
  Daphne
  Euonymus
  Fir
  Fothergilla
  Fringe tree
  Ginkgo
  Holly
  Hornbeam
  Paperbark maple
  Rhododendron
  Yew

Elderberry cultivar

Linden

Boxwood (below)

Getting Started

Before you fall in love with the idea of having a certain tree or shrub in your garden, it's important to consider the growing conditions the plant needs and whether any areas of your garden are appropriate for it. Your plant will need to not only survive, but thrive, in order for its flowers or other features to reach their full potential.

All plants are adapted to certain growing conditions in which they do best. Choosing plants to match your garden conditions is far more practical than trying to alter your garden to match the plants. Yet it is through the use of trees and shrubs that we can best alter the conditions in a garden. Over time a tree can change a sunny, exposed garden into a shaded one, and a hedge can turn a windswept area into a sheltered one. The woody plants you choose must be able to thrive in the garden as it exists now, or they may

not live long enough to produce these changes.

Light, soil conditions and exposure are important factors that will guide your selection. As you plan, look at your garden as it exists now, but keep in mind the changes trees and shrubs will bring.

LIGHT
Buildings, trees, fences, the time of day and the time of year influence the amount of light that gets into your garden. Light levels are often divided into four categories for gardening purposes: full sun, partial shade (partial sun), light shade and full shade. Some plants adapt to a variety of light levels, but most have a preference for a narrower range.

Full sun locations receive direct sunlight over most of the day. An example would be an open location along a south-facing wall. Heat from the sun may be more intense in one spot than another, depending on, for example, the degree of shelter from the wind. **Partial shade** locations receive direct sun for part of the day and shade for the rest. An east- or west-facing wall gets only partial shade. **Light shade** locations receive shade most or all of the day, but with some sun getting through to ground level. The ground under a small-leaved tree is often lightly shaded, with dappled light visible on the ground underneath the tree. **Full shade** locations receive no direct sunlight. The north wall of a house is often in full shade.

Deutzia needs full sun for the best blooming.

SOIL

Plants have a unique relationship with the soil they grow in. Many important plant functions take place underground. Soil holds air, water, nutrients and organic matter. Plant roots depend upon these resources for growth, while using the soil to anchor the plant body. In turn, plants influence soil development by breaking down large clods with their roots and by increasing soil fertility when they die and decompose.

Soil is made up of particles of different sizes. Sand particles are the largest. Water drains quickly from a sandy soil, and nutrients can be rapidly washed away. Sand has lots of air spaces and doesn't compact easily. Clay particles are the smallest, visible only through a microscope.

Yew grows equally well in full sun or full shade.

Potentilla adapts well to clay soils.

Water penetrates clay very slowly and drains away even more slowly. Clay holds the most nutrients, but there is very little room for air and a clay soil compacts quite easily. Silt particles are smaller than sand particles and larger than clay particles. Most soils are made up of a combination of different particle sizes and are called loams.

Particle size is one influence on the drainage and moisture-holding properties of soil; slope is another. Knowing how quickly the water drains out of your soil will help you decide whether you should plant moisture-loving or drought-tolerant plants. Rocky soil on a hillside will probably drain quickly and should be reserved for those plants that prefer a very well-drained soil. Low-lying areas tend to retain water longer, and some areas may rarely drain at all. Moist areas suit plants that require a consistent water supply; constantly wet areas should be reserved for plants that are adapted to boggy conditions.

Drainage can be improved in very wet areas by adding organic matter to the soil, by installing some form of drainage tile or by building raised beds. Avoid adding sand to clay soils, or you may create something much like concrete. Consult with nursery professionals before adding sand to your garden's heavy soil to prevent potential problems. Working some gypsum into a clay soil along with organic matter will help break it up and allow water to penetrate and drain more easily. Water retention in sandy soil can also be improved by adding organic matter.

Another aspect of soil that is important to consider is the pH, or the measure of acidity or alkalinity. Soil pH influences the availability of nutrients for plants. A pH of 7 is neutral; lower values (down to 0) indicate acidic conditions; and higher values (up to 14) indicate alkaline conditions. Most plants prefer a neutral soil pH of 6.5 to 7.5. Ask your Illinois cooperative extension agent about your local soils. The agent can make general recommendations or instruct you on getting your soil tested. A soil test is useful in letting you know the exact pH and other conditions of your particular soil.

If a soil test reveals a pH problem, your soil can be made more acidic by adding horticultural sulfur or more alkaline by adding horticultural lime. The test results should include recommendations for quantities of additives needed to amend your soil.

Keep in mind that it is much easier to amend soil in a small area than it is in an entire garden. The soil in a raised bed or planter can be adjusted quite easily to suit a few plants that need soil very different from that in your garden.

EXPOSURE

Exposure is a very important consideration in all gardens that include woody plants. Wind, heat, cold, rain and snow are the main elements to which your garden may be exposed, and some plants are more tolerant than others of the potential damage these forces can cause. Buildings, walls, fences, hills and hedges or other woody plants can all influence your garden's exposure.

Wind can cause extensive damage to plants, particularly to evergreens in winter. Plants can become dehydrated in windy locations because they may not be able to draw water out of the soil fast enough to replace that lost through the leaves. Evergreens in areas where the ground freezes can often face this problem because they are unable to draw any water out of the frozen ground. While the standard recommendation is to keep them well watered in fall until the ground freezes, it is just as important to prevent drought stress during the heat of summer. Tests have shown that if a plant is water deprived in summer, it suffers greater winter burn. The goal is to avert stress to the plant throughout the growing season. Broad-leaved evergreens, such as rhododendron and holly, are most at risk from dehydration in winter, so grow them in a sheltered site.

Strong winds can cause physical damage by breaking weak branches or by blowing over entire trees. However, woody plants often make

The flowers of bigleaf hydrangea tend to be blue in acidic soils and pink in alkaline soils.

Hedges are excellent windbreaks.

Dwarf Alberta spruce and Japanese maple appreciate a sheltered site.

Shore juniper has a Zone 6 designation but may survive given shelter in Zone 5.

Linden viburnum is hardy mainly in southern Illinois but is worth trying in a sheltered spot in the north.

sheltered spots in Zone 3. Don't be afraid to try species that are not listed as hardy for your area. Plants are incredibly adaptable.

Here are some tips for growing out-of-zone plants:

- Before planting, observe your garden on a frosty morning. Are there areas that escape frost? These are potential sites for tender plants. Keep in mind that cold air tends to collect in low spots and can run down-hill, through breaks in plant-ings and structures, the same way that water does.
- Shelter tender plants from the prevailing wind.
- Plant in groups to create wind-breaks and microclimates. Rhododendrons, for instance, grow better if they are planted in small groups or grouped with plants that have similar growing requirements.
- Mulch young plants in fall with a thick layer of clean organic mulch, such as bark chips, com-posted woodchips, composted leaves or compost mixed with peat moss. Ensure that organic mulches have a minimum depth of 6–8" for good winter protection. Mulch over at least the first two winters.
- Water thoroughly before the ground freezes for the winter.
- Cover or screen frost-tender shrubs with a layer of burlap or horticultural cloth. You can also use special insulating blankets available at garden centers. If the plant is being grown in a container or planter, dig it into the vegetable garden, or place it under shelter or against a house for protection.

excellent windbreaks that shelter other plants. Hedges and trees tem-per the effect of the wind without the turbulence created on the lee-ward side of a more solid structure, such as a wall or fence. Windbreak trees should be species that can flex in the wind or should be planted far enough from buildings to avoid extensive property damage if the branches or trees fall.

Hardiness zones (see map, p.15, and Quick Reference Chart, p. 334) give an indication of whether a species can tolerate conditions in your area, but they are only guide-lines. Daphne is generally listed as a Zone 4 plant but often thrives in

Purchasing Trees & Shrubs

Now that you have thought about the features you like and the range of growing conditions your garden offers, you can select the plants. Any reputable garden center should have a good selection of popular woody plants. Finding more unusual specimens could require a few phone calls and a trip to a more specialized nursery. Mail-order nurseries are often a great source of the newest and most unusual plants.

Developing better plants for Illinois has become an industry-wide initiative. Throughout this book, you will find references to plants that have been introduced as selections of Chicagoland Grows. This consortium of woody-plant professionals seeks to develop and promote trees and shrubs uniquely suited to Illinois soils and weather.

STATE STREET ('Morton') maple is a Chicagoland Grows selection.

Avoid purchasing root-bound plants.
Purchasing plants in fall lets you see the fall color.

Many garden centers and nurseries offer a one-year warranty on trees and shrubs, but because trees take a long time to mature it is always in your best interest to choose the healthiest plants. Never purchase weak, damaged or diseased plants, even if they cost less. Examine the bark and avoid plants with visible damage. Check that the growth is even and appropriate for the species. Shrubs should be bushy and branched right to the ground, while trees should have a strong leader. Observe the leaf and flower buds. If they are dry and fall off easily, the plant has been deprived of moisture. The stem or stems should be strong, supple and unbroken. The rootball should be soft and moist when touched. Do not buy a plant with a dry rootball.

Woody plants are available for purchase in three forms:

Bare-root stock has roots surrounded by nothing except moist sawdust or peat moss within a plastic wrapping. The roots must be kept moist and cool, and planting should occur as soon as possible in spring. Avoid planting stock that appears to have dried out during shipping. See p. 34 for information on planting bare-root stock.

Balled-and-burlapped (B & B) stock comes with the roots surrounded by soil and wrapped in burlap, often secured with a wire cage for larger plants. The plants are usually field grown and then dug up, balled and burlapped the year they are sold. It is essential that the rootball remain moist. Large trees are available in this form, but be aware that the soil and rootball can

The program began in 1986 as a partnership of the Morton Arboretum, the Chicago Botanic Garden and the Ornamental Growers Association of Northern Illinois.

After plant evaluations over as many as 10 years have yielded positive results, and after enough plants have been produced to make them readily available in garden centers, the Chicagoland Grows selections are introduced. Look for them— they are tested Illinois tough.

be very heavy and there may be an extra expense for delivery and planting. See p. 35 for information on planting balled-and-burlapped stock.

Container plants are grown in pots filled with potting soil and have established root systems. This form is the most common at garden centers and nurseries. Container stock establishes quickly after planting and can be planted almost any time during the growing season. It is also easy to plant (see p. 36).

When choosing a plant, make sure it hasn't been in the container too long. If the roots are densely encircling the inside of the pot, then the plant has become root-bound. A root-bound tree or shrub will not establish well, and as the roots mature and thicken, they can choke and kill the plant. Note that sometimes field-grown stock is dug and sold in containers instead of burlap; ask if you aren't sure. Such plants must be treated like balled-and-burlapped stock when planting.

Bigger is not always better when it comes to choosing woody plants. Smaller plants of a given species often end up healthier and more robust than larger stock, particularly in the case of field-grown (as opposed to container-grown) plants. When a plant is dug up out of the field, the roots are severely cut back. The smaller the plant, the more quickly it can recover from the shock of being uprooted.

Improper handling can damage woody plants. You can lift bare-root stock by the stem, but do not lift any other trees or shrubs by the trunk or branches. Rather, lift by

Temporary winter storage for container stock

the rootball or container, or if the plant is too large to lift, place it on a tarp or mat and drag it.

Care during transport is also critical. Even a short trip home from the nursery can be traumatic for plants. The heat produced inside a car can quickly dehydrate a tree or shrub. If you are using a truck for transport, lay the plant down or cover it to shield it from the wind. Avoid mechanical damage such as rubbing or breaking branches during transport.

Once home, water the plant if it is dry and keep it in a sheltered location until you can plant it. Remove any damaged growth and broken branches, but do no other pruning. Plant your tree or shrub as soon as possible. A bare-root tree or shrub should be planted in a large container of potting soil if it will not be planted outdoors immediately. If you must store a container plant over a cold winter before planting, bury the entire container until spring.

Planting Trees & Shrubs

Before you pick up a shovel and start digging, step back for a moment and make sure the site you are considering is appropriate. The most important thing to check is the location of any underground wires or pipes. Even if you don't damage anything by digging, the tree roots may in the future cause trouble, or if there is a problem with the pipes or wires you may have to cut down the tree in order to service them. JULIE (Joint Utility Locating Information for Excavators) is a not-for-profit corporation that provides contractors, excavators, homeowners and others with a toll-free phone number (1-800-892-0123) to call for help locating and marking underground utilities.

Check also the mature plant size. The plant you have in front of you is most likely pretty small. Once it reaches its mature height and spread, will it still fit the space you have chosen? Is it far enough away from the house, the driveway and walkways? Will it hit the overhang of the house or any overhead power lines?

If you're planting several shrubs, make sure that they won't grow too close together once they are mature. The rule of thumb for spacing: add the mature spreads and then divide by two. For example, when planting a shrub with an expected spread of 4' next to another shrub with an expected spread of 6', you would plant them 5' apart. For hedges and windbreaks, the spacing should be one-half to two-thirds the spread of the mature plant to ensure there is no observable space between plants when they are fully grown.

Finally, double-check the conditions. Will the soil moisture and drainage be adequate? Will the plant get the right amount of light? Is the

Nicely planted shrub border

site very windy? It's important to start with the plant in the right location and in the best conditions you can possibly give it.

WHEN TO PLANT

For the most part, trees and shrubs can be planted at any time of year, though some seasons will be better for the plants and more convenient than others. Preferred planting times are indicated at the beginning of each plant entry in this book.

Spring is a great time to plant. It gives the tree or shrub an entire growing season to become established before winter sets in, and gets it started before the weather turns really hot. Many gardeners avoid planting during the hottest and driest part of summer, mainly because of the extra work involved with supplemental watering. However, even a spring-planted tree or shrub will require watering during hot, dry weather.

Bare-root stock must be planted in spring because it is generally available only at that time, and it must be planted as soon as possible to avoid moisture loss.

Balled-and-burlapped and container stock can usually be planted at any time, as long as you can get a shovel into the ground. They can even be planted in frozen ground if you had the foresight to dig the hole before the ground froze and to keep the backfill (the dirt from the hole) in a warm place.

The time of day to plant is also a consideration. Avoid planting in the heat of the day. Planting in the morning, in the evening or on a cloudy, calm day will be easier on both you and the plant.

It's a good idea to plant as soon as possible after you bring your specimen home. If you have to store the tree or shrub for a short time before planting, keep it out of direct sunlight and ensure that the rootball remains moist.

PREPARING THE HOLE

Trees and shrubs should always be planted at the depth at which they were growing, or just above the roots if you are unsure of the depth for bare-root stock. The depth in the center of the hole should be equal to the depth of the rootball or container, whereas the depth around the

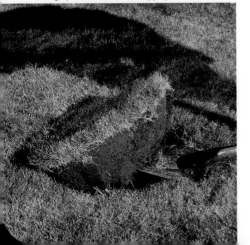

Sizing up the hole (above), digging the hole (below)

edges can be greater than this. Making the center higher prevents the plant from sinking as the soil settles and encourages excess water to drain away from the new plant.

Be sure that the plant is not set too deep. Planting even 2–4" too deep can cause problems. Most potted field-grown trees are planted deeply in the pot in order to help keep the freshly dug tree from tipping over, and there may be mulch on top of the soil as well. Planting such a tree to the same depth as the level in the pot may not be a good idea. Scrape off the soil until you find the root mass, and then plant to just above it.

Make the hole for bare-root stock big enough to completely contain the expanded roots with a bit of extra room on the sides. Make the hole for balled-and-burlapped and container stock about twice the width of the rootball or container.

The soil around the rootball or in the container is not likely to be the same as the soil you just removed from the hole. The extra room in the hole allows the new roots an easier medium (backfill) to grow into than undisturbed soil, providing a transition zone from the rootball soil to the existing on-site soil. It is good practice to rough up the sides and bottom of the hole to aid in root transition and water flow. It is also good practice to loosen the soil outside the hole with a garden fork or power tiller.

PLANTING BARE-ROOT STOCK

Remove the plastic and sawdust from the roots. Fan out the roots and center the plant over the central mound in the hole. The mound for bare-root stock is often made cone

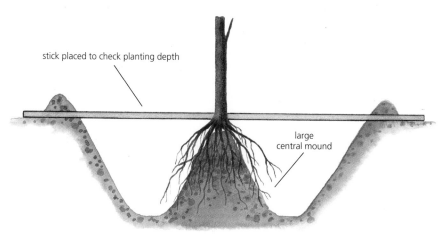

stick placed to check planting depth

large
central mound

Planting bare-root stock

shaped and larger than the mound for other types of plants. Use the cone to help spread out and support the roots. Make sure the hole is big enough to allow the roots to fully extend.

PLANTING BALLED & BURLAPPED STOCK

Burlap was originally made out of natural fibers. It could be loosened and left wrapped around the root-ball to eventually decompose. Modern burlap may or may not be made of natural fibers, and it can be difficult to tell the difference. Synthetic fibers will not decompose and will eventually choke the roots. It is always best to remove any type of burlap to prevent girdling and to maximize contact between the roots and soil. If roots are already growing through the burlap, remove as much burlap as you can while avoiding damage to the new roots. If you know the burlap is natural and decide to leave it, loosen it from the rootball and tuck it below the

soil line so it won't wick water into the air away from the roots.

If a wire basket holds the burlap in place, it should be removed as well. Strong wire cutters may be needed to get the basket off. If the tree is very heavy, it may not be possible to remove the base of the basket, but cut away at least the sides, where most of the important roots will be growing.

With the basket removed, set the still-burlapped plant on the center mound in the hole. Lean the plant over to one side and roll the burlap down to the ground. When you lean the plant in the opposite direction, you should be able to pull the burlap out from under the roots. As with the basket on a heavy tree, just remove as much burlap as you can if the tree is difficult to move.

Past horticultural wisdom suggested removing some top branches when planting to make up for roots lost when the plant was dug out of the field. The theory was that the roots could not provide enough water to the leaves, so top growth should be removed to achieve 'balance.' We now know that the top growth—where photosynthesis occurs and thus where energy is produced—is necessary for root development. The new tree or shrub might drop some leaves, but don't be alarmed; the plant is doing its own balancing. A very light pruning will not adversely affect the plant, but remove only those branches that have been damaged during transport and planting. Leave your new plant to settle in for a year or two before you start any formative pruning.

PLANTING CONTAINER STOCK

Containers are usually made from plastic or pressed fiber. Both kinds should be removed before planting. Although some containers appear to be made of peat moss, they do not decompose well. The roots may have difficulty penetrating the pot sides, and the fiber will wick moisture away from the roots.

Container stock is very easy to plant (see photos, p. 37). Gently remove or cut off the container and observe the root mass to check whether the plant is root-bound. If roots are circling around the inside of the container, they should be loosened or sliced. Any large roots encircling the soil or growing into the center of the root mass instead of outward should be removed before planting. A sharp pair of hand pruners or a pocketknife will work well for this task.

BACKFILLING

With your bare-root, balled-and-burlapped or container plant in the

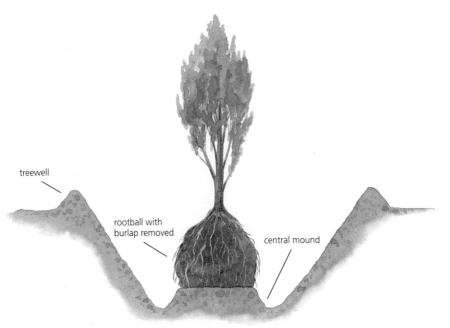

treewell

rootball with
burlap removed

central mound

Planting balled-and-burlapped stock

1. Gently remove container.

2. Ensure proper planting depth.

3. Backfill with amended soil.

4. Settle backfilled soil with water.

5. Ensure newly planted shrub is well watered.

6. Add a layer of mulch.

Young tree in its new home

Adding organic matter to backfill

venture beyond the immediate area of the hole, the tree or shrub will be weaker and much more susceptible to problems, and the encircling roots could eventually choke the plant. Such a tree will also be more vulnerable to blowing down in a strong wind.

Backfill should generally reach the same depth the plant was grown at previously, or just above the root-ball. If planting into a heavy soil, raise the plant about 1" to help improve surface drainage away from the crown and roots. Graft unions of grafted stock are generally kept above ground to make it easy to spot and remove suckers sprouting from the rootstock.

When backfilling, it is important to have good root-to-soil contact for initial stability and good establishment. Large air pockets remaining after backfilling could result in excessive settling and root drying. Use water to settle the soil gently around the roots and in the hole, being careful not to drown the plant. It is a good idea to backfill in small amounts rather than all at once. Add some soil, then water it down, repeating until the hole is full. Stockpile any soil that remains after backfilling and use it to top up the soil around the plant as the backfill settles.

If you are working with a heavy clay soil, ensure that the surface drainage slopes away from your new transplant. Build a temporary 2–4" high, doughnut-like mound of soil around the perimeter of the hole to capture extra water. Water into this reservoir for at least the whole first season. Doing so ensures that water will percolate down through the new root mass. The ring of soil,

hole and standing straight up, it is time to replace the soil. A small amount of organic matter can be well mixed into the backfill. This small amount will encourage the plant to become established, but too much creates a pocket of rich soil that the roots may be reluctant to move beyond. If the roots do not

called a *treewell,* is an excellent way to conserve water, especially during dry spells. In periods of heavy rain, you may need to breach the treewell to prevent the roots from becoming waterlogged. The treewell can be rebuilt when drier conditions resume. Once the tree or shrub has become established, after a year or two, the treewell will no longer be needed and should be permanently removed.

To conserve water, mulch around the new planting. Composted wood chips or shredded bark will stay where you put them, unlike pebble bark or peat moss. Two to four inches of mulch is adequate. Do not use too much, and avoid mulching directly against the trunk or base of the plant; otherwise, you may encourage disease problems.

STAKING

Some trees may need to be staked in order to provide support while the roots establish. Staking is recommended only for bare-root trees; for tall, top-heavy trees over 5' tall; and for trees planted in windy locations,

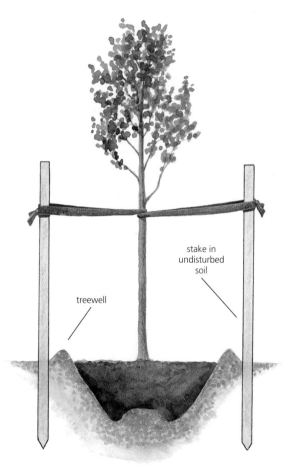

stake in
undisturbed
soil

treewell

Two-stake method

particularly evergreens because they tend to catch winter winds. Stakes should be removed as soon as the roots have had a chance to become established, which normally takes about a year.

Growing trees and shrubs without stakes is preferable because unstaked trees develop more roots and stronger trunks. Most newly planted trees are able to stand on their own without staking. You can always stake later if you find it's needed.

Two common methods are used for staking newly planted trees. For both methods you can use either wood or metal stakes.

The **two-stake** method is suitable for small trees (about 5–6' tall) and trees in low-wind areas. Drive the stakes into the soil just outside of the planting hole on opposite sides of your tree, 180° apart and in line with the prevailing wind. Driving stakes in near the tree can damage the roots and will not provide adequate support. Tie string, rope, cable or wire to the stakes. The end that goes around the trunk should be a wide, belt-like strap of material that will not cut into the trunk.

treewell

Three-stake method

Your local garden center should have ties designed for this purpose, or you can cushion the rope or wire with a section of rubber hose. Attach the straps to the tree about 3–4' above the ground.

The **three-stake** method is used for larger trees and for trees in areas subject to strong or shifting winds. This technique is much the same as the two-stake method, but with three thicker, shorter stakes evenly spaced around the tree. Attach heavy wire or cable to each stake, again with wide strapping or padding on the end that comes into contact with the trunk. Position the straps just above the lower branches to keep them in place.

Here are a few points to keep in mind, regardless of which staking method is used:

- Never wrap rope, wire or cable directly around a tree trunk. Always use a nondamaging type of material. Reposition the strapping every two to three months to prevent any rubbing or girdling injury.
- Never tie trees so firmly that they can't move. Young trees need to be able to move in the wind to produce strong trunks and to develop roots more thickly in appropriate places to compensate for the prevailing wind.
- Don't leave the stakes in place too long. One year is sufficient for almost all trees. The stakes should be there only long enough to allow the roots some time to grow and establish. The tree will actually be weaker if the stakes are left for too long, and over time the ties can damage the trunk and weaken or kill the tree.

Magnolia dislikes being transplanted.

TRANSPLANTING

If you plan your garden carefully, you should rarely need to move trees or shrubs. Some woody plants (indicated as such in the individual species entries) resent being moved once established, and you should avoid transplanting these species whenever possible. For all species, the younger the tree or shrub, the more likely it is to reestablish successfully when moved to a new location. A rule of thumb is that it takes one year for every inch of trunk diameter for a tree to become well established after transplanting.

American beech (above) and bald-cypress (below) should be transplanted only when young.

Generally, you can transplant evergreens in spring before growth starts or later in the season after it stops, as long as you avoid transplanting during a spell of hot weather. Deciduous plants should be transplanted only while dormant—when the branches are bare of leaves in spring, fall or early winter.

When woody plants are transplanted, they inevitably lose much of their root mass. Care should be taken to dig a rootball of an appropriate size. The size of the tree or shrub will determine the minimum size of the rootball that must be dug out in order for the plant to survive. As a general guideline, for every 1" of main stem width, which is measured 6–12" above the ground, you need to excavate a rootball at least 12" wide, and preferably larger.

Rootballs are heavy, and a 24" rootball is probably the most the average gardener can manage without heavy equipment. Trees with trunks more than 2" wide should be moved by professionals. Shrubs cannot always be measured as easily as trees, so you will need to use your best judgment. Because shrubs mature fairly quickly, you may find it easier to start with a new one rather than try to move a very large specimen.

If it is necessary and feasible to transplant a shrub or small tree, follow these steps:
1) Calculate the width of the rootball to be removed, as described above.
2) Water the rootball area to a depth of 12" and allow excess water to drain away. The moist soil will help hold the rootball together.

3) Wrap or tie the branches to minimize branch damage and to ease transport from the old site to the new one.

4) Slice a long spade or shovel into the soil vertically, cutting a circle around the plant as wide as the calculated rootball width. Cut down to about 12". This depth should contain most of the roots for the size of tree or shrub that can be transplanted manually.

5) At this point, most small, densely rooted trees and shrubs can be carefully removed from the hole by leaning on the spade or shovel and prying the plant up and out. If you encounter resistance, you may have missed some roots and should repeat step 4. Once the plant has been freed, place it on a tarp and continue with step 10.

Larger trees and shrubs require additional steps; continue with step 6.

6) Cut another circle one shovel-width outside the first circle, to the same depth.

7) Excavate the soil between the two cut circles.

8) When the appropriate rootball depth is reached, carefully cut horizontally under the rootball. When you encounter a root, cut it with a pair of hand pruners or loppers. The goal is to sculpt out a rootball that is standing on a pedestal of undisturbed earth.

9) Spread a tarp in one side of the hole. Gently remove the pedestal and lean the rootball over onto the tarp. Carefully cut any remaining roots in the pedestal. Lift the tree and rootball out of the hole with the tarp, not by the stem or branches.

10) Lift or drag the tarp to the new location and plant immediately. See planting instructions given in preceding sections for information on when to plant, how to plant, staking, etc. Transplanted trees and shrubs can be treated as balled-and-burlapped stock.

European beech tolerates transplanting well.

Caring for Trees & Shrubs

WEEDING

Weeds can rob young plants of light, water and nutrients, so keep weeds under control to encourage optimal growth of your trees and shrubs. Avoid deep hoeing under woody plants because it may damage the shallow roots of some species. A layer of mulch is a good way to suppress weeds. If you feel that you must use commercial weed killers, consult your local nursery or extension agent for advice, and follow the label directions carefully.

MULCHING

Mulch is an important gardening tool. It helps soil retain moisture, it buffers soil temperatures, and it prevents soil erosion during heavy rain or strong winds. Mulch prevents weed seeds from germinating by blocking out the light, and it can deter pests and help prevent diseases. It keeps lawn mowers and line trimmers away from plants, reducing the chance of damage. Mulch can also add aesthetic value to a planting.

Organic mulches can consist of compost, composted wood chips, bark chips, shredded bark, composted leaves and dry grass clippings. These mulches are desirable because they add nutrients to the soil as they break down. Because they break down, however, they must be replenished on a regular basis.

Inorganic mulches, such as stones, crushed brick or gravel, do not break down and so do not have to be replenished. These types of mulches don't provide nutrients and

The care you give your new tree or shrub in the first year or two after planting is the most important. During this period of establishment, it is critical to remove competing weeds, to keep the plant well watered and to avoid all mechanical damage. Be careful with lawn mowers and string trimmers, which can quickly girdle the base of the plant. Whatever you do to the top of the plant affects the roots, and vice versa.

Once woody plants have established, they generally require minimal care. A few basic maintenance tasks, performed regularly, will save time and trouble in the long run.

they can also adversely increase soil temperatures. Some books recommend using black plastic or ground cloth under the mulch, but doing so can disrupt the microbial balance of the soil. The plastic or ground cloth prevents worms and other important soil organisms from moving freely to the surface, as well as restricting oxygen and water movement into the soil.

For good weed suppression, the mulch layer should be 2–4" thick. Avoid piling mulch up around the base of the plant, or you may risk encouraging fungal decay and rot. Try to maintain a mulch-free zone immediately around the trunk or stem bases.

Keep mulch from the base of your tree or shrub.

WATERING

The weather, type of plant, type of soil and time of year all influence the amount of water your shrubs and trees need. If your area is naturally dry or if there has been a stretch of hot, dry weather, you will need to water more often than if you garden in a naturally wet area or if your area has received a lot of rain recently. Pay attention to the wind; it can dry out soil and plants quickly. Different plants require different amounts of water. Some, such as willow and some birch, will grow in a temporarily waterlogged soil; others, such as pine, prefer a dry, sandy soil. Plants need more water when they are on slopes, when they are flowering and when they are producing fruit.

Plants are good at letting us know when they are thirsty. Wilted, flagging leaves and twigs are a sign of water deprivation, but excessive water can also cause a plant to wilt. Test for soil moisture by checking at least 2" down with your fingers or with a soil probe (purchased or homemade; see sidebar). If you detect moisture, don't water.

Make sure your trees and shrubs are well watered in fall. Continue to water as needed until the ground freezes. Fall watering is very important for evergreen plants because

You can make a soil probe from a 3/8" to 1/2" diameter wooden dowel. Carve one end into a point, then cut a groove or paint a mark 12" up from that end. Do not finish the wood, because you want it to discolor as it absorbs the soil moisture. Push the rod into the soil 12" deep, leave it for up to a minute, then remove it. If it has darkened with moisture, you don't need to water. If it is dry, water immediately. It is quite possible for heavy clay soils to be dry down to 3" but plenty wet enough farther down. Many a plant has been saved from drowning through the use of this simple probe.

once the ground has frozen, the roots can no longer draw moisture from it, leaving the foliage susceptible to desiccation.

Once trees and shrubs are established, they will likely need watering only during periods of excessive drought. To keep water use to a minimum, avoid watering in the heat of the day because much will be lost to evaporation. Work organic matter into the soil to help the soil absorb and retain water, and apply mulch to help prevent moisture loss. Collect and use rainwater whenever possible.

FERTILIZING

Most garden soils provide all the nutrients plants need, particularly if you use an organic mulch and mix compost into the soil before planting your garden. Simply allowing leaf litter to remain on the ground after the leaves drop in autumn promotes natural nutrient cycling of nitrogen and other elements in the soil.

Not all plants have the same nutritional requirements, however. Some plants are heavy feeders, while others thrive in poor soils. Pay attention to the leaf color of your plants as an indicator of nutritional status. Yellowing leaves, for example, may be a sign of nutrient deficiency.

When you do fertilize, use only the recommended quantity because too much can be very harmful. Roots are easily burned by fertilizer applied in too high a concentration. Synthetic fertilizers are more concentrated and therefore have the potential to cause more problems than organic fertilizers.

Granular fertilizers consist of small, dry particles that can be spread with a fertilizer spreader or by hand. Consider using a slow-release type of granular fertilizer. It may cost a bit more but will save you time and reduce the risk of burn because the nutrients are released gradually over the growing season. One application per year is normally sufficient. Applying the fertilizer in early spring provides nutrients for spring growth.

Tree spikes are slow-release fertilizers that are quick and easy to use. Pound the spikes into the ground around the dripline (see diagram, p. 47). These spikes work especially well for fertilizing trees in lawns, because the grass tends to consume most of the nutrients released from surface applications.

If fertilizer is not applied correctly or not needed, your plant will not benefit. In fact, it will make a tree or shrub more susceptible to some pests and diseases and can accelerate a plant's decline.

Fertilizing should be done to correct a visible nutrient deficiency, to correct a deficiency identified by a soil and tissue test, to increase vegetative, flower or fruit growth, or to increase the vigor of the plant that is flagging.

Do not fertilize trees or shrubs
• when there are sufficient nutrients in the soil as determined by a soil and tissue test
• if your plants are growing and appear healthy
• if your plants are sufficiently large and you want to reduce pruning and shearing
• during times of drought. Roots will not absorb nutrients during drought, and excess partially wetted fertilizer can burn root hairs.

If you do not wish to encourage fast growth, do not fertilize. Remember, most trees and shrubs do not need fertilizer, and fast growth may make plants more prone to problems. In particular, avoid fall fertilizing with chemical fertilizers, which can encourage new growth late in the season. This growth is easily damaged in winter. Organic fertilizers can be applied in fall because they are activated by soil organisms that are not as active in cool weather.

Unnecessary or excessive fertilizer pollutes our local lakes, streams and groundwater. Many homes in Illinois obtain their drinking water from wells, which can be contaminated by fertilizers. Use fertilizers wisely, and both your plants and our environment will benefit.

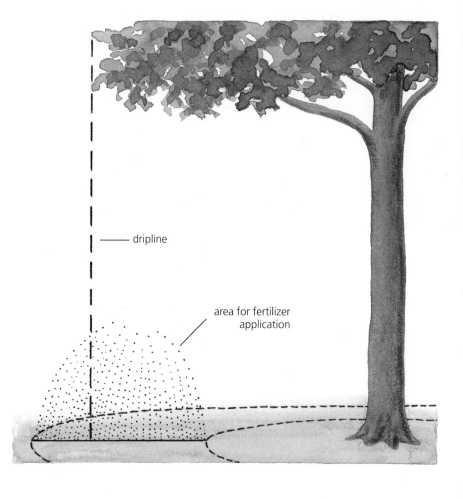

dripline

area for fertilizer application

Pruning

Pruning helps to maintain the health and attractive shape of a woody plant. It also increases the quality and yield of fruit, controls and directs growth, and creates interesting plant forms, such as espalier, topiary and bonsai. Pruning is perhaps the most important maintenance task when growing trees and shrubs—and the easiest to mess up. Fortunately for new gardeners, it is not difficult to learn and can even be enjoyable if done correctly from the beginning and continued on a regular basis.

Proper pruning combines knowledge and skill. General knowledge about how woody plants grow and specific knowledge about the growth habits of your particular plant will help you avoid pruning mistakes that can ruin a plant's shape or make it prone to disease and insect damage.

If you are unsure about pruning, take a pruning course. Courses may be offered by a local garden center, botanical garden, community college or master gardener. Excellent books are also available on the subject.

Another option is to hire a professional, such as an arborist certified by the International Society of Arboriculture (ISA); see Resources (p. 342). Certified professionals understand the plants and have the special pruning training and equipment to do a proper job. They might even be willing to show you some pruning basics. *Always* call a professional to prune trees growing near power lines or other hazardous areas, and to prune or cut down large branches and trees that could fall and damage buildings, fences, cars or pedestrians. Many gardeners have injured themselves or others, or caused significant property damage, because they simply didn't have the equipment or the know-how to remove a large branch or tree.

Genetically programmed to grow to a certain size, plants will always try to reach that potential. If you are doing a lot of pruning to keep a tree or shrub in check, the plant may be too large for that site. We cannot emphasize enough how important it is to consider the mature size of a plant before you put it into the ground.

Professional tree service

WHEN & HOW MUCH TO PRUNE

Aside from removing damaged growth, do not prune for the first year after planting a tree or shrub. After that time, the first pruning should develop the plant's structure. For a strong framework, do not prune branches that have a wide angle at the crotch (where the branch meets another branch or the trunk), because these branch intersections are the strongest. Prune out branches with narrower crotches, while ensuring an even distribution of the main (scaffold) branches. These branches will support all future top growth.

Trees and shrubs vary greatly in their pruning needs. Some plants, such as boxwood, tolerate or thrive on heavy shearing, while others, such as cherry, may be killed if given the same treatment. Pruning guidelines are given in each species entry in this book.

The amount of pruning also depends on your reasons for doing it. Much less work is involved in simply tidying the growth, for

Sheared boxwood hedge

example, than in creating an intricate topiary specimen.

Many gardeners are uncertain about what time of year they should prune. Knowing when a plant flowers is the easiest way to know when to prune. (See p. 54 for information on pruning conifers.)

Trees and shrubs that flower before about July, such as rhododendron and forsythia, should be pruned after they are finished flowering. These plants form flower buds for the following year over summer and fall. Pruning just after the current year's flowers fade allows plenty of time for the next year's flowers to develop and avoids taking away any of the current year's blooms.

Proper hand pruner orientation

causing organisms are active, or in fall, when many wood-rotting fungi release their spores. These are times when the weather is cool and plants are fairly inactive, making it difficult for them to fight off invasion.

Inspect trees and shrubs annually for any dead, damaged, diseased or awkwardly growing branches and to determine what other pruning, if any, is needed. Always remove dead, diseased and damaged branches as soon as you discover them, at any time of year.

THE KINDEST CUT

Trees and shrubs have a remarkable ability to repair their wounds, but it is critical to make proper pruning cuts. A proper pruning cut, while still a wound, minimizes the area where insect and disease attack can occur and takes advantage of the areas on a plant where it can best deal with wounds. The tree or shrub can then heal as quickly as possible, preventing disease and insect damage.

Using the right tools makes pruning easier and more effective. The size of the branch being cut determines the type of tool to use.

Hand pruners should be used for cutting branches up to 3/4" in diameter. Using hand pruners for larger

Trees and shrubs that flower in about July or later, such as peegee hydrangea and rose-of-Sharon, can be pruned early in the year. These plants form flower buds on new stems as the season progresses, and pruning in spring just before or as new growth develops will encourage the best growth and flowering.

Some plants, such as maple, have a heavy spring flow of sap. As long as proper pruning cuts are made, these trees can still be pruned in spring. If the excessive bleeding is aesthetically unappealing or is dripping on something inappropriately, wait until these species are in full leaf before pruning.

Take care when pruning any trees in early spring, when many canker-

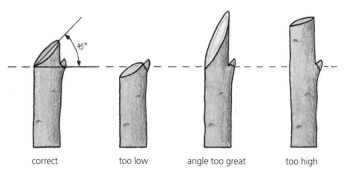

correct   too low   angle too great   too high

Cutting back to a bud

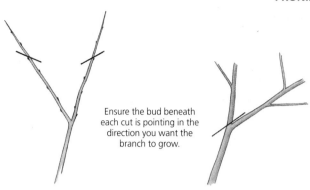

Ensure the bud beneath each cut is pointing in the direction you want the branch to grow.

Cutting back to a bud   Cutting to a lateral branch

stems increases the risk of damage, and it can be physically strenuous.

Loppers are long-handled pruners used for branches up to 1¹/₂" in diameter. Loppers are good for removing old stems. Hand pruners and loppers must be properly oriented when making a cut (see photo, p. 50). The blade should be to the plant side of the cut and the hook to the side being removed. If the cut is made with the hook toward the plant, the cut will be ragged and slow to heal.

Pruning saws have teeth specially designed to cut through green wood. They can be used to cut branches up to 6" in diameter and sometimes larger. Pruning saws are easier to use and much safer than chainsaws.

Hedge clippers, or shears, are intended only for shearing and shaping hedges.

Make sure your tools are sharp and clean before you begin any pruning task. If the branch you are cutting is diseased, sterilize the tool before using it again. Use denatured alcohol or a solution of 1 part bleach to 10 parts water.

TYPES OF PRUNING CUTS

You should be familiar with the following types of pruning cuts.

Cutting back to a bud is used for shortening a branch, redirecting growth or maintaining the size of a tree or shrub. Each cut should be made slightly less than ¹/₄" above a bud (see diagram, p. 50). If the cut is too far away from or too close to the bud, the wound will not heal properly. Cut back to buds that are pointing in the direction you want the new growth to grow in (see diagram, above).

Cutting to a lateral branch is used to shorten limbs and redirect growth. The diameter of the branch to which you are cutting back must be at least one-third of the diameter of the branch you are cutting. As with cutting back to a bud, cut slightly less than ¹/₄" above the lateral branch and line up the cut with the angle of the branch that is to remain (see diagram, above). Make cuts at an angle whenever possible so that rain won't sit on the open wound.

Removing limbs can be a complicated operation. Because the wound is large, it is critical to cut in the correct place—at the branch collar—to ensure quick healing. The cut must be done in steps (see diagram, below) to avoid damaging the bark.

The first cut is on the bottom of the branch to be removed. This cut should be 12–18" up from the crotch and should extend one-third of the way through the branch. The purpose of the first cut is to prevent bark from peeling down the tree when the second cut causes the main part of the branch to fall. The second cut is made a bit farther along the branch from the first cut and is made from the top of the branch. This cut removes most of the branch. The final cut should be made just above the branch collar. The plant tissues at the branch collar quickly create a barrier against insects and diseases. Do not make flush cuts and do not leave stubs; both can be slow to heal.

The use of pruning paint or paste has been much debated. The current consensus is that these substances do more harm than good. Trees and shrubs have a natural ability to create a barrier between living wood and dead or decaying sections. An unpainted cut will eventually heal over, but a cut that has been treated with paint or paste may never heal properly.

Shearing is used to trim and shape hedges. Only plants that can handle heavy pruning should be sheared, because some of the normal pruning rules (such as being careful where you cut in relation to buds) are disregarded here.

Informal hedges take advantage of the natural shape of the plant and require only minimal trimming. These hedges generally take up more room than formal hedges, which are trimmed more severely to assume a neat, even appearance. Formal hedges are generally sheared a minimum of twice per growing season.

For both informal and formal hedges, trim all sides to encourage even growth. The base of the hedge should be wider than the top (see diagram, p. 53) to allow light to reach the entire hedge and to prevent it from thinning at the base. Hedges gradually increase in size despite shearing, so allow room for this when planting.

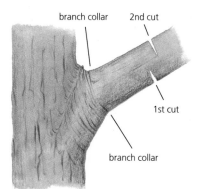

branch collar   2nd cut

1st cut

branch collar

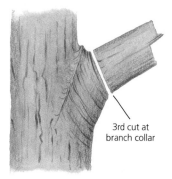

3rd cut at
branch collar

Limb removal steps

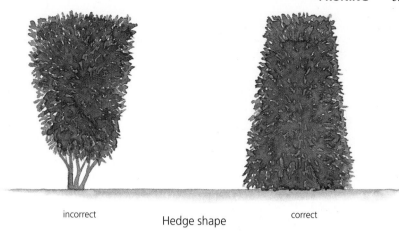

incorrect

Hedge shape

correct

Thinning, or renewal pruning, is a rejuvenation process that maintains the shape, health and productivity of shrubs. It opens up space for air and light to penetrate and provides room for young, healthy branches and selected suckers to grow. Thinning often combines the first two cuts discussed above, and it is the most frequently performed pruning practice. Plants that produce new growth from ground level (either from the crown or by suckers) can be pruned this way.

A shrub that is thinned annually should have one-quarter to one-third of the growth removed. Cutting the oldest stems encourages new growth without causing excess stress from loss of top growth. Although some plants can be cut back completely to the ground and seem to suffer no ill effects, it is generally better to remove no more than one-third of the growth.

Follow these four steps to thin most multi-stemmed shrubs:
1) Remove all dead, diseased, damaged, rubbing and crossing branches to branch junctions, buds or ground level.
2) Remove up to one-third of the growth each year, leaving a mix of old and new growth, and cutting unwanted stems at or close to the base. Do not cut stems below ground level because many disease organisms are present in soil.
3) Thin the top of the shrub to allow air and light penetration and to balance the shape. This step is not always necessary because removing the oldest stems generally thins out the top as well.

Thinning cuts

Sheared arborvitae cultivars

4) Repeat the process each year on established, mature shrubs. Regular pruning of shrubs will keep them healthy and productive for many years.

Fully extended mugo pine candles

PRUNING CONIFERS

Many coniferous trees and shrubs, such as spruce, pine and juniper, require little or no pruning other than to fix damage or to correct wayward growth. Proper pruning procedures do differ, however, for different conifers.

Spruce trees have buds all along their stems and can be pruned at almost any time of year. Branches can be pruned back into the last two or three years of growth.

Pines, on the other hand, must be shaped and directed in mid- to late spring, after the danger of frost has passed. At this time, the new growth, called candles, should have almost fully extended but should still be pliable. Pinch the candles by up to half their length before they are fully extended. Pines do not have side buds along their stems, but when pinched at the proper time new buds will set near the pinched end. For bushy, dense growth, pinch all candles by half. Pinching should be done by hand and not with shears or hand pruners. This technique can be time consuming and has a limited effect. It is better to choose a cultivar that is expected to reach an appropriate size for the space you have and that already has a dense, bushy habit.

Yews, junipers and arborvitae can be lightly sheared for hedging. It is best to begin training hedge plants when they are very young. Yews can be pruned heavily during dormancy, but it is better to shear them on an ongoing basis. As specimens, yews can be heavily hand pruned at almost any time to enhance their natural shape.

When removing a coniferous branch, cut it back to the branch collar at the trunk. Take a good look at a few branches before you start cutting because the collar can be difficult to find on a conifer. There is no point in cutting a branch back partway because most coniferous species, including pine and fir, will not regenerate from old wood. Juniper can regenerate from old wood, but it takes a long time and may result in an oddly shaped plant. Make sure you really need to remove a branch before you do so, to avoid disfiguring the plant. Here is another reason to think about mature size before you plant any tree or shrub.

If the central leader on a young conifer is broken or damaged, cleanly remove it and train a new leader in its place. In doing so you reduce the chance of infection and prevent many opportunistic leaders from competing. Gently place a straight stake next to the main trunk. Do not insert the stake into the ground. Tie the stake to the main trunk, being careful not to girdle the tree by tying it too tightly. Bend the chosen new leader as upright as possible and tie it to the stake. Remove the stake when the new leader is growing strongly upright. Remove any other leaders that attempt to form, or cut their tips.

Older, larger trees may be irreparably damaged by the loss of a leader.

TREE TOPPING
One pruning practice that should never be performed is tree topping. Topping is done in an attempt to control height or size, to prevent trees from growing into overhead power lines, to allow more light

Topping disfigures and stresses trees.

onto a property or to prevent a tall tree from potentially toppling onto a building.

Topped trees are ugly, weak and potentially hazardous. A tree can be killed by the stress of losing so much of its live growth, or by the gaping, slow-to-heal wounds that are vulnerable to attack by insects and wood-rotting fungi. The heartwood of a topped tree rots out quickly, resulting in a weak trunk. The crotches on new growth also tend to be weak. Topped trees, therefore, are susceptible to storm damage and blowdown. Hazards aside, topping a tree spoils its aesthetic value and that of the surrounding landscape.

It is much better to completely remove a tree, and start again with one that will grow to a more appropriate size, than to attempt to reduce the size of a large, mature specimen.

Boxwood topiary (above)

Espaliered apple
Spruce and juniper bonsai

SPECIALTY PRUNING

Custom pruning methods are used to create interesting plant shapes.

Topiary is the shaping of plants into animal, abstract or geometric forms. True topiary uses hedge plants sheared into the desired shape. Species that can handle heavy pruning, such as boxwood, are chosen. A simpler form of topiary involves growing vines or other trailing plants over a wire frame to achieve the desired form. Small-leaved ivy and other flexible, climbing or trailing plants work well for this kind of topiary.

Espalier involves training a tree or shrub to grow in two dimensions instead of three, with the aid of a solid wire or other framework. The plant is commonly trained against a wall or fence, but it can also be free-standing. This method is popularly applied to fruit trees, such as apple, when space is at a premium. Many gardeners consider the forms attractive and unusual, and you may wish to try your hand at espalier even if you have lots of space.

Bonsai is the art of developing miniature versions of large trees and landscapes. A gardener prunes the top growth and roots and uses wire to train the plant to the desired form. The severe pruning creates a dwarfed form of the species. Many books are available on the subject, and courses may be offered at colleges or by horticultural or bonsai societies.

Propagating Trees & Shrubs

Many gardeners enjoy the art and science of starting new plants. Although some gardeners are willing to try growing annuals from seeds and perennials from seeds, cuttings or divisions, they may be unsure how to go about propagating their own trees and shrubs. Yet many woody plants can be propagated with ease, allowing the gardener to buy a single specimen and then clone it, rather than buying additional plants.

Do-it-yourself propagating does more than cut costs. It can become an enjoyable aspect of gardening and an interesting hobby in itself. As well, it allows gardeners to add to their landscapes species that may be hard to find at nurseries.

A number of methods can be used to propagate trees and shrubs. Many species can be started from seed; this can be a long, slow process, but some gardeners enjoy the variable and sometimes unusual results. Simpler techniques include cuttings, ground layering and mound layering.

CUTTINGS

Cut segments of stems can be encouraged to develop their own roots and form new plants. Cuttings are treated differently depending on the maturity of the growth.

Cuttings taken in spring or early summer from new growth are called *greenwood* or *softwood* cuttings. They can actually be the most difficult

Willow cultivar
False cypress

cuttings to start because they require warm, humid conditions that are as likely to cause the cuttings to rot as to root.

Cuttings taken in fall from mature, woody growth are called *hardwood* or *ripe* cuttings. In order to root, these cuttings require a coarse, gritty, moist and preferably warm soil mix and cold, but not freezing, air temperatures. They may take all winter to root. These special conditions make it difficult to start hardwood cuttings unless you have a cold frame, heated greenhouse or plant propagator.

The easiest cuttings for most gardeners to start are those taken in late summer or early fall from new, but mature, growth that has not yet become completely woody. These are called *semi-ripe, semi-mature* or *semi-hardwood* cuttings.

Follow these steps to take and plant semi-ripe cuttings:

1) Take cuttings about 2–4" long from the tip of a stem, cutting just below a leaf node (the node is the place where a leaf meets the stem). There should be at least two nodes on the cutting. The tip of each cutting will be soft, but the base will be starting to harden.

2) Remove the leaves from the lower half of the cutting. Moisten the stripped end and dust it lightly with rooting hormone powder. Consult your local garden center to find an appropriate rooting hormone for your cutting.

3) Plant cuttings directly in the garden, or in a cold frame or pots. The soil mix should be well drained but moist. Firm the cuttings into the soil to ensure there

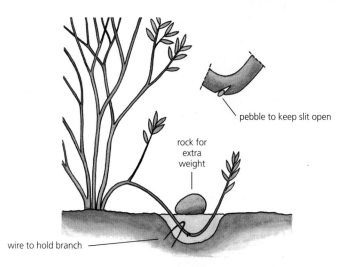

pebble to keep slit open

rock for
extra
weight

wire to hold branch

Ground layering

are no air spaces that will dry out roots as they emerge.
4) Keep the cuttings out of direct sunlight and keep the soil moist.
5) Make sure roots are well established before transplanting. Plants should root by the time winter begins.
6) Protect the new plants from extreme cold for the first winter. Plants in pots should be kept in a cold but frost-free location.

Plants for Semi-Ripe Cuttings
Butterfly bush
Cotoneaster
Dawn redwood
Deutzia
False cypress
Forsythia
Honeysuckle
Hydrangea
Katsura-tree
Kerria
Ninebark
Potentilla
Willow

GROUND LAYERING
Layering, and ground layering in particular, is the easiest propagation method and the one most likely to produce successful results. Layering allows future cuttings to form their own roots before being detached from the parent plant. In ground layering, a section of a flexible branch is buried until it produces roots. The method is quite simple.

1) Choose a branch or shoot growing low enough on the plant to reach the ground. Remove the leaves from the section of at least four nodes that will be underground. At least another four should protrude above ground at the new growth end.
2) Twist the leafless section of the branch, or make a small cut on the underside near a leaf node. This damage will stimulate root growth. A toothpick or small pebble can be used to hold the cut open.

Smokebush (above)

Euonymus (center), viburnum (below)

3) Bend the branch down to see where it will touch the ground, and dig a shallow trench about 4" deep in this position. The end of the trench nearest the shrub can slope gradually upwards, but the end where the branch tip will be should be vertical in order to force the tip up.

4) Use a peg or bent wire to hold the branch in place. Fill the soil back into the trench, and water well. A rock or brick on top of the soil will help to keep the branch in place.

5) Keep the soil moist but not soggy. Roots may take a year or more to develop. Once roots are well established, the new plant can be severed from the parent and planted in a permanent location.

The best shrubs for layering have low, flexible branches. Spring and fall are the best times to start the layer, and many species respond better in one season or the other. Some, such as rhododendron, respond equally well in spring and fall.

Plants to Layer in Spring
Chokeberry
Dogwood
Lilac
Magnolia
Smokebush
Virginia creeper
Witchhazel

Plants to Layer in Fall
Arborvitae
Euonymus
Filbert
Forsythia
Fothergilla
Honeysuckle
Viburnum

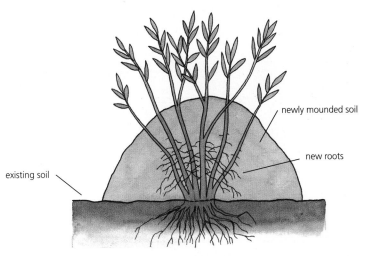

newly mounded soil

new roots

existing soil

Mound layering

MOUND LAYERING

Mound layering is a simple way to propagate low, shrubby plants. With this technique, the shrub is partially buried in a mound of well-drained soil mix. The buried stems will then sprout roots along their lengths. This method can provide many new plants with little effort.

Mound layering should be initiated in spring, once new shoots begin to grow. Make a mound from a mixture of sand, peat moss and soil over half or more of the plant. Leave the branch tips exposed. More soil can be mounded up over the course of the summer. Keep the mound moist but not soggy.

At the end of the summer (or in the following season, for large plants), gently wash the mound away and detach the rooted branches. Plant them out either directly where you want them or in a protected, temporary spot if you want to shelter them for the first winter.

Plants to Mound Layer

Cotoneaster
Dogwood
Euonymus
Forsythia
Lilac
Potentilla

Lilac

Problems & Pests

We take the trees of our landscape for granted because they seem so permanent. Yet in the natural world, change is constant, even for woody plants. Our native American chestnut *(Castanea dentata)*, once a dominant forest tree, was almost entirely wiped out by disease. Similarly, Dutch elm disease has taken a toll on the American elm, although disease-resistant cultivars, many bred by Dr. George Ware at the Morton Arboretum, are now becoming common. Many of them are cataloged in this volume.

The global community brings problems to local tree populations. An example in recent years is the Asian long-horned beetle. This large insect decimated huge numbers of trees in just a few years in areas of Chicago and surrounding suburbs. The spread of this pest to a wider area was feared, and extensive efforts were mounted to control it. These efforts appear successful for now, but as trade continues with China and Korea, there is always the opportunity for accidental importation of more of these beetles in shipping crates.

Illinois was initially spared the scourge of the gypsy moth that denuded the foliage in entire forests along the northeastern United States. It has now spread to Illinois, a result of our movable society—people unwittingly brought gypsy moth egg masses with them when they moved here, relocating the dormant eggs and allowing these pests a new home.

In gardens, tree and shrub plantings can be both assets and liabilities when it comes to pests and diseases. Many insects and diseases attack only one plant species. Mixed plantings can make it difficult for pests and diseases to find their preferred hosts and establish a population. At the same time, because woody plants are in the same spot for many years, any problems can become permanent. The advantage is that beneficial birds, insects and other pest-devouring organisms can also develop permanent populations.

For many years pest control meant spraying or dusting, with the goal to eliminate every pest in the landscape. A more moderate approach advocated today is known as IPM (Integrated Pest Management or Integrated Plant Management). For an interesting overview of IPM, consult the University of Illinois Extension website at <www.ipm.uiuc.edu/ipm/index.html>.

The goal of IPM is to reduce pest problems to levels at which only negligible damage is done. You must determine what degree of damage is acceptable to you. Consider whether a pest's damage is localized or covers the entire plant. Will the damage being done kill the plant or is it affecting only the outward appearance? Are there methods of controlling the pest without chemicals?

IPM is an interactive system in which observation, identification and assessment are the primary tools. Observing your plants on a regular basis will allow you to assess the severity of any infestation. It will also allow you to catch problems early, when they are easier to control with minimal effort. But seeing an insect does not mean you have a problem. Most insects do no harm at all, and many are beneficial

'Morton' elm has excellent disease resistance.

to your garden as pollinators or predators. Take immediate action against the well-known garden pests you are already familiar with, but wait until you have identified any other insects as harmful before attempting to control them. You may find that an insect you are concerned about is actually eating the ones you don't want.

Chemicals should always be the last resort. They can endanger gardeners and their families and pets, and they kill as many good organisms as bad ones, leaving the whole garden vulnerable to even worse attacks.

A good IPM program includes learning about the following aspects of your plants: the conditions they need for healthy growth; what pests might affect your particular plants; where and when to look for those pests; and how and when to best control them. Keep records of pest damage because such observations frequently reveal patterns useful in

Frogs eat many insect pests.

competing for light, nutrients and space. Remove plants that are decimated by the same pests every year. Dispose of diseased foliage and branches by burning the material or by taking it to a permitted dump site. Prevent the spread of disease by keeping your gardening tools clean and by tidying up dead plant matter at the end of every growing season.

Physical controls are generally used to combat insect and mammal problems. An example of such a control is picking insects off shrubs by hand, which is not a daunting task if you catch the problem when it is just beginning. Simply drop the offenders into a bucket of soapy water kept around for that purpose (soap prevents them from floating and climbing out and may suffocate them).

Other physical controls for insects and mammals include traps, barriers, scarecrows and natural repellents that make a plant taste or smell bad to pests. Garden centers offer a wide array of such devices. Physical control of diseases usually involves removing the infected plant or parts of the plant in order to keep the problem from spreading.

Biological controls make use of predators that like to eat pests. Animals such as birds, snakes, frogs, spiders, ladybird beetles, bats and certain bacteria can play an important role in keeping pest populations manageable. Encourage these creatures to take up permanent residence in your garden. A birdbath and birdfeeder will encourage birds to enjoy your yard and feed on a wide variety of insect pests. Beneficial insects most likely already live

spotting recurring problems and in planning a maintenance regime. Most problems strike at about the same time each year.

There are four steps in effective and responsible pest management. Cultural controls are the most important. Physical controls should be attempted next, followed by biological controls. Resort to chemical controls only when the first three possibilities have been exhausted.

Cultural controls are the gardening techniques you use in the day-to-day care of your garden. Perhaps the best defense against pests and diseases is to grow your woody plants in the conditions for which they are adapted. It is also very important to keep your soil healthy, with plenty of organic matter added.

Other cultural controls are equally straightforward. Choose resistant varieties of trees and shrubs that are not prone to problems. Space your plants so they have good air circulation in and around them and are not stressed from

in your landscape, and you can encourage them to stay by planting appropriate alternate food sources. Many beneficial insects eat nectar from plants such as yarrow and daisies. In many cases it is the young and not the adult insects that are predatory.

Another form of biological control is the naturally occurring soil bacterium *Bacillus thuringiensis* var. *kurstaki,* or *B.t.* for short, which breaks down the gut lining of some insect pests. It is commonly available in garden centers.

Sticky trap, a physical control

Chemical controls should rarely be necessary, but if you must use them, many low-toxicity and organic options are available. Organic sprays are no less dangerous than synthetic ones, but they break down more readily into harmless compounds. The main drawback to using any chemical is that it may also kill the beneficial insects you have been trying to attract.

Organic chemicals are available at most garden centers, and you should follow the manufacturer's instructions very carefully. A larger amount or concentration of the insecticide is not any more effective in controlling insect pests than the recommended dosage. Always practice target application, or 'spot spraying'; very rarely does the whole area or even the whole plant need to be sprayed.

Note that if a particular pest is not listed on the package, it will probably not be controlled by that product. It is also important to find out at what stage in an insect's life cycle you will get the best control. Some can be controlled only at particular stages. Accurate and early identification of pests is vital for finding a quick solution.

Consumers are demanding effective pest-control products that do not harm the environment, and less toxic, more precisely targeted pesticides are becoming available. Alternatives to commercial chemical pesticides are also available or can be made easily at home. Horticultural oils and insecticidal soaps, for example (see p. 73), are effective and safer to use for pest control.

Cultural, physical, biological and chemical controls are all possible defenses against insect pests. Many diseases, however, can be dealt with only culturally. It is most often weakened plants that succumb to diseases, although some diseases can infect plants regardless of their level of health. Some diseases, such as powdery mildew, are largely a cosmetic concern, but they may weaken a plant enough to make it susceptible to other pests and diseases. Prevention is often the only hope. Once a plant has been infected, it should generally be destroyed in order to prevent the disease from spreading.

GLOSSARY OF PESTS & DISEASES

Anthracnose

Fungus. Yellow or brown spots on leaves; sunken lesions and blisters on stems; can kill plant.

What to Do. Choose resistant varieties and cultivars; keep soil well drained; thin out stems to improve air circulation; avoid handling wet foliage. Remove and destroy infected plant parts; clean up and destroy debris from infected plants at end of growing season. Applying liquid copper can minimize damage.

Aphids

Tiny, pear-shaped insects, wingless or winged; can be green, black, brown, red or gray. Cluster along stems, on buds and on leaves. Example: woolly adelgids. Suck sap and cause distorted or stunted growth. Sticky honeydew forms on surfaces, encouraging sooty mold.

What to Do. Squish small colonies by hand; dislodge with brisk water spray from hose. Predatory insects and birds feed on aphids. Spray serious infestations with insecticidal soap (see p. 73) or neem oil according to directions.

Beetles

Many types and sizes; usually rounded in shape with hard, shell-like outer wings over membranous inner wings. Some are beneficial; e.g., ladybird beetles ('ladybugs'). Others are not; e.g., Japanese beetles, leaf skeletonizers, bark beetles, weevils. Larvae: see Borers, Grubs. Leave wide range of chewing damage: make small or large holes in or around margins of leaves; consume entire leaves or areas between leaf veins ('skeletonize'); may also chew holes in flowers and eat through root bark. Some bark beetles carry deadly plant diseases.

What to Do. For shrubs, pick beetles off at night and drop them in soapy water; spread an old sheet under small trees and shrubs and shake off beetles to collect and dispose of them; use a broom to reach tall branches. The Hot Pepper Wax brand of insect repellent discourages beetles and may also repel rabbits and deer.

Blight

Fungal or bacterial diseases, many types; e.g., leaf blight, needle blight, petal blight, snow blight, twig blight. Leaves, stems and flowers blacken, rot, die. See also Fire Blight, Gray Mold.

What to Do. Thin out stems to improve air circulation; keep mulch away from base of plants; remove debris from garden at end of season. Remove and destroy infected plant parts. Sterilize equipment after each cut to avoid reinfecting plant and spreading fungus.

Borers

Larvae of some moths, wasps and beetles; among the most damaging of plant pests. Burrow into plant stems, leaves or roots, destroying

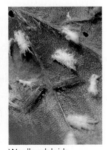

Green aphids   Woolly adelgids

conducting tissue and structural strength. Worm-like; vary in size and get bigger as they bore under bark and sometimes into heartwood. Tunnels left by borers create sites for infection and decomposition to begin; some borers carry infection.

What to Do. Site tree or shrub properly and keep as healthy as possible with proper fertilizing and watering. May be able to squish borers within leaves. Remove and destroy bored parts; may need to remove entire plant.

Bugs (True Bugs)
Small insects up to $1/2$" long; green, brown, black or brightly colored and patterned. Many beneficial; a few pests, such as lace bugs, pierce plants to suck out sap. Toxins may be injected that deform plants; sunken areas left where tissue pierced; leaves rip as they grow; leaves, buds and new growth may be dwarfed and deformed.

What to Do. Remove debris and weeds from around plants in fall to destroy overwintering sites. Spray plants with insecticidal soap (see p. 73) or neem oil according to directions.

Canker
Swollen or sunken lesions on stems or branches, surrounded by living tissue. Caused by many different bacterial and fungal diseases. Most canker-causing diseases enter through wounded wood. Woodpeckers may unwittingly infect plants when they drill for insects.

What to Do. Maintain vigor of plants; avoid wounding or injuring trees (e.g., string trimmer damage), especially in spring when canker-causing organisms most active;

Caterpillar on hawthorn   Japanese beetle

control borers and other bark-dwelling insects. Prune out and destroy infected material. Sterilize pruning tools before, during and after use on infected plants.

Case Bearers
see Caterpillars

Caterpillars
Larvae of butterflies, moths, sawflies. Include bagworms, budworms, case bearers, cutworms, leaf rollers, leaf tiers, loopers, webworms. Chew foliage and buds. Can completely defoliate a plant if infestation severe.

What to Do. Removal from plant is best control. Use high-pressure water and soap or pick caterpillars off by hand if plant is small enough. Cut off and burn large tents or webs of larvae. Control biologically using *B.t.* (see p. 65). Apply horticultural oil in spring. Wrap or band tree trunks to prevent caterpillars from climbing tree to access leaves.

Dieback
Plant slowly wilts, browns and dies, starting at branch tips. Can be caused by wide range of disease organisms, cultural problems and nutrient deficiencies.

What to Do. Keep plants healthy by providing them optimal growing

Fuzzy oak galls   Leaf miner damage

conditions. Cut off dead tips below dead sections.

Fire Blight

Highly destructive bacterial disease of the rose family, which includes crabapple, cherry, pear, cotoneaster, hawthorn and serviceberry. Infected areas appear to have been burned. Look for bent twig tips (resembling shepherd's hooks), branches that retain leaves over winter and cankers on lower parts of plant. Disease usually starts at young tips and kills its way down stems.

What to Do. Choose resistant plant varieties. Remove and burn infected parts, making cuts at least 24" below infected areas. Sterilize tools after each cut on infected plant. Reinfection is possible because fire blight is often carried by pollinating birds and insects and enters plant through flowers. If whole plant is infected it must be removed and burned.

Galls

Unusual swellings of plant tissues caused by insects or diseases. Can affect leaves, buds, stems, flowers, fruit or trunks. Often a specific gall affects a single genus or species.

What to Do. Cut galls out of plant and destroy them. Galls caused by insects usually contain the insect's eggs and juvenile forms. Prevent these galls by controlling insect before it lays eggs; otherwise, try to remove and destroy infected tissue before young insects emerge. Generally insect galls more unsightly than damaging to plant. Galls caused by diseases often require destruction of plant. Avoid placing other plants susceptible to same disease in that location.

Gray Mold (Botrytis Blight)

Fungal disease. Gray fuzz coats affected surfaces. Leaves, flowers or fruit may blacken, rot and die. Common on dead plant matter and on damaged or stressed plants in cool, damp, poorly ventilated areas.

What to Do. Thin stems for better air circulation; keep mulch away from base of plant, particularly in spring when plant starts to sprout; remove debris from garden at end of growing season; do not overwater. Remove and destroy infected plant parts.

Grubs

Larvae of different beetles, commonly found below soil level; usually curled in C shape. Body white or gray; head may be white, gray, brown or reddish. Problematic in lawns; may feed on roots of shallow-rooted trees and shrubs. Plant wilts despite regular watering; may pull easily out of ground in severe cases.

What to Do. Throw any grubs found while digging onto a stone path or patio for birds to devour; apply parasitic nematodes or milky disease spore to infested soil (ask at your local garden center).

Leafhoppers & Treehoppers

Small, wedge-shaped insects; can be green, brown, gray, multi-colored. Jump around frantically when disturbed. Suck juice from plant leaves and cause distorted growth. Carry diseases such as aster yellows. Treehoppers also damage bark when they slit it to lay eggs. **What to Do.** Encourage predators by growing nectar-rich species such as yarrow. Wash insects off with strong spray of water; spray insecticidal soap (see p. 73) or neem oil according to directions.

Leaf Miners

Tiny, stubby larvae of some butterflies and moths; may be yellow or green. Tunnel within foliage leaving winding trails; tunneled areas lighter in color than rest of leaf. Unsightly rather than health risk to plant. **What to Do.** Remove debris from area in fall to destroy overwintering sites; attract parasitic wasps with nectar plants such as yarrow. Remove and destroy infected foliage.

Leaf Rollers

see Caterpillars

Leaf Scorch

Yellowing or browning of leaves beginning at tips or edges. Most often caused by drought or heat stress but can also be caused by bacteria. **What to Do.** Water susceptible plants during droughts, and avoid siting them where excessive heat reflects from pavement or buildings. For bacterial leaf scorch, remove plant and don't replace with susceptible species. To help prevent or ameliorate bacterial leaf scorch: control the insect carriers (leafhoppers and spittlebugs) of scorch bacteria; prune out scorched shoots as soon as symptoms appear; inject bactericide into the trunk of lightly damaged specimens; fertilize and irrigate as appropriate.

Leaf Spot

Two common types. *Bacterial:* small brown or purple speckles grow to encompass entire leaves; leaves may drop. *Fungal:* black, brown or yellow spots develop; leaves wither; e.g., scab, tar spot. **What to Do.** Bacterial infection more severe; must remove entire plant. For fungal infection, remove and destroy infected plant parts. Sterilize removal tools; avoid wetting foliage or touching it when wet; remove and destroy debris at end of growing season. Spray compost tea (see p. 73) on leaves.

Mealybugs

Tiny crawling insects related to aphids; appear covered with white fuzz or flour. Sucking damage stunts and stresses plant. Mealybugs excrete honeydew that promotes sooty mold. **What to Do.** Remove by hand on smaller plants; wash plants with soap and water; wipe with alcohol-soaked swabs; remove heavily infested leaves; encourage or introduce natural predators such as mealybug destroyer beetle and parasitic wasps; spray with insecticidal soap (see p. 73) or horticultural oil. Keep in mind larvae of mealybug destroyer beetles look like very large mealybugs.

Mildew

Two types, both caused by fungus, but with slightly different symptoms. *Downy mildew:* yellow spots on upper sides of leaves and downy fuzz on undersides; fuzz may be yellow, white or gray. *Powdery mildew:* leaf surfaces have white or gray powdery coating that doesn't brush off.

What to Do. Choose resistant cultivars; space plants well; thin stems to encourage air circulation; tidy any debris in fall. Remove and destroy infected leaves or other parts. For powdery mildew, spray foliage with compost tea (see p. 73) or very dilute fish emulsion (1 tsp. per qt. of water). For downy mildew, spray foliage with mixture of 5 tbsp. horticultural oil, 2 tsp. baking soda and 1 gal. water. Apply once a week for three weeks.

Mites

Tiny, eight-legged relatives of spiders; do not eat insects, but may spin webs. Almost invisible to naked eye; red, yellow or green; usually found on undersides of plant leaves. Examples: bud mites, spider mites, spruce mites. Suck juice out of leaves. May see fine webbing on leaves and stems; may see mites moving on leaf undersides. Leaves become discolored, speckled; then turn brown and shrivel up.

What to Do. Wash off with strong spray of water daily until all signs of infestation are gone; introduce predatory mites available through garden centers. Spray plants with insecticidal soap (see p. 73), or spray horticultural oil at a rate of 5 tbsp. to 1 gal. of water. Another application may be needed after a month.

Mosaic

see Viruses

Needle Cast

Fungal disease causing premature needle drop. Spotty yellow areas turn brown; infected needles drop up to a year later.

What to Do. Ensure good air circulation. Clean up and destroy fallen needles. Prune off damaged growth. To prevent recurrence the following year, treat plants twice with bordeaux mix (available at garden centers), two weeks apart, as candles elongate the next spring.

Nematodes

Tiny, translucent worms; some, such as predatory and decomposer nematodes, are beneficial. Pest nematodes give plants disease symptoms. Different nematodes infect foliage, stems and roots. *Foliar and stem:* yellow spots that turn brown on leaves; leaves shrivel and wither; lesions appear on stems; problem starts low on plant and works upward. *Root-knot:* plant is stunted; may wilt; yellow spots on leaves; roots have tiny bumps or knots.

What to Do. Mulch soil, mix in organic matter, clear garden debris in fall. Avoid wetting the leaves, and don't touch wet foliage of infected

Powdery mildew   Skeletonizer damage

plants. Can add parasitic nematodes to soil. Remove infected plants in extreme cases.

Psyllids
Plant lice; treat as for aphids (see Aphids).

Rot
Several different fungi and bacteria that cause decay of different plant parts and can kill plant. *Crown rot:* affects base of plant; stems blacken and fall over; leaves yellow and wilt. *Heart rot (wood rot):* decay of a tree's heartwood; damage often evident only after high winds cause branches or whole tree to come down. *Root rot:* leaves yellow and plant wilts; digging up plant shows roots rotted away.

What to Do. Keep soil well drained; don't damage plant if you are digging or working around it; keep mulches away from plant base. Destroy infected plant if whole plant affected. Replant area with only rot-resistant species or cultivars, not the same species that died.

Rust
Fungi. Pale spots on upper leaf surfaces; orange, fuzzy or dusty spots on leaf undersides. Examples: blister rust, cedar-apple rust, cone rust.

What to Do. Choose varieties and cultivars resistant to rust; avoid handling wet leaves; provide plant with good air circulation; clear up garden debris at end of season. Remove and destroy infected plant parts. A late-winter application of lime-sulfur can delay infection the following year.

Sawflies
see Caterpillars

Slug

Scab
see Leaf Spot

Scale Insects (Scale)
Tiny, shelled insects that suck sap, weakening and possibly killing plant or making it vulnerable to other problems. Once female scale insect has pierced plant with mouthpart, it is there for life. Juvenile scale insects are called crawlers.

What to Do. Wipe plant with alcohol-soaked swabs; spray with water to dislodge crawlers; prune out heavily infested branches; encourage natural predators and parasites; spray dormant oil in spring before bud break.

Skeletonizers
see Beetles

Slugs & Snails
Both are mollusks; slugs lack shells whereas snails have spiral shells. Slimy, smooth skin; can be up to 8" long, though many are smaller; gray, green, black, beige, yellow or spotted. Leave large, ragged holes in foliage and silvery slime trails on and around plants.

What to Do. Attach strips of copper to wood around raised beds or to smaller boards inserted around susceptible plants; slugs and snails

Mosaic virus

get shocked if they touch copper surfaces. Pick off by hand in the evening and squish with boot or drop in soapy water. Spread wood ash or diatomaceous earth (available in garden centers) around plants; it will pierce mollusks' soft bodies and cause them to dehydrate. *Do not* use diatomaceous earth intended for swimming pool filters. Lay damp cardboard on the ground in the evening, then dispose of it and the resting slugs the next morning. Beer in a shallow dish may be effective. Slug baits containing iron phosphate are not harmful to humans or animals and control slugs when used according to directions. If slugs damaged garden late in season, begin controls in spring as soon as green shoots appear.

Sooty Mold
Fungus. Thin black film forms on leaf surfaces and reduces amount of light getting to leaves.

What to Do. Wipe mold off leaf surfaces; control aphids, mealybugs, whiteflies (honeydew they deposit on leaves encourages sooty mold).

Tar Spot
see Leaf Spot

Thrips
Tiny, slender insects with narrow, fringed wings; yellow, black or brown. Difficult to see; may be visible if you disturb them by blowing gently on an infested flower. Thrips suck juice out of plant cells, particularly in flowers and buds, resulting in mottled petals and leaves, dying buds and distorted and stunted growth.

What to Do. Remove and destroy infected plant parts; encourage native predatory insects with nectar plants such as yarrow; spray severe infestations with insecticidal soap (see p. 73) or neem oil according to directions. Use blue sticky cards to prevent recurrence. Horticultural oil controls adult thrips.

Viruses
Plant may be stunted and leaves and flowers distorted, streaked or discolored. Examples: mosaic virus, ringspot virus.

What to Do. Viral diseases in plants cannot be treated. Control disease-spreading insects, such as aphids, leafhoppers and whiteflies. Destroy infected plants.

Weevils
see Beetles

Whiteflies
Tiny flying insects that flutter up into the air when plant is disturbed. Moth-like, white; live on undersides of leaves. Suck juice out of leaves, causing yellowed foliage and weakened plants; leave behind sticky honeydew on foliage, encouraging sooty mold.

What to Do. Destroy weeds that may be home to insects. Attract native predatory beetles and parasitic wasps with nectar plants such as yarrow and sweet alyssum; spray severe cases with insecticidal soap (see below). Can make a sticky flypaper-like trap by mounting tin can on stake; wrap can with yellow paper and cover with clear sandwich bag smeared with petroleum jelly; replace bag when full of flies. Apply horticultural oil.

Wilt

If watering hasn't helped a wilted plant, a wilt fungus may be at fault. *Fusarium wilt:* plant wilts, leaves turn yellow then die; symptoms often appear first on one part of plant before spreading. *Verticillium wilt:* plant wilts; leaves curl up at edges, turn yellow then drop or may stay on plant; plant may die. **What to Do.** Both wilts difficult to control. Choose resistant varieties; clean up debris at end of growing season. Destroy infected plants; solarize (sterilize) soil before replanting (this may help if you've lost an entire bed of plants to these fungi)—contact local garden center for assistance. Do not replant same or other susceptible species.

Witches'-Broom

Twigs become densely clustered together, resembling a broom. Can develop on many types of plants and can be caused by various microorganisms or insects. Witches'-brooms caused by fungi can afflict cherry *(Prunus)* and blackberry *(Rubus)*. The organisms that cause elm or ash yellows can also cause this symptom. Honeysuckle witches'-broom is caused by an aphid. Black locust witches'-broom is caused by a virus. Many of the twigs in a broom will die back in winter. **What to Do.** Cut out the affected portions. Determine the cause and try to provide better growing conditions for the plant.

Woolly Adelgids

see Aphids

Worms

see Caterpillars, Nematodes

PEST CONTROL RECIPES

Compost 'Tea'

Mix 1–2 lb. compost in 5 gal. of water. Let sit four to seven days, then strain off liquid and add remaining solids back to compost. Store liquid out of direct sunlight. For use, dilute until it resembles weak tea. Use during normal watering or apply as a foliar spray to prevent or treat fungal diseases.

Horticultural Oil

Mix 5 tbsp. horticultural oil per 1 gal. water and apply as a spray for a variety of insect and fungal problems. If purchased, follow package directions.

Insecticidal Soap

Mix 1 tsp. mild, fragrance- and color-free dish detergent (preferably biodegradable) with 1 qt. water in a clean spray bottle. Spray surfaces of insect-infested plants, and rinse well within an hour to avoid foliage discoloration.

About This Guide

The trees and shrubs in this book are organized alphabetically by common name. Alternative common names and scientific names are given beneath the main headings and in the index. The illustrated Trees & Shrubs at a Glance (pp. 5–9) allows you to become familiar with the different plants quickly, and it will help you find a tree or shrub if you aren't sure what it's called.

Clearly displayed at the beginning of each entry are the special features of the woody plant, height and spread ranges, preferred planting forms (bare-root, balled-and-burlapped or container), optimal planting seasons and plant hardiness zones (see map, p. 15).

Our favorite species, hybrids and cultivars are listed in each entry's Recommended section. Many more types are often available, so check with your local garden center. Some cultivated varieties are known by only the cultivar name proper, shown in single quotation marks (e.g., 'Little Gem'); others are known instead or also by a trade name registered by a particular company. Trade names are shown in small capitals (e.g., AUTUMN PURPLE). For all plants, we present the most commonly used name first, with any alternative names following in parentheses.

Where height, spread and hardiness zones are not indicated in the Recommended section, refer to the information under the main heading. The ranges at the beginning of each entry always encompass the measurements for all plants listed in the Recommended section.

Common pests and problems, if any, are also noted for each entry in the book. Consult the Problems & Pests section of the introduction (pp. 62–73) for information on how to address these problems.

The Quick Reference Chart at the back of the book (pp. 334–39) is a handy guide to planning a diversity of features, forms, foliage types and blooming times in your garden.

We refer to seasons only in a general sense. Keep in mind the timing and duration of seasons in your particular area when planning your garden. Hardiness zones, too, can vary locally; consult your local extension agent, horticulturist or garden center.

The Trees
& Shrubs

American Yellowwood

Yellowwood

Cladrastis

Features: summer and fall foliage, spring flowers, bark, habit **Habit:** rounded, low-branching, deciduous tree **Height:** 30–50' **Spread:** 30–55' **Planting:** B & B; spring **Zones:** 4–8

NAMED FOR THE YELLOW WOOD IT PRODUCES, THIS NATIVE TREE of extreme southern Illinois matures into a broad, domed shape. Its low-branching pattern partially cloaks the handsome smooth, gray bark. Because of its spread, American yellowwood is most often seen on large properties or in park settings. The fragrant white flowers, borne in clusters up to 15" long, appear in June of every other year. The flowers are followed by broad seed-pods that are shed during the winter.

Growing

American yellowwood grows best in **full sun**. The soil should be **fertile, moist** and **well drained**. Alkaline soil is preferable, but yellowwood adapts well to acidic soil. It will also tolerate clay. Plant trees when they are young and don't move them because they resent having their roots disturbed.

Remove dead, diseased, damaged or awkward growth in summer. The sap tends to run profusely if yellowwood is pruned in winter or spring. This tree will need care as it matures—the appearance can be compromised if it is not pruned properly.

Tips

American yellowwood is best used in a large setting such as a park, or as a specimen in a large garden. Do not plant it close to houses or other buildings because the wood can break in a strong wind.

The bean-like seedpods and the seeds they contain are not edible.

Recommended

C. kentukea (C. lutea) is an attractive, wide-spreading tree with bright yellowish green leaves that turn bright yellow in fall. The bark is smooth and gray, much like beech bark. This tree blooms in late spring and early summer of alternating years. It may take a few years after planting for the tree to mature enough to begin blooming.

American yellowwood is rarely afflicted by pest or disease problems.

Like many other members of the pea family, this tree has roots that fix nitrogen in the surrounding soil.

Arborvitae
Cedar
Thuja

Features: foliage, bark, form **Habit:** small to large, evergreen shrub or tree
Height: 18"–50' **Spread:** 18"–12' **Planting:** B & B, container; spring or fall
Zones: 2–9

AS A NEW HOMEOWNER, I WAS INTRIGUED BY AN EVERGREEN
shrub that did not have sharp needles and seemed to have a self-maintained,
rounded shape—a globe arborvitae. Our next home needed a screening
device, and 'Techny' arborvitae was recommended—upright in shape, dense,
not overly tall, again soft-needled. Many years have gone by and the trio I'd
planted still does its job. Now to remember to keep heavy snows off—I'm
still nursing a main trunk that was bent down a winter or so ago.

Growing

Arborvitae prefer **full sun**. The soil should be of **average fertility, moist** and **well drained**. These plants enjoy humidity and are often found growing near marshy areas. *T. orientalis*, however, requires good drainage. Arborvitae will perform best in a location with some **shelter** from the wind, especially in winter, when the foliage can easily dry out and give the entire plant a rather brown, drab appearance.

These plants take very well to pruning and are often grown as hedges. Though they may be kept formally shaped, they are also attractive if just clipped to maintain a loose but compact shape and size.

Tips

Large varieties of arborvitae make excellent specimen trees, and smaller cultivars can be used in foundation plantings, shrub borders and formal or informal hedges.

Deer enjoy eating the foliage of eastern arborvitae. If deer are a problem in your area, you may wish to avoid using this plant. Alternatively, consider using western arborvitae, which is relatively resistant to deer browsing.

Recommended

T. occidentalis (eastern arborvitae, American arborvitae) is native to much of the Midwest and northeastern U.S. In the wild this tree can grow to about 60' tall and 10–15' wide. In cultivation it grows about half this size or smaller. '**Danica**' is a dwarf globe form growing up to about 18" tall and wide. It features emerald

T. plicata SPRING GROVE

Crush some foliage between your fingers to enjoy the wonderful aroma. Be cautious, though, if you have sensitive skin; the pungent oils may irritate.

T. occidentalis 'Rheingold'

green foliage. **'Emerald'** ('Smaragd') can grow 10–15' tall, spreading about 4'. This cultivar is small and very cold hardy; the foliage does not lose color in winter. **'Holmstrup'** is small and upright, with whorls of tightly compact foliage. It grows 6–10' tall and 24–36" wide. **'Little Gem'** is a globe-shaped dwarf with dark green foliage. It grows 36" tall and 4–6' wide. **'Nigra'** ('Nigra Dark Green') has a neat pyramidal habit and keeps its dark green foliage color in winter. It grows 20–30' tall and 8' wide. **'Rheingold'** has bright golden yellow foliage that turns coppery gold in winter. It grows to about 6' tall and 5' wide and is popular for hedges. **'Techny'** is a very hardy cultivar with a broad pyramidal form. It grows 10–20' tall and 5–8' wide and keeps its bluish green color all winter. (Zones 2–7; cultivars may be less cold hardy)

T. occidentalis 'Little Gem' (above), 'Nigra' (below)

T. orientalis (*Platycladus orientalis*; oriental arborvitae) can grow as high as 50' but usually grows 15–25' high in the garden, with a spread of 8–12'. Many cultivars are available, including **'Aurea Nana'** (Berkman's golden arborvitae), a popular dwarf cultivar. It grows up to 5' tall and 3–5' wide. The new foliage emerges a golden color that fades to yellow-green as it matures. (Zones 5–9)

T. plicata (western arborvitae, western redcedar) can grow up to 200' tall in its native Pacific Northwest but usually stays under 50' in Illinois. This narrowly pyramidal evergreen grows quickly and maintains good foliage color all winter. 'Excelsa' grows 6' tall and 6–8' wide, with a loose habit, horizontal branching and dark green foliage. It is deer proof and cold hardy. 'Hillier' has blue-green foliage that turns bronzy in winter. It grows 7–10' tall and wide and tolerates alkaline conditions. SPRING GROVE ('Grovepli') is a very narrow, very hardy cultivar with bright green foliage. It grows about 20' tall and up to 10' wide. 'Virescens' is deer proof. It grows 5–6' tall, spreads 4–5' and has bright green foliage year-round. 'Zebrina' has foliage variegated yellow and green. This pyramidal cultivar can grow more than 30' tall and 12' wide. (Zones 4–7)

Problems & Pests

Bagworm, leaf miners, red spider mites, scale insects, blight, canker and heart rot are possible, though not frequent, problems. Leaf miner damage may resemble winter browning—hold branch tips up to the light and look for tiny caterpillars feeding inside. Trim and destroy infested foliage before June.

T. occidentalis *was grown in Europe as early as 1536. It was named* arborvitae *(Latin for 'tree of life') because a vitamin C–rich tea made from its foliage and bark saved Jacques Cartier's crew from scurvy.*

T. plicata 'Zebrina'

Many diverse arborvitae cultivars are available, from pyramidal forms that make excellent specimens, to yellow types that add color to the winter landscape, to dwarf, globe-shaped forms for the mixed border or rock garden.

T. occidentalis 'Emerald'

Ash

Fraxinus

Features: fall color, adaptability, fast growth **Habit:** upright or spreading, deciduous tree **Height:** 40–80' **Spread:** 25–80' **Planting:** B & B, container, bare-root; spring or fall **Zones:** 3–9

ASHES HAVE BECOME WELL REPRESENTED IN THE URBAN-SUBURBAN landscape. Some have been planted, while others started as property-line survivors and have matured into fine shade-producing specimens. The negatives: fall color is often a timid yellow; ashes are among the earliest trees to shed their foliage; and weak branch crotches sometimes force homeowners to install cables that prevent limbs from breaking free. The pluses, fortunately, are many: adaptability, few pest and disease problems and a good selection of cultivars.

Growing

Ashes grow best in **full sun**. Young plants tolerate partial shade. The soil should be **fertile** and **moist,** with lots of room for root growth. These native trees tolerate drought, poor soil, salt and pollution. White ash is more ornamental but less adaptable than green ash.

Little pruning is required. Remove dead, damaged, diseased and wayward branches as needed.

Tips

Ashes are popular, quick-growing shade trees. They grow well in the moist soil along streams and ponds.

Recommended

F. americana (white ash) is a large, wide-spreading tree. It grows 50–80' tall, with an equal spread. Fall color ranges from yellow to purple. **'Autumn Applause'** is a male (seedless) cultivar growing 40–50' tall and spreading 25–30', with a straight trunk and deep red, maroon or purple fall foliage. **AUTUMN PURPLE** ('Jungiger,' 'Junginger') is a seedless selection growing to 50' tall and 45' wide. It has deep purple fall color. **WINDY CITY** ('Tures') is a Chicagoland Grows selection. It has an upright habit, features fall colors ranging from bronze to burgundy, and resists frost cracking.

F. americana cultivar

F. pennsylvanica (green ash, red ash) is an irregular, spreading tree 50–70' tall and wide. The fall foliage is yellow, sometimes with orange or red. **CIMMARON** ('Cimmzam') is an upright, oval tree 40–60' tall and 30–40' wide. It leafs out later in spring and holds its leaves later in fall than the species. Fall color is burgundy to orange. **'Patmore'** is a disease-resistant, seedless selection with a large oval crown. It grows 45' tall and 35' wide. **SHERWOOD GLEN** is an upright, oval tree reaching a height of 55' and a spread of 30'. **'Summit'** is a neat, upright tree that grows up to 50' tall and 25' wide. Fall color is bright yellow.

Problems & Pests

Possible problems include borers, leaf miners, sawflies, scale insects, webworm, canker, dieback, flower gall, leaf spot, powdery mildew and rust. Plants grown in appropriate conditions generally resist problems.

Emerald ash borer is a serious pest expected to appear in Illinois. Affected trees must be removed. Grow ashes in combination with other woody plants, so that an attack of this pest won't affect the entire planting.

F. pennsylvanica fruit

Bald-Cypress
Taxodium

Features: summer and fall foliage, habit, cones, trunk **Habit:** conical, deciduous, coniferous tree **Height:** 50–75' **Spread:** 15–30' **Planting:** B & B, container; spring or fall **Zones:** 4–9

SEEING THE 'KNEES' OF A BALD-CYPRESS POKING THROUGH THE waterline of a southern swamp is a sight to behold. Equally impressive are the signature plantings at the Chicago Botanic Garden in Glencoe. Designers planted bald-cypress around the entry garden. The twist is that these deciduous trees are sheared yearly to form a loosely formal hedge. This garden is said to be the only place where a pollarding form of pruning has been applied to bald-cypress.

Growing

Bald-cypress grows well in **full sun** or **partial shade**. The soil should preferably be **moist** and **acidic**, but these trees adapt to most soils and conditions. Bald-cypress develops a deep taproot but transplants fairly easily when young. Pruning is rarely required.

Tips

Bald-cypress can be used as a specimen tree or in a group planting. This is a fairly large tree that looks best with plenty of space. It is ideal in a swampy or frequently wet area where few other trees would thrive.

When grown in waterlogged soil or near a water feature, bald-cypress develops gnome-like 'knees' (pneumatophores), which are knobby roots that poke up from the water. These structures are thought to help the roots breathe in wet conditions.

T. distichum (both photos)

To the uninitiated, bald-cypress appears to be an evergreen. Great gasps are often heard when this deciduous conifer turns color in fall and defoliates.

Recommended

T. distichum is a slender, conical tree that becomes irregular and more rounded as it matures. In the wild it may grow over 100' tall, but in gardens it grows 50–70' tall and 15–30' wide. In fall the blue-green foliage turns a rusty orange before falling. The trunk becomes buttressed with age. 'Shawnee Brave' has a narrow, pyramidal habit. It matures to about 75' tall and about 18' in spread.

Problems & Pests

Cypress moth, gall mites and wood rot may cause problems. Highly alkaline soil can cause the foliage to turn yellow (chlorotic).

Barberry

Berberis

Features: foliage, flowers, fruit, spines **Habit:** deciduous shrub **Height:** 18"–6'
Spread: 2–6' **Planting:** container; spring or fall **Zones:** 4–8

BARBERRIES CAN BE HORTICULTURAL DOUBLE-EDGED SWORDS. The prickly stems are a nuisance if a shrub is planted close to a walkway. However, a barberry can be very effective if used as a hedge, discouraging foot (or dog) traffic from cutting through. Barberries add a bold reddish contrast in a shrub border, but it's best to put them in the center of the planting. Effective siting will maximize their visual interest while preventing the decidedly unpleasant experience of walking into them.

Growing

Barberries develop the best fall color when grown in **full sun,** but they tolerate partial shade. Any **well-drained** soil is suitable. These plants tolerate drought and urban conditions but suffer in poorly drained, wet soil.

Barberries take heavy pruning well and make excellent hedges, which should be trimmed after they bloom. A plant in an informal border can be left alone or can be lightly pruned.

Remove old wood and unwanted suckers in mid- to late winter. Remove dead wood in summer.

Tips

Grow barberries as hedges, or include them in shrub and mixed borders. Small cultivars can be grown in rock gardens, in raised beds and along rock walls.

B. thunbergii is being noted as an invasive species in shaded, well-drained natural habitats. Its seeds are typically distributed by birds. The cultivars are less invasive.

Recommended

B. 'Tara' (EMERALD CAROUSEL) is a rounded shrub 6' tall and wide, with arching stems and deep green foliage.

B. thunbergii (Japanese barberry) is a dense shrub that develops a broad, rounded habit. It grows 3–5' tall and spreads 4–6'. The bright green foliage turns variable shades of orange, red or purple in fall. Yellow flowers appear in spring, followed by glossy red fruit. '**Aurea**' (golden barberry) grows to 4' tall and wide. It has bright yellow new growth. '**Concorde**' is a dwarf cultivar with purple foliage. It grows about 24" tall and 36" wide. '**Crimson Pygmy**' ('Atropurpurea Nana') is a dwarf cultivar with reddish purple foliage. It grows 18–24" tall and spreads up to 36". '**Helmond Pillar**' is a narrow, upright form with reddish purple leaves that turn bright red in fall. It grows up to 5' tall and 24" wide. '**Rose Glow**' has purple foliage variegated with white and pink splotches. It grows 5–6' tall and wide or slightly wider.

'Rose Glow'

Problems & Pests

Healthy barberries rarely suffer from problems, but stressed plants can be affected by aphids, scale insects, spider mites, weevils, leaf spot, mosaic, root rot and wilt.

Extracts from the rhizomes of Berberis *have been used to treat rheumatic and other inflammatory disorders as well as the common cold.*

'Crimson Pygmy'

Bearberry
Kinnikinnick
Arctostaphylos

Features: late-spring flowers, fruit, foliage **Habit:** low-growing, mat-forming, evergreen shrub **Height:** 4–6" **Spread:** 8"–4' **Planting:** container; spring or fall **Zones:** 2–7

TOLD TO THINK OF A SHRUBBY GROUNDCOVER SPECIES, MANY OF us would imagine a wintercreeper euonymus or one of the spreading cotoneasters—especially *C. dammeri*, whose common name is bearberry cotoneaster. Bearberry not only offers an alternative, it can stand up to soil conditions where other plants would fail. It prefers sandy, infertile settings. But being a member of the heath family of plants, whose members include blueberries and rhododendrons, it needs the soil to be amended to a neutral to acidic condition.

Growing
Bearberry grows well in **full sun** or **partial shade**. The soil should be of **poor to average fertility, well drained, neutral to acidic** and **moist**. Bearberry will adapt to most Illinois soils. Generally no pruning is required.

Tips

Bearberry can be used as a ground-cover or can be included in a rock garden. Once established, it is a vigorous, wide-spreading grower, but it can be slow to get started. Use mulch to keep the weeds down while the plant is becoming established.

Recommended

A. uva-ursi is a low-growing native shrub that grows 4–6" tall and spreads 8–20". White flowers appear in late spring, followed by berries that ripen to bright red. The cultivars share the white flowers and red fruit but also have leaves that turn bright red in winter. '**Vancouver Jade**' is a low-growing plant with arching stems. It grows 6" high and spreads 18". This cultivar is resistant to the leaf spot that can afflict bearberry. '**Wood's Compact**' spreads about 3–4'.

Problems & Pests

Possible problems include bud and leaf galls as well as fungal diseases of the leaves, stems and fruit.

'Vancouver Jade'

This plant's alternative common name, kinnikinnick, is said to be an Algonquian term meaning 'smoking mixture,' reflecting that traditional use for the leaves.

A. uva-ursi

Beech

Fagus

Features: foliage, bark, habit, fall color **Habit:** large, oval, deciduous shade tree
Height: 30–80' **Spread:** 10–65' **Planting:** B & B, container; spring **Zones:** 4–9

IN THE WORDS OF THE LATE JAMES UNDERWOOD CROCKETT
(host of *Crockett's Victory Garden* and author of a series of books based on
that PBS program), 'If the word noble had to be applied to only one kind of
tree, the honor would probably go to the beech.' Several magnificent species
belong to this genus, but the most impressive specimens are grown in an
expansive setting, such as a park, cemetery or woodland. Most have low-
branching habits that affect what can be grown beneath. Look for the distinctive gray, smooth bark in winter.

Growing

Beeches grow equally well in **full sun** or **partial shade**. The soil should be of **average fertility, loamy** and **well drained,** though almost all well-drained soils are tolerated. American beech suffers in alkaline and poorly drained soils.

American beech doesn't like having its roots disturbed and should be transplanted only when very young. European beech transplants easily and is more tolerant of varied soil conditions than American beech.

Very little pruning is required. Remove dead or damaged branches in spring or at any time after the damage occurs. European beech is a popular hedging species and responds well to severe pruning.

F. grandifolia

Beeches retain their very smooth and elastic bark long into maturity.

F. sylvatica 'Pendula'

F. sylvatica 'Pendula'
F. grandifolia

Tips

Beeches make excellent specimens. They are also used as shade trees and in woodland gardens. These trees need a lot of space, but the European beech's adaptability to pruning makes it a reasonable choice in a small garden.

The nuts are edible when roasted.

Recommended

F. grandifolia (American beech) is a broad-canopied tree that can grow 50–80' tall and often almost as wide. This species is native to Illinois and most of the eastern U.S.

F. sylvatica (European beech) is a spectacular tree that can grow 60' tall and wide or even larger. Too massive for most settings, the species is best kept pruned and used as a hedge in smaller gardens. Several cultivars are small enough to use in the home garden. 'Asplenifolia' (cut-leaf beech, fernleaf beech) has lacier foliage than the species and grows in a pyramidal form to 60' tall and 50–60' wide. 'Fastigiata' ('Dawyck') is a narrow, upright tree. It can grow to 80' but spreads only about 10'. Yellow- or purple-leaved forms are available. 'Pendula' (weeping beech) is a dramatic tree whose pendulous branches reach down to the ground. It varies in form; some can spread

Young lovers' initials carved into a beech may, unfortunately, deface the tree for the remainder of its life—an effect that outlasts many young relationships.

widely, resulting in a cascade effect, while other specimens may be rather upright with branches drooping from the central trunk. This cultivar can grow as tall as the species, but a specimen with the branches drooping from the central trunk may be narrow enough for a home garden. **'Purpurea'** (copper beech) has the same habit as the species but has purple leaves. Weeping purple-leaved forms are also available. **'Purpurea Tricolor'** has striking foliage with pink and white variegation that develops best in partial shade. This rare tree grows slowly, maturing to about 30' tall and wide. It can be grown as a smaller tree if constrained to a large planter.

Problems & Pests

Aphids, borers, scale insects, bark disease, canker, leaf spot and powdery mildew can afflict beech trees. None causes serious problems.

F. sylvatica 'Purpurea Tricolor'

Beech nuts provide food for a wide variety of animals, including squirrels and birds. They were a favorite food of the now-extinct passenger pigeon.

Weeping form of *F. sylvatica* 'Purpurea'

Birch
Betula

Features: foliage, fall color, habit, bark, winter and early-spring catkins **Habit:** open, deciduous tree **Height:** 10–90' **Spread:** 10–60' **Planting:** B & B, container; spring or fall **Zones:** 2–9

MANY GARDENERS ARE IN LOVE with trees that have white bark. Perhaps in our state it has something to do with the many Illinoisans who vacation in the north woods of Wisconsin and Michigan. There, native birches line the creek beds, soaking up moisture and living with minimal heat stress. But consider our climate, and it's no wonder these same trees die a slow, agonizing death on our open lawns during the dog days of summer. Enter Illinoisan Earl Cully, who discovered the HERITAGE ('Cully') river birch. That cultivar has peeling bark on a tan or beige trunk and can tolerate many of the stresses that overcome other birches.

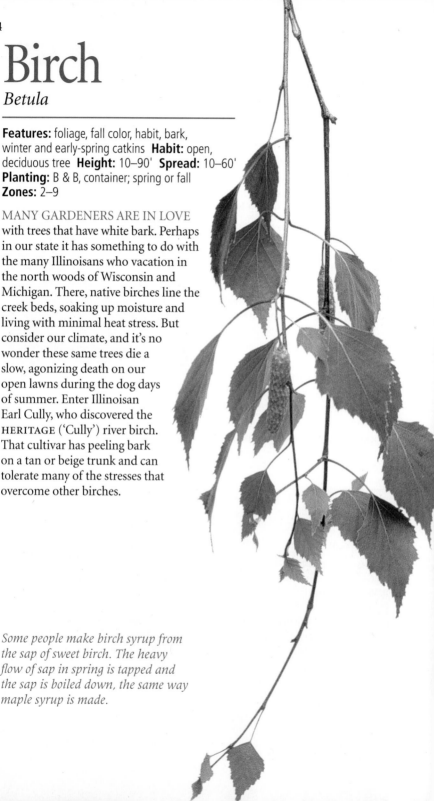

Some people make birch syrup from the sap of sweet birch. The heavy flow of sap in spring is tapped and the sap is boiled down, the same way maple syrup is made.

Growing

Birches grow well in **full sun, partial shade** or **light shade**. The soil should be of **average to rich fertility, moist** and fairly **well drained**. Some birch species naturally grow in wet areas, such as along streams. They don't, however, like to grow in places that remain wet for prolonged periods. Provide supplemental water to all birches during periods of extended drought.

Minimal pruning is required. Remove any dead, damaged, diseased or awkward branches as needed.

Tips

Birch trees are generally grown for their attractive, often white and peeling bark. The bark contrasts nicely with the dark green leaves in summer and with the glossy red or chestnut-colored younger branches and twigs in winter. Yellowish catkins dangle from the branches in early spring.

B. nigra

B. papyrifera

These trees are often used as specimens. With their small leaves and open canopy, birches provide light shade that allows perennials, annuals or lawns to flourish beneath. Birch trees are also attractive when grown in groups near natural or artificial water features. They do need quite a bit of room to grow and are not the best choice in gardens with limited space.

The common and popular European white birch *(B. pendula)* and its weeping cultivars are poor choices for gardens because of their susceptibility to pests and diseases,

B. populifolia 'Whitespire'

B. nigra HERITAGE

particularly the fatal bronze birch borer. If you plan to grow or already have one of these trees, consult a local gardening center or tree specialist to begin a preventive program.

Recommended

B. lenta (sweet birch, cherry birch) has glossy, serrated leaves and brown-black bark. The fall color is a delicate gold. This birch is excellent for naturalizing. It will grow 25–50' tall and 20–45' wide. (Zones 3–7)

B. nigra (river birch, black birch) is native to Illinois. It has shaggy, cinnamon brown bark that flakes off in sheets when it is young but thickens and becomes ridged as it matures. This fast-growing tree attains a height of 60–90' and a spread of 40–60'. The bright green leaves are silvery white on the undersides. *B. nigra* is one of the most disease-resistant species. It also resists bronze birch borer. HERITAGE ('Cully') is a vigorous grower that resists leaf spot and heat stress. It is intolerant of drought conditions and highly alkaline soils. The leaves are larger and glossier than those of the species. The bark begins peeling when the tree is quite young, to show off white or pink areas that mature to salmon brown as the tree ages. 'Little King' (FOX VALLEY) is a dwarf cultivar with a broad, pyramidal habit. In 10 years it will grow to 10–12' tall, with an equal spread. (Zones 3–9)

B. papyrifera (paper birch, canoe birch) is another Illinois native. Its creamy white bark peels off in layers, exposing cinnamon-colored bark beneath. It grows about 70' tall and spreads about 30'. This tree dislikes hot summer weather. (Zones 2–7)

B. populifolia 'Whitespire' (*B. platyphylla* var. *japonica* 'Whitespire') has a distinctive, spire-like habit, with chalky white bark and glossy green leaves that turn yellow in fall. It reaches a mature height of 40–50' and a spread of 15–20'. 'Whitespire' is resistant to bronze birch borer and is only moderately susceptible to leaf miners. Ensure your plant is a cutting or is produced by tissue culture from the original tree. (Zones 4–8)

Problems & Pests

The bronze birch borer is a destructive insect that preys on weakened trees and can kill them quickly. It is most likely to be drawn to white-barked birches. Dieback in the top branches indicates the insects have done their damage. Commercial tree-care companies may be able to stave off the tree's demise but not if wilting is already observed.

Aphids love birch trees. The sticky honeydew aphids secrete may drip off the leaves and onto parked cars, patios or decks. Other potential problems include birch skeletonizer, leaf miners, tent caterpillars and leaf spot.

Birch trees were once a common part of spring fertility rituals in Europe. The maypole, for example, was often a skinned birch.

B. lenta (above)

B. nigra (center), B. papyrifera (below)

Black Locust
False Acacia
Robinia

Features: foliage, flowers, fast growth, spiny branches **Habit:** open, deciduous tree **Height:** 8–90' **Spread:** 10–40' **Planting:** B & B, container; spring or fall **Zones:** 3–8

THIS TREE IS PERHAPS NOT THE BEST CHOICE FOR THE FRONT yard, but if you need a tough customer for a disturbed or recently flooded site, black locust may work. Its dense wood is good for the fireplace. The tree's native range includes southern Illinois. The next time you visit Cantigny Gardens in Wheaton, look for the 'Tortuosa' cultivar, which has interesting contorted branches.

Growing

Black locust prefers **full sun**. It does best in **average to fertile, moist** soil but adapts to any soils that aren't constantly soggy. It tolerates infertile or salty soils, drought and pollution. Avoid growing this tree in exposed locations because heavy wind can cause the weak branches to break.

It is best to train black locust trees when they are young. Prune young trees to have a central leader and well-spaced branches. Remove suckers as well as branches that will form a narrow crotch. Large cuts on *Robinia* species do not heal well and should be avoided. Prune in late summer to avoid excessive bleeding.

Tips

Black locust is best used in difficult situations, where other trees have failed to thrive. It can also be used in shelterbelts and as a firewood source.

All parts of this tree contain poisonous proteins. The bean-like seeds should never be eaten.

Recommended

R. pseudoacacia is an upright, suckering and self-seeding, deciduous tree. It generally grows 30–50' tall and 20–40' wide, but it can reach 90' in open, ideal sites. It has deeply furrowed bark and produces dangling clusters of fragrant white flowers in early summer. **'Frisia'** has golden yellow foliage that turns yellow-green in summer and orange-gold in fall. **TWISTY BABY** ('Lace Lady') is a small, often grafted selection with contorted and twisted branches. It grows 8–10' tall and 10–14' wide and

TWISTY BABY

produces few to no flowers. The twisted branches make a good winter garden feature.

Problems & Pests

Locust borer is the biggest problem for black locust. Occasional problems may also occur with caterpillars, leaf miners, scale insects, twig borers, weevils, whiteflies, canker, leaf spot, powdery mildew, root and heart rot, *Verticillium* wilt and witches'-broom virus.

'Frisia'

Black Tupelo
Blackgum, Sourgum, Pepperidge
Nyssa

Features: habit, summer and fall foliage, bark **Habit:** pyramidal to rounded, decid-uous tree **Height:** 10–50', occasionally more **Spread:** 6–30' **Planting:** B & B, container; spring **Zones:** 4–9

BLACK TUPELO SHINES WITH BRIGHT GREEN FOLIAGE IN SUMMER, giving way to a lovely autumn show in shades of yellow, orange, scarlet and purple. Fall color is fleeting, though, because this tree is quick to drop its leaves once they turn. Somewhat pyramidal in youth, the tree sends out more lateral branches as it matures into a somewhat flattened crown. Black tupelo is a medium-sized native Illinoisan species that can grow in very wet or moderately dry conditions. The mature bark resembles alligator hide.

Growing

Black tupelo grows well in **full sun** or **partial shade**. The soil should be **average to fertile, neutral to acidic** and **well drained**. Provide a location with **shelter** from strong winds. Plant trees when they are young and don't attempt to move them again. They dislike having their roots disturbed and can take a while to get established when they are first planted.

Prune out awkward or damaged growth in fall.

Tips

Black tupelo is a beautiful specimen tree. It can be used as a street tree, but not in polluted situations. Singly or in groups, it is attractive and small enough for a medium-sized property.

Recommended

N. sylvatica is a small to medium-sized, pyramidal to rounded tree. It generally grows 30–50' tall but can reach 100'. It spreads about 20–30'. **'Carolyn'** is a selection from the University of Wisconsin-Madison (Dr. Edward R. Hasselkus, director of the Longnecker Gardens, named it for his granddaughter). It was selected for its hardiness, form and outstanding fall color. It will grow to 10–12' tall and 6–8' wide within 10 years. **RED RAGE** ('Red Fury') has glossy green leaves that turn brilliant red in fall.

Problems & Pests

Occasional problems with caterpillars, leaf miners, scale insects, canker, leaf spot and rot can occur but are rarely serious enough to warrant action.

N. sylvatica cultivar

The fruit attracts birds but is too sour for human tastes.

N. sylvatica

Boxwood
Box
Buxus

Features: foliage, habit **Habit:** dense, rounded, evergreen shrub **Height:** 2–8'
Spread: equal to or slightly greater than height **Planting:** B & B, container; spring
Zones: 4–8

WILLIAM A.P. PULLMAN WAS SUCH A FAN OF BOXWOODS THAT
the selections he made became the original research project of the fledgling
Chicago Botanic Garden in the early 1970s. He wanted a good-looking small
shrub that would not suffer dieback during Chicago-area winters. Boxwoods
define formality in gardens, although the noted horticulturalist Michael A.
Dirr says they are 'too often pruned into a green meatball and allowed to
haunt a foundation planting.' In the right spot, they do anything but haunt
a landscape. They are also immune to deer browsing—a key feature in many
neighborhoods.

Growing

Boxwoods prefer **partial shade** but adapt to full shade or to full sun if kept well watered. The soil should be **fertile** and **well drained**. Once established, boxwoods tolerate drought. *B. sempervirens* has a low tolerance of extremes of heat and cold, so it should be grown in a **sheltered** spot.

A good mulch will benefit these shrubs because their roots grow very close to the surface. For the same reason it is best not to disturb the earth around a boxwood once the shrub is established.

Many formal gardens include boxwoods because they can be pruned to form neat hedges, geometric shapes or fanciful creatures. The dense growth and small leaves form an even green surface, which, along with the slow rate of growth, makes this plant one of the most popular for creating topiary. When left unpruned, a boxwood shrub forms an attractive, rounded mound.

B. microphylla var. *koreana*

The wood of Buxus, *particularly the wood of the root, is very dense and fine-grained, making it valuable for carving. It has been used to make ornate boxes, hence the common name.*

B. sempervirens

'Green Velvet'

Boxwoods will sprout new growth from old wood. A plant that has been neglected or is growing in a lopsided manner can be cut back hard in spring. By the end of summer the exposed areas will have filled in with new green growth.

Tips

These shrubs make excellent background plants in a mixed border. Brightly colored flowers show up well against the even, dark green surface of the boxwood. Dwarf cultivars can be trimmed into small hedges for edging garden beds or walkways. An interesting topiary piece can create a formal or whimsical focal point

in any garden. Larger species and cultivars are often used to form dense evergreen hedges.

Boxwood foliage contains toxic compounds that, when ingested, can cause severe digestive upset.

Recommended

B. microphylla var. *koreana* (Korean littleleaf boxwood) grows to 4' in height and spread. It is cold hardy and quite pest resistant. The foliage tends to lose its green in winter, turning shades of bronze, yellow or brown. (Zones 4–8)

B. sempervirens (common boxwood) is a much larger species, growing to 8' tall and wide. The foliage stays green in winter. Many cultivars are available with interesting features, such as compact or dwarf growth, variegated foliage and pendulous branches. **'Vardar Valley'** is a wide, mounding cultivar, with dark bluish green foliage. It grows to 36" tall and spreads about 5'. It is prone to winter damage in Zone 5. (Zones 5–8)

B. microphylla var. *koreana* with *Thuja* behind

Several cultivars have been developed from crosses between *B. m.* var. *koreana* and *B. sempervirens*. Some of these have inherited the best attributes of each parent—hardiness and pest resistance from one and attractive foliage year-round from the other. **CHICAGOLAND GREEN** ('Glencoe'), a Chicagoland Grows selection, has a neat, rounded habit and grows quickly to a mature height of 3–4' and a spread of 5'. **'Green Gem'** forms a rounded 24" mound. The deep green foliage stays green all winter. **'Green Mountain'** is a large upright shrub with dark green foliage. It grows 5' tall and about 36" wide. **'Green Velvet'** is a hardy cultivar developed in Canada. It has glossy foliage and a rounded habit, growing up to 36" in height and spread. (Zones 4–8)

B. sinica insularis **'Wintergreen'** (*B. microphylla* var. *koreana* 'Winter Green') is a dense, mounding shrub growing 2–4' tall and 3–5' wide. The foliage keeps its light green color through the winter. (Zones 4–8)

B. **'Wilson'** (**NORTHERN CHARM**) is a cold-hardy, compact, oval shrub that reaches $3^1/_2'$ tall and 4' wide. This Chicagoland Grows selection has delicate, semi-glossy, emerald green foliage with a bluish cast. The foliage color holds through the winter. (Zones 4–8)

Problems & Pests
Leaf miners, mites, psyllids, scale insects, leaf spot, powdery mildew and root rot are all possible problems affecting boxwoods.

B. sempervirens

Boxwood hedges were traditionally planted around graves to keep the spirits from wandering.

B. sinica insularis 'Wintergreen'
'Green Velvet'

Butterfly Bush
Summer Lilac
Buddleia (Buddleja)

Features: flowers, habit, foliage **Habit:** large deciduous shrub with arching branches
Height: 3–20' **Spread:** 2–20' **Planting:** container; spring or summer **Zones:** 4–9

IT HARDLY SEEMS FAIR TO CLASSIFY THE BUTTERFLY bushes as shrubs—one can argue they are annuals (often not surviving winter) or herbaceous perennials (dying back to the ground over winter). Yet, if we lose one, we head determinedly to the nursery each spring to get another because of the long, nodding flower stems that give the plant an ethereal feeling as well as providing its namesake function—attracting butterflies. Fragrance is an added bonus. And don't give up on last year's bush too soon. Butterfly bushes are among the latest shrubs to break dormancy.

Butterfly bushes are among the best shrubs for attracting butterflies and bees to your garden. Don't spray your plant for pests—you will harm the beautiful and beneficial insects that make their homes there.

Growing

Butterfly bushes prefer to grow in **full sun**. Plants grown in shady conditions will produce few, if any, flowers. The soil should be **average to fertile** and **well drained**. These shrubs are quite drought tolerant once established.

B. davidii and *B.* x *weyeriana* form flowers on the current year's growth. Early each spring cut your shrub back to within 6–12" of the ground to encourage new growth and plenty of flowers. Pruning of these two species may be unnecessary because the stems often die back to the ground in winter.

B. alternifolia blooms on the previous year's growth, not on new growth. Prune this plant after flowering is complete in mid-summer. Growing this species in a sheltered location may prevent winter dieback.

B. x *weyeriana* 'Honeycomb'

B. davidii 'White Ball' with purple-flowered cultivar

Deadhead all species to encourage new shoots, extend the blooming period and prevent self-seeding.

Tips

These plants make beautiful additions to shrub and mixed borders. The graceful, arching branches make butterfly bushes excellent specimen plants as well. The dwarf forms that stay under 5' are suitable for small gardens.

Recommended

B. alternifolia (alternate-leaved butterfly bush) grows 10–20' tall, with a spread that is equal to or slightly narrower than the height. It can be trained to form a tree, if the branches are given lots of room to arch down

B. davidii 'Pink Delight'

Butterfly bushes have a habit of self-seeding, and you may find tiny bushes popping up in unlikely places in the garden. The seedlings are easily pulled up from places they aren't wanted.

B. davidii

around the trunk. In late spring or early summer, panicles of light purple flowers form at the ends of the branches, flopping around in a wonderful state of disarray. **'Argentea'** has silvery gray leaves. (Zones 4–9)

B. davidii (orange-eye butterfly bush, summer lilac) is the most commonly grown species. It grows 4–10' tall, with an equal spread. This plant has a long blooming period, bearing flowers in bright and pastel shades of purple, white, pink or blue from mid-summer to fall. **'Black Knight'** grows 6–8' tall and 4–6' wide. It has deep purple flowers. **'Ellen's Blue'** has dark blue blooms on plants 4–6' tall and wide. **'Harlequin'** grows 8–10' tall and 6–8' wide. It has red-purple flowers and cream and green variegated leaves. **'Orchid Beauty'** grows 7–9' tall and wide and bears long spikes of lavender purple flowers. **'Pink Delight'** has pink flowers and grows 8–10' tall and 7–9' wide.

'White Ball' bears white flowers. This cultivar grows 3–4' tall and 24–36" wide. (Zones 5–9)

B. x *weyeriana* is a wide-spreading shrub with arching stems. It grows 6–12' tall, spreads 5–10' and bears purple or yellow flowers from mid-summer through fall. 'Honeycomb' bears clusters of attractive yellow flowers. (Zones 5–9)

Problems & Pests

Many insects are attracted to butterfly bushes, but most come just for the pollen and any others aren't likely to be a big problem. Spider mites can be troublesome occasionally. Good air circulation helps keep spider mites at bay and helps prevent the fungal problems that might otherwise afflict these plants.

B. davidii (both photos)

Cherry
Plum, Almond
Prunus

Features: spring to early-summer flowers, fruit, bark, fall foliage **Habit:** upright, rounded, spreading or weeping, deciduous tree or shrub **Height:** 3–75'
Spread: 3–50' **Planting:** bare-root, B & B, container; spring **Zones:** 2–9

MANY *PRUNUS* SPECIES HAVE A DIFFICULT TIME WITH THE CLAY soils, climatic extremes and variations in moisture typical of Illinois gardens. Stressed plants invite infection and insect problems, leading to shortened life spans and frustrated gardeners. Choose resistant species, such as Sargent cherry or Higan cherry. They boast strong flowering, and the trees can be maintained for use in smaller gardens.

Growing

These flowering fruit trees prefer to grow in **full sun**. The soil should be of **average fertility, moist** and **well drained**. Plant on mounds when possible to encourage drainage. Shallow roots will come up from the ground if the tree isn't getting enough water.

Most of the *Prunus* types listed in this entry need little or no pruning when grown as individual shrubs or trees. Simply remove damaged growth and wayward branches. Some species have specific pruning requirements, which are noted in the Recommended section. All pruning should take place after flowering is complete.

Tips

These shrubs or trees are beautiful as specimens, and many are small enough to be included in almost any garden. Small species and cultivars can also be included in borders or grouped to form informal hedges or barriers. Pissard plum, Fuji cherry and purpleleaf sand cherry can be trained as formal hedges.

Because of the pest problems that afflict many cherries, they can be rather short-lived. If you plant a more susceptible species, such as Japanese flowering cherry, enjoy it while it thrives but be prepared to replace it once problems surface.

The flesh of most *Prunus* fruit is edible, but the pits contain hydrocyanic acid and are not. The fruit sometimes has ornamental value, as indicated in the Recommended section.

P. serrulata 'Kwanzan' (both photos)

Pissard plum was one of the first purple-leaved cultivars, introduced into cultivation in 1880.

Recommended

P. cerasifera 'Atropurpurea' (Pissard plum) is a shrubby, often multi-stemmed tree that grows 20–30' tall, with an equal spread. Light pink flowers that fade to white emerge before the deep purple foliage. The leaves turn dark green as they mature. The edible fruit is purple and about 1" in diameter. Pissard plum can be pruned to form a hedge. **'Newport'** was bred by crossing 'Atropurpurea' with *P.* 'Omaha.' It is more cold hardy and flowers earlier than *P. cerasifera*. The fruit is dull purple. (Zones 4–8)

P. x cistena (purpleleaf sand cherry, purpleleaf dwarf plum) is a dainty, upright shrub that grows 5–10' high, with an equal or lesser spread. The deep purple leaves keep their color all season. The fragrant white or slightly pink flowers open in mid- to late spring after the leaves have developed. The fruit ripens to purple-black in July. This hybrid can be trained to form a small tree in space-restricted gardens. It can also be pruned to form a hedge. (Zones 3–8)

P. glandulosa (dwarf flowering almond) grows 3–4' in height and width. The beautiful pink or white, single or double flowers completely cover the stems in early spring, before the leaves emerge. Though very attractive when in flower, this species is best planted with other trees and shrubs, allowing it to fade gracefully into the background as the season wears on. This shrub may spread by suckers; keep an eye open for unwanted plants turning up. Prune one-third of the old wood to the ground each year, after flowering is complete. **'Rosea Plena'** features pink double flowers. (Zones 4–8)

P. subhirtella 'Pendula'

P. incisa (Fuji cherry) is an attractive small tree that grows to about 15' tall and about 10' in spread. It produces white or pink flowers in early spring, followed by small, purple-black fruit. Fuji cherry tolerates the heavy pruning needed to form a hedge. **'Kojo No Mai'** is a dwarf cultivar with an interesting zigzagged and layered branching habit. It grows 3–4' tall, with an equal spread. Pink flowers appear in spring, and the leaves turn bright orange in fall. (Zones 4–8)

P. maackii (Amur chokecherry) grows 30–45' tall and spreads 25–45'. It tolerates cold winter weather and does well in central and northern parts of Illinois. White, mid-spring flowers are followed by red fruit that ripens to black. The glossy, peeling bark is a reddish or golden brown and provides interest in the garden all year. (Zones 2–6)

P. x cistena
P. tomentosa

P. sargentii (Sargent cherry) is a rounded or spreading tree that grows 20–40' tall, with a spread of 20–30'. Fragrant light pink or white flowers appear in mid- to late spring, and the fruit ripens to a deep red by mid-summer. The orange fall color and glossy, red-brown bark are very attractive. **'Columnaris'** is a narrow, upright cultivar suitable for tight spots and small gardens. (Zones 4–9)

P. serrulata (Japanese flowering cherry) is a large tree that grows up to 75' tall, with a spread of up to 50'. It bears white or pink flowers in mid- to late spring. **'Kwanzan'** (Kwanzan cherry) is a popular culti-var with drooping clusters of pink

double flowers. It is sometimes grafted onto a single trunk, creating a small, vase-shaped tree. Grown on its own roots it becomes a large, spreading tree 30–40' tall and wide. **'Mount Fuji'** ('Shirotae') bears pink buds that open to fragrant white flowers in early spring. It has a spreading habit and grows 15–30' tall and wide. **'Shirofugan'** is a spreading, vigorous tree that grows 25' tall and 30' wide. Pink flower buds appear in mid-spring and open to fragrant white flowers. The leaves are bronze when young and mature to dark green, turning orange-red in fall. (Zones 5–8)

Many important fruit and nut crops belong to the genus Prunus, *including apricot* (P. armeniaca), *garden plum* (P. domestica), *almond* (P. amygdalus) *and peach and nectarine (both* P. persica).

P. **SNOW FOUNTAIN** ('Snofozam') is hardier than most flowering cherries. It grows about 10–15' tall, with an equal spread. The graceful cascading branches are covered in white double flowers in early spring, before the foliage emerges. (Zones 3–8)

P. glandulosa

P. subhirtella (Higan cherry) grows 20–40' tall and spreads 15–25'. It bears light pink or white flowers in early to mid-spring. **'Autumnalis'** (autumn flowering cherry) bears light pink flowers sporadically in fall and prolifically in mid-spring. It grows up to 25' tall, with an equal spread. **'Pendula'** (weeping Higan cherry) has flowers in many shades of pink, appearing before the leaves in mid-spring. The graceful weeping branches make this tree a cascade of pink when in flower. It is sometimes grafted onto a standard trunk, creating a small weeping tree about 7' tall. **'Whitcomb'** blooms early, with pink flowers fading to white. It grows into a flat-topped, horizontal shape 15–25' tall and slightly wider than tall. It has good orangy fall color. (Zones 4–8)

P. tomentosa (Nanking cherry, Manchu cherry) is a hardy shrub cherry that is popular for its tart, edible fruit. Fragrant white flowers appear in mid-spring from pink buds, followed by bright red fruit that ripens by the middle of summer. The shiny, exfoliating, reddish bark is an attractive winter feature. This species grows 6–10' tall and spreads up to 15'. (Zones 2–7)

Problems & Pests

The many possible problems include aphids, borers, caterpillars, leafhoppers, mites, nematodes, scale insects, canker, crown gall, fire blight, powdery mildew and viruses. Root rot can occur in poorly drained soils. Stress-free plants are less likely to have problems.

P. sargentii in fall color

Cut cherry stems in February, mash the ends with a hammer and arrange the stems in a vase indoors for an early burst of fragrant blooms.

P. incisa 'Kojo No Mai'

Chokeberry

Aronia

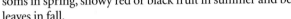

Features: flowers, fruit, fall foliage **Habit:** suckering, deciduous shrub **Height:** 3–8'
Spread: 3–8' **Planting:** B & B, container, bare-root; spring or fall **Zones:** 3–8

CHOKEBERRY IS A GOOD EXAMPLE OF WHAT CULTIVATION CAN
do for a plant. The species *A. melanocarpa* is an upright, multi-stemmed shrub
with a rounded top—it looks like a typical native shrub. The Chicagoland
Grows cultivar IROQUOIS BEAUTY is a selection from the Morton Arboretum
with a dense, compact, full appearance, making it a neat border shrub. Choose
your plant to match the look you are seeking, whether untamed native or tidy
formal. All chokeberries offer multi-season interest—abundant white blossoms in spring, showy red or black fruit in summer and beautiful orange to red
leaves in fall.

Growing

Chokeberries grow well in **full sun** or **partial shade,** with the best flowering and fruiting in full sun. The soil should be of **average fertility** and **well drained,** but these plants adapt to most soils and generally tolerate wet, dry or poor soil. *A. arbutifolia* 'Brilliantissima' prefers moist to wet soil.

When a chokeberry shrub is mature, up to one-third of its oldest stems can be pruned out annually.

IROQUOIS BEAUTY

Tips

These plants are useful in a shrub or mixed border. They also make interesting, low-maintenance specimens. Left to their own devices, they will colonize a fairly large area.

Recommended

A. arbutifolia 'Brilliantissima' ('Brilliant') is an upright, suckering plant that grows 8' tall and 3–5' wide. The glossy, dark green foliage turns a bright reddish purple in autumn. This cultivar bears clusters of white flowers in profusion in late spring, followed by shiny red fruit.

A. melanocarpa (black chokeberry) is an upright, suckering shrub that is native to Illinois. It grows 3–6' tall and 6–8' wide, bearing white flowers in late spring and early summer, followed by dark fruit that ripens in fall and persists through the winter. The foliage turns bright red to purplish red in fall. **IROQUOIS BEAUTY** ('Morton') is a compact cultivar that grows only 36" tall and slightly wider than tall. 'Viking' grows 3–5' tall and 6–8' wide. It has glossy dark green foliage that turns dark red in fall.

Problems & Pests

Chokeberries rarely suffer from major problems, though fungal leaf spot is possible.

The bitter fruit of these plants persists into winter because even birds won't eat it until it is well fermented. Copious amounts of sugar are needed to make it into jam or juice.

A. melanocarpa with immature fruit

Cotoneaster

Cotoneaster

Features: foliage, early-summer flowers, persistent fruit, variety of forms
Habit: evergreen or deciduous groundcover or shrub **Height:** 6"–6'
Spread: 2–8' **Planting:** container; spring or fall **Zones:** 4–8

COTONEASTERS COME IN MANY SHAPES AND SIZES, THE MOST
remarkable being the groundcover species that spill into layers of pendulous
branches. All cotoneasters have multi-season interest, from spring flowering
through fruit formation in summer to fall, by which time the glossy green,
button-shaped leaves have turned a charming orangy red. The fruit persists
into winter. Larger cotoneasters can be grown as small specimen trees.

Growing

Cotoneasters grow well in **full sun** or **partial shade**. The soil should be of **average fertility** and **well drained**.

Though pruning is rarely required, these plants tolerate even hard pruning. Pruning cotoneaster hedges in mid- to late summer will let you see how much you can trim off while still leaving some of the ornamental fruit in place. Hard pruning encourages new growth and can rejuvenate plants that are looking worn out.

Tips

Cotoneasters can be included in shrub or mixed borders. The low spreaders work well as ground-covers, and shrubby species can be used to form hedges. Some low growers are grafted onto standards and grown as small weeping trees.

Although cotoneaster berries are not poisonous, they can cause stomach upset if eaten in large quantities. The foliage may be toxic.

C. horizontalis
C. dammeri 'Mooncreeper'

Recommended

C. adpressus (creeping cotoneaster) is a low deciduous species used as a groundcover. It grows only 12" high and spreads up to 7'. Red-tinged white flowers are produced in summer, followed by fruit that ripens to red in fall. The foliage turns reddish purple in fall. (Zones 4–6)

C. apiculatus (cranberry cotoneaster) is a deciduous species that forms a mound of arching, tangled branches. It grows about 36" high and spreads up to 7'. Small pink flowers bloom in late spring. The bright red fruit persists into winter. This species is sometimes available in a tree form. (Zones 4–7)

C. dammeri (bearberry cotoneaster) is evergreen. Its low-growing, arching stems gradually stack up on top of one another as the plant matures. This species grows 12–24" in height and spreads to 7'. Small white flowers

blanket the stems in early summer and are followed by bright red fruit in fall. 'Coral Beauty' is a ground-cover with abundant, bright orange to red fruit. 'Lowfast' grows 6–12" tall and 24" in spread. It features glossy green foliage and red fruit. 'Mooncreeper' is a low-growing cultivar with large white flowers and tiny red fruit. (Zones 4–8)

C. divaricatus (spreading cotoneaster) grows 5–6' in height and 5–8' in spread. It is a rounded to spreading, deciduous shrub with dense, somewhat arched branching and glossy, dark green foliage. Small reddish pink to white flowers bloom in late spring and are often concealed by the foliage. The fruit is red to dark red and ovoid. Fall leaf color is maroon to bright red, sometimes yellow, and is long lasting. This species takes clipping very well, so it can be used in a hedge border. (Zones 4–7)

C. horizontalis

C. x 'Hessei' is a tidy, low-growing, deciduous cultivar with an irregular branching habit. It grows 12–24" tall and spreads 5–6'. The dark pink, late-spring flowers are followed by fruit that ripens to bright red. The leaves turn burgundy in fall. This cultivar is resistant to spider mites and fire blight. It is recommended by Chicagoland Grows. (Zones 4–7)

C. horizontalis (rockspray cotoneaster) is a low-growing, deciduous species with a distinctive, attractive herringbone branching pattern. It grows 24–36" tall and 5–8' in spread. Light pink, early-summer flowers are followed by red fall fruit. The leaves turn a bright red in fall. (Zones 5–7)

Problems & Pests

These plants are generally problem free, but occasional attacks of lace bugs, scale insects, slugs, snails, spider mites, canker, fire blight, powdery mildew and rust are possible.

C. x 'Hessei' (above)

C. dammeri (center), C. apiculatus (below)

Crabapple
Malus

Features: spring flowers, late-season and winter fruit, fall foliage, habit, bark
Habit: rounded, mounded or spreading, small to medium, deciduous tree
Height: 5–30' **Spread:** 6–30' **Planting:** B & B, container; spring or fall **Zones:** 4–8

FOR WINTER-SAPPED ILLINOISANS, FEW FLOWERS OF SPRING present quite as magnificent a display as a crabapple tree in full array. The trees seem to change color from one day to the next as buds of one shade open to flowers of a different hue. The fruit is often yet another color, adding further interest. Good fall foliage color gives way to persistence of the fruit into winter. Crabs are probably the finest small trees in the Illinois landscape. If you're nursing a crabapple tree from a couple of generations ago, consider replacing it.

Some gardeners use crabapple fruit to make preserves, cider or even wine.

Growing

Crabapples prefer **full sun** but tolerate partial shade. The soil should be of **average to rich fertility, moist** and **well drained**. These trees tolerate damp soil.

Crabapples require very little pruning but adapt to aggressive pruning. Remove damaged or wayward branches and suckers when necessary. Branches that shoot straight up should be removed because they won't flower as much as horizontal branches. The next year's flower buds form in early summer, so any pruning done to shape the tree should be done by late spring, or as soon as the current year's flowering is finished.

Tips

Crabapples make excellent specimen plants. Many varieties are quite small, so there is one to suit almost any size of garden. Some forms are even small enough to grow in large containers. Crabapples' flexible young branches make them a good choice for creating espalier specimens along walls or fences.

Recommended

The following are just a few suggestions from among the hundreds of crabapples available. When choosing a species, variety or cultivar, look for disease resistance. Even the most beautiful plant will never look good if ravaged by pests or diseases. We in Illinois are very fortunate— the Morton Arboretum is a leader in research on crabapple cultivars.

All of the following crabapples flower in mid- to late spring, unless otherwise noted.

M. 'Snowdrift'

M. SUGAR TYME

M. 'Adirondack' resists all diseases. It is an upright oval tree that grows about 10' tall and spreads about 6'. Red buds open to red-tinged white flowers. The fruit is reddish orange. (Zones 4–8)

M. CENTURION ('Centzam') is highly resistant to all crabapple diseases. This upright tree becomes rounded as it matures. It grows to 25' in height, with a spread of 20'. Dark pink flowers appear in late spring. The bright red fruit persists for a long time. (Zones 5–8)

M. 'Donald Wyman' is resistant to all diseases except apple scab and powdery mildew, which can be prevented by pruning out enough growth to allow good air circulation. This cultivar has an open, rounded habit and grows to 20' tall and 25' in spread. Dark pink buds open to white flowers in mid-spring. Flowering tends to be heavier in alternating years. The persistent fruit is bright red. (Zones 5–8)

M. floribunda (Japanese flowering crabapple, showy crabapple) is a medium-sized, densely crowned, spreading tree. It grows up to 30' in both height and width. This species is fairly resistant to crabapple problems. It has pink buds that open to pale pink flowers, followed by small, yellow apples. (Zones 4–8)

M. 'Golden Raindrops' (*M. transitoria* 'Schmidtcutleaf') is a vase-shaped, fast-growing tree 15–20' tall and 10–15' wide. It has deeply cut foliage, white flowers and tiny golden yellow fruit. It is susceptible to fire blight. (Zones 4–8)

M. 'Liset' grows 15–20' tall and wide. The foliage is deep red to purple-red when young, maturing to green tinged with bronze. This cultivar bears dark reddish pink flowers and dark purple-red fruit. Japanese beetle may be a problem. (Zones 5–8)

M. 'Prairifire' is very disease resistant. This rounded tree grows about 20' tall, with an equal spread. The new leaves have a reddish tinge but mature to dark green. The red buds and flowers are followed by persistent, purplish red fruit. (Zones 4–8)

M. sargentii (Sargent crabapple) is a small, mounding tree that is fairly resistant to disease. It grows 6–10' tall and spreads 8–15'. In late spring, red buds open to white flowers. The fruit is dark red and long lasting. FIREBIRD ('Select A') is a slow-growing, rounded cultivar that is superior to the species, with fruit that persists even longer and good disease resistance. 'Tina' is a dwarf form that closely resembles the species, except that it grows only 5' tall and spreads up to 10'. With a bit of pruning to control the spread, this cultivar makes an interesting specimen for a large container on a balcony or patio. (Zones 4–8)

M. 'Sinai Fire' is very disease resistant. This tree has a broad, weeping habit, growing about 12' tall, with an equal spread. The red buds and white flowers are followed by persistent orangy red fruit. (Zones 4–8)

An espalier specimen

Though crabapples are usually grown as trees, their excellent response to training makes them good candidates for bonsai and espalier.

M. SPRING SENSATION

M. 'Snowdrift' is a dense, quick-growing, rounded tree that resists apple scab diseases. It grows 15–20' tall, with an equal spread. Red buds open to white flowers in late spring or early summer. The foliage is dark green and the fruit is bright orange. (Zones 5–8)

M. SPRING SENSATION ('Hub Tures') has a dense, wide-spreading habit, excellent disease resistance, dark rose flower buds, pink-tinted flowers with excellent weather resistance, and attractive red-tinted foliage. Fruit production is minimal to none. This Chicagoland Grows selection grows 8–10' tall and 10–12' wide. It is a good choice for espalier hedges. It was selected by Hub Tures and Sons Nursery in Kingston, Illinois. (Zones 4–8)

M. SUGAR TYME ('Sutyzam') is very disease resistant. This upright tree grows about 18' tall and spreads about 15'. The buds are pale pink and the flowers are white. The bright red fruit persists through the winter. (Zones 4–8)

M. WHITE ANGEL ('Inglis') is quite disease resistant and is admired for the masses of white flowers and red fruit that it produces. The habit is rounded, but the branches often bend down with the weight of the fruit. This cultivar grows about 20' tall, with an equal spread. (Zones 4–8)

M. x *zumi* is a small pyramidal tree, rarely grown in favor of its cultivars. 'Calocarpa' (var. *calocarpa*) grows 20–25' tall and wide. It has red buds, fragrant white flowers and plentiful, bright red, persistent fruit. 'Wooster' is similar in size to 'Calocarpa' and bears orange-red fruit. Both are highly resistant to scab but prone to fire blight. (Zones 4–8)

Problems & Pests

Aphids, Japanese beetle, leaf rollers, leaf skeletonizers, scale insects and tent caterpillars are insect pests to watch for, though they cause damage that is largely cosmetic. Leaf drop caused by apple scab is the most common problem with susceptible varieties. Cedar-apple rust, fire blight, leaf spot and powdery mildew can also be problematic, depending on the weather.

M. SPRING SENSATION (center)

Be sure to properly prune crabapples while they are young to help them become the unique mature specimens that are so universally admired.

Daphne

Daphne

Features: foliage, fragrant spring flowers **Habit:** upright, rounded or low-growing, evergreen, semi-evergreen or deciduous shrub **Height:** 6"–5' **Spread:** 3–5'
Planting: container; early spring or early fall **Zones:** 4–7

NOT SHRUBS FOR THE FAINT OF HEART, DAPHNES REWARD THE patient, attentive gardener with a wonderful, fragrant floral display in late spring or early summer. Most cultivars have variegated foliage and are semi-evergreen for year-round interest. Proper drainage is crucial to survival of daphnes; stress of any other type should be avoided as well. All are slow growing, so don't worry about them crossing their boundaries.

Growing

Daphnes prefer **partial shade.** The soil should be **moist, well drained** and of **average fertility.** A layer of mulch will keep the shallow roots cool. Avoid overfertilizing and over-watering.

These plants have neat, dense growth that needs very little pruning. Remove damaged or diseased branches as soon as they are noticed. Spent inflorescences can be removed if desired, once flowering is finished. Cut flowering stems back to where they join main branches in order to preserve the natural growth habit of the shrub.

D. caucasica

Tips

Daphnes can be included in shrub or mixed borders. Rose daphne also makes an attractive groundcover in rock gardens or woodland gardens. Plant daphnes near paths, doors, windows or other places where the wonderful scent can be enjoyed.

In late winter cut a few stems and arrange them in a vase indoors—they should come into bloom in a warm, bright room. Enjoy both the sweet scent and the delicately beautiful flowers.

D. cneorum var. variegata

D. x burkwoodii 'Somerset'

Once you've successfully installed a daphne and it is growing well, the best advice is to leave it alone.

D. x burkwoodii 'Carol Mackie'

Though daphnes are usually said to be hardy to Zone 4, they often thrive as smaller plants in even colder climates. These plants do, however, have a strange habit of dying suddenly. Experts have various theories about why this happens and how to avoid it, but the best advice seems to be to plant daphnes in well-drained soil and then leave them alone. Any disturbance that could stress them should be avoided. Don't move daphnes after they are established.

All parts of these plants are toxic if eaten, and the sap may cause skin irritation. Avoid planting daphnes where children may be tempted to sample the berries.

Recommended

D. x *burkwoodii* (Burkwood daphne) is a semi-evergreen, upright shrub that grows 3–5' in height and spread. It bears fragrant white or light pink flowers in late spring and sometimes again in fall. **'Brigg's Moonlight'** has creamy yellow foliage with green margins and bears clusters of fragrant pink flowers. **'Carol Mackie'** has pale pink, star-shaped flowers. Its dark green leaves have creamy margins. **'Somerset'** has darker pink flowers than *D.* x *burkwoodii*.

D. caucasica (Caucasian daphne) is a rounded, upright, deciduous shrub 4–5' tall, with an equal spread. It bears clusters of fragrant white flowers in a main flush in late spring and sporadically all summer.

D. cneorum (rose daphne, garland flower) is a low-growing evergreen shrub. It grows 6–12" tall and can spread to 4'. The fragrant pale to deep pink or white flowers are borne in late spring. **'Alba'** has white flowers. **'Ruby Glow'** (sometimes attributed to *D. mezereum*) has reddish pink flowers. **Var.** *variegata* ('Variegata') has yellow-edged foliage.

Problems & Pests

Aphids, scale insects, crown or root rot, leaf spot, twig blight and viruses affect daphnes. Poor growing conditions can result in greater susceptibility to these problems. A plant may wilt and die suddenly if diseased.

D. cneorum var. *variegata*
D. x *burkwoodii* 'Somerset'

Daphnes have wonderfully fragrant flowers and attractive, often evergreen foliage, giving these shrubs appeal all year round.

D. x *burkwoodii* 'Brigg's Moonlight'

Dawn Redwood
Metasequoia

Features: foliage, bark, cones, buttressed trunk **Habit:** narrow, conical, deciduous conifer **Height:** 70–125' **Spread:** 15–25' **Planting:** bare-root, B & B, container; spring or fall **Zones:** 5–8

DAWN REDWOOD IS AN ANCIENT PLANT THOUGHT TO BE EXTINCT until it was observed growing in China in the 1940s. It has enjoyed a horticultural revival because of its fast growth, uniform, conical shape and interesting seasonal cycle. This tree grows soft, evergreen-type foliage, but the fern-like needles turn a unique pinkish tan in autumn and drop, leaving behind box-like cones hanging on long stalks. The bark is reddish brown and peels in strips to create a rope-like appearance.

Don't worry when this tree drops its needles each fall: it's a deciduous conifer.

Growing

Dawn redwood grows well in **full sun** or **light shade**. The cultivar 'Gold Rush' prefers **partial shade**. The soil should be **humus rich,** slightly **acidic, moist** and **well drained**. Dawn redwood is intolerant of drought. This tree likes humid conditions and should be mulched and watered regularly until it is established.

Pruning is not necessary. The lower branches must be left in place in order for the buttressing to develop. A buttressed trunk is flared and grooved, and the branches appear to be growing from deep inside the grooves.

'Gold Rush'

Tips

This large tree needs plenty of room to grow. Large gardens and parks can best accommodate it. As a single specimen or in a group planting, dawn redwood is attractive and impressive. The cones may not develop in many Illinois gardens because the tree matures very slowly in cold-winter climates.

Recommended

M. glyptostroboides has a pyramidal, sometimes spire-like form. The needles turn gold, orange or pinkish tan in fall before dropping. The cultivars do not differ significantly from the species. **'Gold Rush'** has attractive yellow-green foliage. This cultivar grows more slowly than the species and doesn't grow quite as large. **'National'** is narrower than the species. It has not been in cultivation long enough to have reached its mature height, but it is expected to be as tall as the species.

Problems & Pests

Dawn redwood is not generally prone to problems, although it can be killed by canker infections. Spider mites may be problematic in dry conditions. The foliage may be attacked by Japanese beetle.

M. glyptostroboides

Deutzia
Deutzia

Features: early-summer flowers **Habit:** bushy, deciduous shrub **Height:** 1–8'
Spread: 3–8' or more **Planting:** container; spring to fall **Zones:** 4–9

DEUTZIAS ARE GROWN FOR THEIR SHOW OF FLOWERS, TYPICALLY
on arching branches in late spring. The blooms vary from white to pink to
striped (in the cultivar 'Magician'). These low-maintenance shrubs stay in
bounds. The standard is 'Nikko,' with its white double flowers and a burgundy to purple fall color. It can be used as a groundcover with a mature
height of 12–24".

D. gracilis *is lovely as a small, easily managed,
informal hedge or in a mid-border planting.*

Growing

Deutzias grow best in **full sun**. They tolerate light shade but will not bear as many flowers. The soil should be of **average to high fertility, moist** and **well drained**.

These shrubs bloom on the previous year's growth. After flowering is complete, cut flowering stems back to strong buds, main stems or basal stems as required to shape the plant. Remove one-third of the old stems on established plants at ground level for strong new growth.

D. x *hybrida* 'Magician'

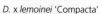
D. x *lemoinei* 'Compacta'

Tips

Include deutzias in shrub or mixed borders or in rock gardens. You can also use them as specimen plants.

Deutzias are quite frost hardy. If you live in a colder area than is generally recommended for these plants, try growing them in a sheltered spot where they will be protected from the worst extremes of weather.

Recommended

D. gracilis (slender deutzia) is a low-growing, mounding species 2–4' high and 3–7' wide. In late spring the plant is completely covered with white flowers. The species is hardy in Zones 5–8. 'Nikko' has white double flowers, and its foliage turns purple in fall. This compact cultivar grows 12–24" tall and spreads about 5'. It is hardy to Zone 4.

D. x *hybrida* '**Magician'** ('Magicien') is a large, arching shrub that grows 6–8' tall, with an equal or greater spread. The pink-and-white-streaked flowers are borne in loose clusters in early to mid-summer. (Zones 5–9)

D. x *lemoinei* is a dense, rounded, upright hybrid 5–7' tall, with an equal spread. The early-summer blooms are white. '**Avalanche**' has arching branches and abundant white flowers in dense clusters. '**Compacta**' ('Boule de Neige') has denser, more compact growth than *D.* x *lemoinei*. It bears large clusters of white flowers. (Zones 5–9)

Problems & Pests

Problems are rare, though these plants can have trouble with aphids, leaf miners and fungal leaf spot.

Dogwood
Cornus

Features: late-spring to early-summer flowers, fall foliage, fruit, habit
Habit: deciduous large shrub or small tree **Height:** 5–30' **Spread:** 5–30'
Planting: B & B, container; spring **Zones:** 2–9

THE GLORIOUS SPRING SHOW OF THE AMERICAN OR FLOWERING
dogwood *(C. florida)* is a sight reserved for those in the lower half of our
state. Up north, a better choice is the Kousa dogwood, with superior winter
survival and less susceptibility to leaf blight. Both of these small trees produce fruit and good fall color. The shrubby dogwoods include three species
recommended by the Morton Arboretum: pagoda dogwood *(C. alternifolia),*
gray dogwood *(C. racemosa)* and red-osier dogwood *(C. sericea).* Red-osier
dogwood and Tatarian dogwood *(C. alba)* are red-twigged types that are
popular for their winter interest after the foliage drops.

Growing

Tree dogwoods grow well in **light shade** or **partial shade**. Shrub dogwoods prefer **full sun** or **partial shade**, with the best stem colors developing in full sun. For all dogwoods, the soil should be of **average to high fertility**, rich in **organic matter, neutral to slightly acidic** and **well drained**. Shrub dogwoods adapt to most soils but prefer moist soil. *C. sericea* tolerates wet soil.

Tree dogwoods and *C. alternifolia* require very little pruning. Simply remove damaged, dead or awkward branches in early spring.

C. alba and *C. sericea,* which are grown for the colorful stems that are so striking in winter, need regular rejuvenation pruning because the color is best on young growth. *C. racemosa* and *C. sanguinea* 'Winter Flame' will also respond well to rejuvenation pruning. There are two ways to encourage new growth. A drastic, but effective, method is to cut back all stems to within a couple of buds of the ground, in early spring. To make up for the loss of top growth, feed the plant once it starts growing. The second, less drastic, method is to cut back about one-third of the old growth to within a couple of buds of the ground in early spring. This procedure leaves most of the growth in place, and branches can be removed as they age and lose their color.

Tips

The tree species make wonderful specimen plants and are small enough to include in most gardens. Use them along the edge of a

C. sericea

Ornamental dogwoods fall into two main categories: the tree or flowering dogwoods (including C. florida *and* C. kousa*), with large, showy blooms; and the shrubby dogwoods (including* C. alba *and* C. sericea*), which often have colorful stems.*

C. kousa var. *chinensis*

C. kousa
C. florida 'Cherokee Chief'

woodland garden, in a shrub or mixed border, alongside a house, or near a pond, water feature or patio. Shrub dogwoods can be included in a shrub or mixed border. They look best in groups rather than as single specimens.

Recommended

C. alba (Tatarian dogwood, red-twig dogwood) is a shrub dogwood grown for its bright red winter stems. The stems are green during the summer, turning red as winter approaches. This species can grow 5–10' tall, with an equal spread. It prefers cool climates and can develop problems with leaf scorch and canker in hot weather. The cultivar **'Argenteo-marginata'** ('Elegantissima') has gray-green leaves with creamy margins. **'Sibirica'** (Siberian dogwood) has pinkish red to bright red winter stems. (Zones 2–7)

C. alternifolia (pagoda dogwood, alternate-leaf dogwood) is native to Illinois. It can be grown as a large, multi-stemmed shrub or a small, single-stemmed tree. It grows 15–25' in height and spreads 10–25'. The branches have an attractive layered appearance. Clusters of small white flowers appear in early summer. This species prefers light shade. **GOLDEN SHADOWS** ('W. Stackman') has leaves variegated yellow and green. (Zones 3–8)

C. x **CONSTELLATION** ('Rutcan') is an upright to somewhat spreading tree dogwood that grows 15–25' tall and spreads 15–20'. This hybrid was developed from crosses between *C. kousa* and *C. florida*. It grows quickly and resists anthracnose and borers.

The white blossoms are borne in late spring and early summer, and the leaves become reddish in fall. (Zones 5–9)

C. florida (flowering dogwood, American dogwood) is native to Illinois. It is usually grown as a small tree 20–30' tall, with an equal or greater spread. It features horizontally layered branches and showy pink or white blossoms that appear in late spring. The species and its cultivars are susceptible to blight. **'Apple Blossom'** has light pink bracts with white at the bases. **'Cherokee Chief'** has dark pink bracts. **'Cloud Nine'** has large white bracts. **Forma *rubra*** (var. *rubra*, 'Rubra') has pale pink to dark pink-red bracts. **'Spring Song'** has rose pink bracts. (Zones 5–9)

C. kousa (Kousa dogwood) is grown for its flowers, fruit, fall color and interesting bark. This tree dogwood grows 20–30' tall and spreads 15–30'.

C. sericea 'Cardinal'

The showy parts of tree dogwood blooms are actually bracts, not petals; the true flowers are small and clustered in the center of the four bracts.

C. kousa

C. sericea (above)

C. florida in fall color (center) & flowering (below)

It is more resistant to leaf blight and other problems than *C. florida*. The white-bracted, early-summer flowers are followed by bright red fruit. The foliage turns red and purple in fall. **Var.** *chinensis* (Chinese dogwood) grows more vigorously and has larger flowers. (Zones 5–9)

C. racemosa (gray dogwood) is an erect, multi-stemmed shrub that grows 8–10' tall and wide and spreads by rhizomes to form colonies. It has dark green foliage and attractive gray bark on mature stems. In late spring it bears abundant clusters of white flowers at the stem tips. The fruit of this Illinois native is white and is enjoyed by many bird species. This dogwood grows in sun or shade and is especially good for dry shade situations. (Zones 3–8)

C. sanguinea 'Winter Flame' ('Midwinter Fire,' 'Winter Beauty') is a great selection for winter interest. The stems are yellow at the base, turning to orange and red at the tips. Fall foliage colors are bright yellow and orange. This cultivar grows 5–8' tall and wide and spreads by suckers to form thickets. White flowers are borne in spring. 'Winter Flame' is sometimes attributed to *C. alba* or to *C. sericea*. You may also see 'Winter Flame' and 'Midwinter Fire' listed as separate cultivars. (Zones 4–8)

C. sericea (*C. stolonifera;* red-osier dogwood, red-twig dogwood) is a widespread, vigorous shrub with bright red stems. This Illinois native grows about 6' tall, spreads up to 12' and bears clusters of small white flowers in early summer. The fall color is red or orange. The species and many cultivars are hardy in Zones 2–8. **Forma *baileyi*** (var. *baileyi, C. baileyi,* 'Baileyi'; Bailey redosier dogwood) grows more erect than the species. It grows 6–9' tall and wide, with dark red stems and purple-red fall color. It is hardy in Zones 3–9. **'Cardinal'** has pinkish red stems that become bright red in winter. It is resistant to leaf spot. **'Flaviramea'** (yellow-twig dogwood) has bright yellow-green stems. **'Silver and Gold'** has excellent white and green variegated leaves and yellow-green stems.

C. florida 'Cherokee Chief' (above), *C. kousa* (center)

Problems & Pests
The many possible problems include aphids, borers, leafhoppers, nematodes, scale insects, thrips, weevils, anthracnose, blight, canker, leaf spot, powdery mildew and root rot.

Use the strong horizontal branching of pagoda dogwood for contrast with vertical lines in the landscape.

C. sericea 'Silver and Gold'

Elderberry
Elder
Sambucus

Features: early-summer flowers, fruit, foliage **Habit:** large, bushy, deciduous shrub
Height: 5–15' **Spread:** 8–15' **Planting:** bare-root, container; spring or fall
Zones: 3–9

ELDERBERRIES HAVE WHAT WE ALL WANT IN A SHRUB—FLOWERS
(often fragrant), berries and interesting foliage. On the other hand, most
need pruning to keep them looking tidy. Cultivars with varied leaf character-
istics and habits are bringing a new level of awareness to this group of plants.
Be the first on your block to plant the intriguing BLACK BEAUTY, with its
deep burgundy foliage and lemon-scented pink blossoms.

Growing

Elderberries grow well in **full sun** or **partial shade**. Cultivars grown for burgundy or black leaf color develop the best color in full sun, while cultivars with yellow leaf color develop the best color in light or partial shade. The soil should be of **average fertility, moist** and **well drained**. These plants tolerate dry soil once established.

S. racemosa (both photos)

Elderberry fruit attracts birds to the garden.

Though elderberries do not require pruning, they can become scraggly and untidy if ignored. They will tolerate even severe pruning. Plants can be cut back to within a couple of buds of the ground in early spring. This treatment controls the spread of these vigorous growers and encourages the best foliage color on specimens grown for this purpose.

Plants cut right back to the ground will not flower or produce fruit that season. If you desire flowers and fruit as well as good foliage color, remove only one-third to one-half of the growth in early spring. Fertilize or apply a layer of compost after pruning to encourage strong new growth.

Tips

Elderberries can be used in shrub or mixed borders, in natural woodland gardens or next to ponds or other water features. Plants with interesting or colorful foliage can be used as specimen plants or to create focal points in the garden.

Both the blossoms and the fruit of *S. canadensis* can be used to make wine. The berries are also popular for pies and jelly. The raw berries

S. nigra 'Madonna'

These versatile shrubs can be cut back hard each year or trained into a small tree form.

S. nigra 'Pulverulenta'

are marginally edible but not palatable and can cause stomach upset, particularly in children. Cooking the berries before eating them is recommended. Try them in place of blueberries in pies, scones or muffins. Berries of other species are not edible.

All parts of elderberries other than the berries are toxic.

Recommended

S. canadensis (*S. nigra* subsp. *canadensis;* American elderberry) is a shrub about 12' tall, with an equal spread. White mid-summer flowers are followed by dark purple berries. A widespread native across the eastern and central U.S., this species is generally found growing in damp ditches and alongside rivers and streams. 'Aurea' has yellow foliage and red fruit. 'Goldfinch' has finely cut, yellow foliage. (Zones 4–9)

S. nigra (*S. nigra* subsp. *nigra;* European elderberry, black elderberry) is a large shrub that can grow 15' tall and wide. The yellowish white to creamy white, early-summer flowers are followed by purple-black fruit. BLACK BEAUTY ('Gerda') has dark foliage that gets blacker as the season progresses. The flowers are pink. It grows 8–12' tall, with an equal spread. 'Laciniata' has deeply dissected leaflets that give the shrub a feathery appearance. It grows up to 10' tall and wide. 'Madonna' has dark green foliage with wide, irregular, yellow margins. 'Pulverulenta' has unusually dark green and white mottled foliage. It grows slower than other cultivars but reaches 10' in height and spread. (Zones 4–8)

S. racemosa (red elderberry, European red elderberry) grows 8–12' tall, with an equal spread. This shrub bears pyramidal clusters of white flowers in spring, followed by bright red fruit. **'Sutherland Gold'** has deeply cut, yellow-green foliage. It grows 5–10' in height and spread. (Zones 3–7)

Problems & Pests
Borers, canker, dieback, leaf spot and powdery mildew may occasionally affect elderberries.

The genus name Sambucus *is derived from the Greek word for a musical instrument made from elderberry wood.*

S. nigra BLACK BEAUTY

S. nigra cultivar

Elm
Ulmus

Features: habit, fall color, bark **Habit:** variable, rounded to vase-shaped, deciduous tree **Height:** 10–80' **Spread:** 20–60' **Planting:** container, B & B, bare-root; spring or fall **Zones:** 2–9

AMERICAN ELM WAS THE CLASSIC street tree of Illinois for generations. With its nearly perfect vase shape, the tree once created archways along many urban and suburban streets— scenes now remembered only in black-and-white photographs. American elm has been dealt a devastating blow by Dutch elm disease, caused by an introduced fungus and spread by a small insect called the elm bark beetle. The Morton Arboretum has become an international leader in breeding resistant varieties, leading the fight to reestablish this important tree.

Elm wood is used for making furniture, crates, barrels, agricultural implements and caskets. The Iroquois used elm bark to make canoes, rope and utensils.

Growing

Elms grow well in **full sun** and in **partial shade**. They adapt to most soil types and conditions but prefer a **moist, fertile** soil. They are tolerant of urban conditions, including salt from roadways.

These trees rarely need pruning, but it can be done in fall. Remove damaged, diseased or dead growth as needed.

Tips

Elms are often large trees, attractive where they have room to grow on large properties and in parks. Smaller species and cultivars make good specimen and shade trees.

Recommended

U. americana (American elm) is a large, long-lived, vase-shaped native tree that has pendulous branches and a large, rounded to oval crown. It grows 60–80' tall and spreads 30–60'. It can reach heights well over 100' in the wild. The shiny, dark green foliage turns an attractive golden yellow in fall. The thick gray bark is deeply furrowed. This species is susceptible to Dutch elm disease, but disease-resistant cultivars are now becoming available. **'New Harmony'** has a broad, vase-shaped habit. **'Princeton'** is a narrow, vase-shaped selection with attractive foliage. It grows quickly and is becoming more common in commerce. **'Valley Forge'** is an upright tree with arching branches.

Dutch elm disease was discovered by seven female Dutch scientists in 1917.

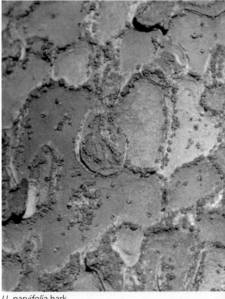

U. parvifolia bark

A single elm tree on the south side of your house can provide the same summer cooling as five air-conditioning units.

U. americana

U. 'Morton Glossy'
U. americana

It is probably the best American elm cultivar, with high resistance to Dutch elm disease. (Zones 2–9)

U. glabra 'Camperdownii' (umbrella elm, weeping elm) is a rounded, wide-spreading tree with pendulous branches that reach the ground. It grows 10–15' tall and 20–30' wide and has dark green foliage. It is often grafted to a standard to create an attractive small, weeping tree. (Zones 4–7)

U. 'Homestead' is an upright, vase-shaped tree with arching branches. It grows 50–80' tall and 30–40' wide. This hybrid is resistant to Dutch elm disease. (Zones 5–8)

U. 'Morton' (ACCOLADE) is a vigorous, upright tree with an oval to vase-shaped crown and arching branches. It grows 60–70' tall, spreads 45–60' and has shiny, dark green foliage that turns bright yellow in fall. It has excellent disease resistance, and the foliage is resistant to the elm leaf beetle. It is very drought tolerant. (Zones 4–7)

U. 'Morton Glossy' (TRIUMPH) is an upright tree 50–60' tall and 40–50' wide, with an oval to vase-shaped crown. It has glossy, dark green foliage and excellent disease and pest resistance. The bark of this cultivar is dark gray and deeply fissured. (Zones 4–7)

U. 'Morton Red Tip' (DANADA CHARM) is a very graceful, vase-shaped tree 70' tall and 60' wide. The new foliage is tinged with red. This tree is resistant to Dutch elm disease. (Zones 4–9)

U. 'Morton Stalwart' (COMMENDA-TION) is a vigorous tree that forms an upright, oval crown. It grows 60' tall, spreads 40–50' and has excellent drought tolerance and good disease resistance. The green foliage turns yellow in fall. (Zones 4–9)

U. parvifolia ALLEE ('Emer II') is a broadly vase-shaped tree 40–50' tall and wide. It has attractive, exfoliating, mottled bark and pendulous branches. It also has good disease resistance and drought tolerance. Its foliage may turn red in fall. This elm is hardy in the southern half of Illinois. (Zones 5–9)

U. 'Pioneer' is a fast-growing, vigorous, rounded tree growing 50' tall and wide. It has dark green foliage, yellow fall color and good disease resistance. (Zones 5–7)

U. 'Morton' (both photos)

U. 'Regal' is a European elm hybrid introduced by the University of Wisconsin. It has a pyramidal to oval shape, grows to 60' tall by 35' wide, tolerates stress and has good disease resistance. (Zones 4–7)

Problems & Pests
In addition to the fatal fungal Dutch elm disease, elms can suffer attack from aphids, bark and leaf beetles, borers, caterpillars, Japanese beetle, leafhoppers, leaf miners, canker, dieback, leaf spot, powdery mildew, rot and *Verticillium* wilt.

Elm seeds provide food for many birds and small mammals, and the trees provide shelter and nest sites.

Euonymus

Euonymus

Features: foliage, corky stems *(E. alatus)*, habit **Habit:** deciduous or evergreen shrub, small tree, groundcover or climber **Height:** 18"–20' **Spread:** 2–20' **Planting:** B & B, container; spring or fall **Zones:** 3–9

OF THE MANY *EUONYMUS* SPECIES AVAILABLE IN THE TRADE, burning bush *(E. alatus)*, also known as winged euonymus, is the one to which most homeowners are drawn. And while we may prefer the smaller size of the cultivar 'Compacta,' it does not provide as dramatic 'wings' on its branches as the species does. The foliar display of burning bush in autumn is truly one of our best shows of color—deep red, reliable and enhanced by attractive fruit.

Growing

Euonymus prefer **full sun** but tolerate light or partial shade. They will also tolerate heavy shade but with diminished fall color. Soil of **average to rich fertility** is preferable, but any **moist, well-drained** soil will do.

E. alatus requires very little pruning except to remove dead, damaged or awkward growth as needed. It tolerates severe pruning and can be used to form a hedge. *E. fortunei* is a vigorous, spreading plant that can be trimmed as required to keep it within the desired growing area. It too tolerates severe pruning.

Tips

E. alatus adds season-long color in a shrub or mixed border, as a specimen, in a naturalistic garden or as a hedge. Dwarf cultivars can be used to create informal hedges. *E. fortunei* can be grown as a shrub in a border or as a hedge. It is an excellent substitute for boxwood. Its trailing habit also makes it suitable as a groundcover or climber.

Recommended

E. alatus (burning bush, winged euonymus) is an attractive, open, mounding, deciduous shrub. It grows 15–20' tall, with an equal or greater spread. The foliage turns a watermelon pink in fall. The small, red fall berries are somewhat obscured by the bright foliage. Winter interest is provided by the corky ridges, or 'wings,' that grow on the stems and branches. This wide-spreading plant is often pruned into a neat, rounded form. The species can be invasive. **CHICAGO FIRE** ('Timber Creek') grows 8–10' tall

E. alatus (both photos)

Burning bush achieves the best fall color when grown in full sun.

E. fortunei 'Emerald Gaiety' with *Hosta*

E. fortunei BLONDY

and 6–8' wide. It has early, bright red fall foliage and conspicuous orange fruit. It is hardier than the species and has superior branch structure. 'Compacta' ('Compactus'; compact winged euonymus) is a popular cultivar. It has more dense, compact growth, reaching up to 10' tall and wide, and has less prominently corky ridges on the branches. It may suffer winter damage during unusually cold winters. FIRE BALL ('Select') is a hardier selection of 'Compacta' that grows up to 7' tall and wide. It has brilliant red fall color and suffers no winter damage. (Zones 3–8)

E. fortunei (wintercreeper euonymus) as a species is rarely grown in favor of the wide and attractive variety of cultivars. These can be prostrate, climbing or mounding evergreens, often with attractive, variegated foliage. BLONDY ('Interbolwji') has yellow foliage with narrow, irregular dark green margins. It grows 18–24" tall and 24–36" wide. 'Coloratus' (purpleleaf wintercreeper) is a popular cultivar, usually grown as a groundcover. The foliage turns red or purple over the winter. 'Emerald Gaiety' is a vigorous shrub that grows about 5' tall, with an equal or greater spread. It sends out long shoots that will attempt to scale any nearby wall. This rambling habit can be encouraged, or the long shoots can be trimmed back to maintain the plant as a shrub. The foliage is bright green with irregular, creamy margins that turn pink in winter. 'Emerald 'n' Gold' is a bushy selection 24" tall and 36" wide. It has green leaves with wide gold margins. The foliage turns pinky red during winter and spring. **'Sunspot'** is an upright shrub growing 3–4' tall and slightly less wide. It has dark green foliage with a gold blotch in each leaf center. **'Vegetus'** grows up to 5' in height and width, with large, dark green leaves. It can be trained up a trellis as a climber or trimmed back to form a shrub. (Zones 5–9)

Problems & Pests

The two worst problems are crown gall and scale insects, both of which can prove fatal to the infected plant. Other possible problems include aphids, leaf miners, tent caterpillars, leaf spot and powdery mildew.

E. alatus has become a serious invasive species that is escaping into the wild in southern Illinois. E. fortunei is a problem from the latitude of Chicago southward. Cultivars are much less invasive than the parent species.

E. fortunei 'Emerald 'n' Gold'

E. alatus FIRE BALL

False Cypress

Chamaecyparis

Features: foliage, habit, cones **Habit:** narrow,
pyramidal, evergreen tree or shrub **Height:** 10"–100'
Spread: 1–55' **Planting:** B & B, container; spring
or fall **Zones:** 4–8

FALSE CYPRESSES COME IN BOTH
tree and shrub forms, most of which have
in common the drooping foliage toward
the ends of the branches. These plants are
often confused with their cousins the
arborvitae but can be distinguished by the
drooping tips, twigs that are four-sided
in cross-section (flat to rounded in
arborvitae) and globular seed cones
(more oval in the arborvitae). The false
cypresses include a number of cultivars that thrive in our climate, and they
are diverse enough in form, texture and
color to suit almost every garden.

Most species in the cypress family,
which includes the true cypresses
(genus Cupressus)*, false cypresses,*
junipers and arborvitae, have rot-
resistant, straight-grained wood.

Growing

False cypresses prefer **full sun**. The soil should be **fertile, moist, neutral to acidic** and **well drained**. Alkaline soils are tolerated. In shaded areas, growth may be sparse or thin.

No pruning is required on tree specimens. Plants grown as hedges can be trimmed any time during the growing season. Avoid severe pruning because new growth will not sprout from old wood. To tidy shrubs, pull dry, brown leaves from the base by hand.

Tips

Tree varieties are used as specimen plants and for hedging. The dwarf and slow-growing cultivars are used in shrub or mixed borders, in rock gardens, as foundation plants and as bonsai.

As with the related arborvitae and junipers, the foliage of false cypresses may be irritating to sensitive skin. Wear gloves when planting or pruning.

C. nootkatensis 'Pendula'

In the wild, C. nootkatensis *can grow as tall as 165' and as old as 1800 years.*

C. pisifera 'Vintage Gold'

C. *pisifera* 'Squarrosa'

C. *obtusa* 'Nana Gracilis'

Recommended

C. nootkatensis (yellow-cedar, Nootka false cypress) is native to the Pacific Northwest. It grows 30–100' tall, with a spread of about 25'. The species is rarely grown in favor of the cultivar '**Pendula**,' which has a very open habit and even more pendulous foliage than the species. It grows to 50' in height and 20–25' in spread. (Zones 4–8)

C. obtusa (Hinoki false cypress), a native of Japan, has foliage arranged in fan-like sprays. It grows about 70' tall, with a spread of 20'. '**Minima**' is a very dwarf, mounding cultivar. It grows about 10" tall and spreads 16". '**Nana Aurea**' grows 3–6' in height and spread. The foliage is gold-tipped, becoming greener in the shade and bronzy over the winter. '**Nana Gracilis**' (dwarf Hinoki false cypress) is a slow-growing cultivar that reaches 24–36" in height, with a slightly greater spread. (Zones 4–7)

C. pisifera (Japanese false cypress, Sawara cypress) is another Japanese native. It grows 70–100' tall and spreads 15–25'. The cultivars are more commonly grown than the species. '**Filifera Aurea**' (golden threadleaf false cypress) is a slow-growing cultivar with golden yellow, thread-like foliage. It grows about 40' tall and 10–20' wide. '**Nana**' (dwarf false cypress) is a dwarf cultivar with feathery foliage similar to that of the species. It grows into a mound about 12" in height and width. '**Plumosa**' (plume false cypress) has very feathery foliage. It reaches 30–50' in height, with a 10–20' spread. '**Squarrosa**' (moss false cypress) has less pendulous foliage than the other cultivars. Young plants grow very densely, looking like fuzzy stuffed animals. The growth becomes more relaxed and open with maturity. This cultivar grows about 65' tall, with a spread of about 55'. **'Vintage Gold'** is a dwarf cultivar with bright yellow, feathery foliage that resists fading in summer and winter. It grows 18–30" tall and wide. (Zones 4–8)

Problems & Pests
False cypresses are not prone to problems but can occasionally be affected by spruce mites, blight, gall and root rot.

Chamaecyparis comes from the Greek and means 'low cypress,' even though many species are very tall trees.

C. *nootkatensis* 'Pendula'

C. *obtusa* 'Nana Aurea'

Filbert
Hazelnut
Corylus

Features: early-spring catkins, nuts, foliage, habit **Habit:** large, dense, deciduous shrub or small tree **Height:** 8–50' **Spread:** 6–25' **Planting:** B & B, container; spring or fall **Zones:** 4–8

FILBERTS INCLUDE BOTH SHRUBS AND TREES, WITH THE MOST notable type being the novelty cultivar 'Contorta'—also known by the marvelous common name Harry Lauder's walking stick. Use this cultivar as a specimen plant in an area where its twisted stems and foliage can be appreciated. Other plants recommended by the Morton Arboretum include the shrub *C. americana* (American filbert) and the tree form *C. colurna* (Turkish filbert).

Though all filberts bear edible nuts,
C. avellana and C. maxima are two
of the most common commercial
species. They are grown for the
delicious nuts themselves and for
the extracted oil.

Growing

Filberts grow equally well in **full sun** or **partial shade**. The soil should be **fertile** and **well drained**.

These plants require little pruning but tolerate it well. Entire plants can be cut back to within 6" of the ground to encourage new growth in spring. On grafted specimens of corkscrew hazelnut, suckers that come up from the roots should be cut out. They will be easy to spot because they won't have the twisted habit.

Tips

Use filberts as specimens or in shrub or mixed borders. American filbert is a good choice for naturalized areas and woodland gardens.

Male and female flowers are produced on the same plant, but you should grow at least three plants for good nut production. Male flowers are borne in long, showy, dangling

C. avellana 'Contorta' (both photos)

Forked filbert branches have been used as divining rods to find underground water or precious metals.

C. maxima var. purpurea
C. americana

catkins. The less conspicuous female flowers produce the edible nuts.

Recommended

C. americana (American filbert, American hazelnut) is a rounded, multi-stemmed, suckering native shrub that gets leggy with age. It grows to 10' tall and 6' wide and features showy catkins in early spring. The dark green foliage turns orange-yellow in fall. The edible nuts are enclosed in attractive, hairy, papery, frilled husks that turn from green to brown when ripe. (Zones 4–7)

C. avellana (European filbert, European hazelnut) grows as a large shrub or small tree. It reaches 12–20' in height and spreads up to 15'. Male catkins are borne in late winter and early spring. Cultivars are more commonly grown than the species. 'Contorta' (corkscrew hazelnut, Harry Lauder's walking stick) is perhaps the best known cultivar. It grows 8–10' tall and wide. The stems and leaves are twisted and contorted. This is a particularly interesting feature in winter, when the bare stems are most visible. Keep your eyes open for a selection called 'Red Majestic,' a purple-leaved form of corkscrew hazelnut. The leaves emerge deep red in spring and mature to a purple color that lasts through early summer. (Zones 4–8)

C. colurna (Turkish filbert, Turkish hazelnut) grows 40–50' in height, with a spread of 20–25'. It tolerates a range of soil types and adverse conditions. This species has good yellow fall color and is a species recommended by the Morton Arboretum. (Zones 4–7)

C. maxima (giant filbert) is a large shrub or small tree that is rarely seen in cultivation. More common is **var. *purpurea,*** the purple giant filbert. It makes a fine addition to the spring garden. This variety adds deep purple leaf color and adapts to many soils. It grows 10–12' tall, with an equal spread. The best leaf color develops in full sun, though the rich color usually fades in the heat of summer to dark green. (Zones 4–8)

C. **'Purple Haze'** is a purple-leaved selection that is a hybrid of *C. americana* and *C. maxima* var. *purpurea.* It forms a rounded shrub 8–10' tall and wide, with burgundy new foliage that turns bronze in summer. This plant was discovered and introduced by McKay Nursery in Waterloo, Wisconsin. (Zones 5–7)

Problems & Pests
Bud mites, Japanese beetle, tent caterpillars, webworm, blight, canker, fungal leaf spot, powdery mildew and rust may cause occasional problems.

C. avellana 'Contorta'

The alternative name for corkscrew hazel, Harry Lauder's walking stick, comes from the gnarled, twisted cane the famous vaudeville comedian used.

C. maxima var. *purpurea*

Fir

Abies

Features: foliage, cones, form **Habit:** narrow, pyramidal or columnar, evergreen tree or shrub **Height:** 1–75' **Spread:** 2–30' **Planting:** B & B, container; spring **Zones:** 3–7

LIKE MANY GROUPS OF EVERGREENS, FIRS COME IN MYRIAD TYPES and sizes. The most commonly grown in Illinois is white fir *(A. concolor)*, which tolerates our conditions better than most. Many firs are adapted to cool, moist forests and thrive on acidic soils. For that reason, it is recommended to plant these trees where they will be sheltered from drying winds and hot, midday sun. To distinguish a fir from a spruce, look at the needles: fir needles are typically flat and blunt-tipped, while spruce needles are usually square in cross-section and sharply pointed. Also, fir cones sit on top of the branches and shed their scales individually, while spruce cones hang downwards and are shed whole.

Growing

Firs usually prefer **full sun** but tolerate partial shade. The soil should be **rich, cool, moist, neutral to acidic** and **well drained**. *A. balsamea* tolerates wet soil. *A concolor* prefers a loose, sandy soil and will not tolerate heavy clay. These trees generally do not tolerate extreme heat or polluted, urban conditions. *A. concolor* is far more tolerant of such conditions than other *Abies*.

Tips

Firs make impressive specimen trees in large areas. The species tend to be too large for the average home garden. Several compact or dwarf cultivars can be included in shrub borders or used as specimens.

Recommended

*A. **balsamea*** (balsam fir) is quite pyramidal when young but narrows as it ages. A slow-growing tree native to northern boreal regions, it can reach 45–75' in height, with a spread of 15–25'. **'Hudsonia'** (forma

A. balsamea

The genus name Abies *is derived from the Latin word* abire, *'to rise up,' referring to the great height some fir trees reach.*

A. nordmanniana

A. balsamea 'Hudsonia'
A. concolor

hudsoniana) grows only 24" tall, with a spread of 24–36". It is a natural form of the species, but it is usually sold as a cultivar. 'Nana' is a slow-growing, dense, rounded shrub with dark green needles that are silvery white on the undersides. It grows 12–24" tall and 24–36" wide. These dwarf cultivars are coneless and more suitable to a small garden than the much larger parent species. They benefit from some afternoon shade from the hot sun. (Zones 3–6)

A. concolor (white fir, silver fir) forms an impressive specimen that grows 30–50' tall in garden conditions but can grow up to 130' in unrestricted natural conditions. It spreads 20–30'. The needles have a whitish coating, giving the tree a hazy blue appearance. 'Candicans' is a narrow, upright tree that has silvery blue needles. 'Compacta' is a dwarf cultivar. It has whiter needles than the species and grows to 10' in height and spread. This cultivar makes an attractive specimen tree. 'Violacea' has silvery blue needles and is very attractive. It grows as large as the species. (Zones 3–7)

A. koreana (Korean fir) is slow growing and small, by evergreen standards. It grows 15–30' in height and spreads 10–20'. The unusual, attractive purple-blue cones are produced while the tree is still young. 'Horstmann's Silberlocke' ('Silberlocke') has unusual, twisted needles that show off silvery stripes on the undersides. 'Prostrata' ('Prostrate Beauty') is a low-growing cultivar with bright green needles. It reaches about 24" in height and spreads 3–6'. (Zones 5–7)

A. nordmanniana (Nordmann fir) is a dense, slow-growing, narrowly pyramidal tree, with tiered branches that sweep the ground. In garden settings it grows 40–60' tall and 12–20' wide, but it can reach 200' tall in the wild. This species has smooth, gray-brown bark and black-green needles with two silvery white stripes along the undersides. The upper branches bear 6" long, upright cones that are pinkish when young and red-brown when mature. Nordmann fir dislikes hot, dry summers. (Zones 4–7)

Problems & Pests

Firs are susceptible to problems with aphids, bagworm, bark beetles, spruce budworm, needle blight, root rot and rust.

According to the National Christmas Tree Association, balsam fir and white fir are among the 10 most popular tree Christmas tree species in the world.

A. concolor 'Candicans'

A. koreana

Forsythia

Forsythia

Features: early- to mid-spring flowers **Habit:** spreading, deciduous shrub with upright or arching branches **Height:** 1–10' **Spread:** 2–15' **Planting:** B & B or container in spring or fall; bare-root in spring **Zones:** 4–9

SUNNY YELLOW BLOOMS EXTENDING ALONG A FORSYTHIA'S STEMS announce a triumphant return to spring. Little touches of yellow at the base of the plant, on the other hand, are a sign the winter was harsh and the flower buds were frozen down to wherever the snow protected the stems. Recent introductions bring hardier cultivars, providing a spring show no matter what the winter's severity. Well-pruned forsythias give a great appearance during the spring show and through the rest of the season. Unpruned shrubs appear raggedy, especially when their uneven stems are full of flowers.

Growing

Most forsythias grow best in **full sun** but tolerate light shade. *F. viridissima* var. *koreana* 'Suwan Gold' prefers **partial shade**. The soil should be of **average fertility, moist** and **well drained**.

Correct pruning is essential to keep forsythias attractive. Flowers are usually produced on growth that is at least two years old. Prune minimally when forsythia plants are young. Mature plants should be thinned annually, removing older wood back to vigorous shoots, and removing one or two of the oldest stems to the ground. Pruning should take place after flowering is finished.

Trimming these shrubs into formal hedges often results in uneven flowering. An informal hedge allows the plants to grow more naturally. Size can be restricted by cutting shoots back to strong junctions.

Tips

These shrubs are gorgeous while in flower, with yellow blooms that cover the stems before the leaves appear. Include one in a shrub or mixed border where other plants will take over once the forsythia's early-season blooms have passed.

Forsythia plants are very cold hardy, surviving in Zone 3 quite happily. The flowers, however, are not as hardy because the buds form in summer and are then vulnerable to winter cold. Hardiness zones listed in the following section apply to bud and flower hardiness.

F. x intermedia 'Fiesta'

Allow a clematis to twine through your forsythia for an ongoing display of flowers and color.

F. x intermedia GOLD TIDE

Recommended

F. 'Arnold Dwarf' is a low, mounding shrub with long, trailing branches. It is sometimes listed as a cultivar of *F. x intermedia*. It generally grows about 36" tall but can reach 6', with a spread up to 7'. The flowers are a slightly greenish yellow

F. viridissima var. koreana 'Kumson'

Forsythias can be used as hedging plants, but they look most attractive when grown informally.

F. x intermedia GOLDILOCKS

and are rather sparse on young plants, becoming more abundant as plants mature. This cultivar blooms in early to mid-spring. It makes an interesting groundcover and can be used to prevent erosion on steep banks. (Zones 5–8)

F. x intermedia (border forsythia) is a large shrub with upright stems that arch as they mature. It grows 5–10' tall and spreads 5–12'. Yellow flowers emerge in early to mid-spring. 'Fiesta' has bright yellow and green variegated foliage and red young stems. GOLDILOCKS ('Courtacour') is a dwarf cultivar that grows to 4' tall, with an equal spread. The flowers are densely clustered along the stems. GOLD TIDE ('Courtasol') is a unique low, spreading cultivar that grows only 24–30" tall but can spread up to 4'. 'Lynwood' ('Lynwood Gold') grows to 10' in both height and width. The light yellow flowers open widely and are distributed evenly along the branches. 'Spectabilis' grows to 10' in height and width. Its bright yellow flowers are more cold tolerant than those of the parent hybrid. 'Week End' is a neat, upright shrub with abundant large flowers that bloom several weeks later than those of most other forsythias. It grows 8' tall and wide. (Zones 6–9)

F. ovata (early forsythia) is a low, spreading shrub that grows up to 6' tall and 8' wide. This species has the hardiest buds, and its flowers open in early spring. It has been crossed with other species to create attractive, floriferous, hardy hybrids. 'Meadowlark' is a complex hybrid having *F. ovata* as one of its parents.

It was bred to have extremely hardy flower buds. The flowers are bright yellow. 'New Hampshire Gold' is an attractive compact cultivar with very hardy buds. It grows 4–6' tall, with an equal spread, and has the added attraction of developing red-purple fall color. 'Northern Gold' was developed in Canada to bloom after –28° F winter temperatures. It has golden yellow blooms on upright plants that reach 5–8' in height and can spread up to 10'. 'Northern Sun' is hardy to –30° F and bears clear yellow flowers. It has a spreading habit and can reach 8–10' in height and 8–15' in width. 'Ottawa' is a hardy cultivar with a neat, compact growth habit and light yellow flowers. It grows to 4–5' tall and as much as 9' wide. (Zones 4–7)

F. viridissima (greenstem forsythia) is a low, spreading plant with shoots that stay green for several years. The species is rarely found. The following cultivars share the green stems and have flowers that appear in early to mid-spring. 'Bronxensis' is a low, mounding plant with pale yellow blooms. It generally grows 12–24" tall and 24–36" wide, but it can reach 30" in height and 5' in width. **Var. *koreana* 'Kumson'** has bright yellow flowers and features silvery veins on the green leaves. It grows 4–6' tall and wide. **Var. *koreana* 'Suwan Gold'** has bright yellow flowers and foliage. It grows 3–4' tall, with an equal spread. (Zones 5–8)

F. x *intermedia* (both photos)

Problems & Pests

Most problems are not serious but may include root-knot nematodes, leaf spot and stem gall.

Fothergilla
Bottlebrush
Fothergilla

Features: spring flowers, scent, fall foliage **Habit:** dense, rounded or bushy, deciduous shrub **Height:** 2–10' **Spread:** 2–10' **Planting:** B & B, container; spring or fall **Zones:** 4–9

THE SCENT OF HONEY IS JUST ONE OF MANY REASONS TO GROW fothergillas. The unique spring blooms often appear ahead of the foliage and look like little bottlebrushes, inspiring one of the common names for these shrubs. Good summer color gives way to vibrant fall hues that hold off until late in the season and include yellow, orange and red, often on the same leaf.

Growing

Fothergillas grow well in **full sun** or **partial shade**. In full sun they bear the most flowers and have the most vivid fall color. The soil should be of **average fertility, acidic, humus rich, moist** and **well drained**.

These plants require little pruning. Remove any wayward and dead branches as needed.

F. gardenii cultivar in fall color (above)

Tips

Fothergillas are attractive and useful in shrub or mixed borders, in woodland gardens and in combination with evergreen groundcovers.

Recommended

F. gardenii (dwarf fothergilla) is a bushy shrub that grows 24–36" tall, with an equal spread. In mid- to late spring, fragrant white flowers appear before the foliage. The foliage turns yellow, orange and red in fall.

F. major (center & below)

F. major (large fothergilla) is a rounded shrub that grows 6–10' tall, with an equal spread. In late spring it produces erect clusters of fragrant, white flowers just before or with the emerging foliage. The flowers are larger and appear a little later than those of *F. gardenii*. The fall colors are yellow, orange and scarlet. **'Mount Airy'** is a more compact, upright-branching cultivar, growing 5–6' in height and width. It bears abundant flowers and has more consistent fall color than the species.

Fothergilla flowers have no petals. The showy parts are the white stamens.

Fringe Tree
Chionanthus

Features: early-summer flowers, fall and winter fruit, bark, habit **Habit:** rounded or spreading, deciduous large shrub or small tree **Height:** 10–25' **Spread:** 10–25' **Planting:** B & B, container; spring **Zones:** 4–9

TREE OR SHRUB? GENERALLY GROWN AS MULTI-STEMMED PLANTS, fringe trees tend toward a shrubby appearance but may reach 25' in height—the size of many small trees. The first part of the common name derives from the 4–10" long flower clusters that appear to be fringed with white at the base. The pure white blooms are fragrant and appear in early summer as the foliage begins to emerge. Dark purplish berries form on female plants, and in fall, fringe trees turn golden yellow.

Growing
Fringe trees prefer **full sun** but will grow in partial shade. They do best in soil that is **fertile, moist** and **well drained** but adapt to most soil conditions. They tolerate salt and pollution. In the wild they are often found along streams and in rock crevices near water.

Little pruning is required on mature fringe trees. Thin out the stems when the plant is young to encourage an attractive habit. Prune after flowering, or in spring for young plants that aren't yet flowering.

Tips

Fringe trees work well as specimen plants, in borders or beside water features. Plants begin flowering at a very early age. They are among the latest woody plants to leaf out each year.

Both male and female plants must be present for the females to set fruit. Some trees have both male and female flowers. The fruit attracts birds.

Recommended

C. retusus (Chinese fringe tree) is a rounded, spreading shrub or small tree. It grows 15–25' tall, with an equal spread. In early summer it bears erect, fragrant white flowers followed in late summer by dark blue fruit. (Zones 5–9)

C. virginicus (white fringe tree) is a spreading small tree or large shrub that is native to the eastern and southern U.S. (not to Illinois). It grows 10–20' tall, with an equal or greater spread. In early summer it bears drooping, fragrant white flowers, followed only occasionally by dark blue fruit. (Zones 4–9)

Problems & Pests

Fringe trees rarely have any serious problems but can be affected by borers, canker, leaf spot and powdery mildew.

C. virginicus

Your pruning technique can shape a fringe tree into a large, full shrub or a lovely small, multi-stemmed specimen tree.

C. retusus

Ginkgo
Maidenhair Tree
Ginkgo

Features: summer and fall foliage, habit, bark **Habit:** deciduous tree; conical in youth, variable with age **Height:** 40–100' **Spread:** 10–100' or more
Planting: B & B, bare-root, container; spring or fall **Zones:** 3–9

THERE'S NOT A LEAF IN THE TREE KINGDOM AS DISTINCTIVE AND elegant as the ginkgo's. Even though a ginkgo tree may not have a perfect crown, just getting close enough to discern the fan-like leaves brings joy to tree lovers. Ginkgo has been a horticultural specimen far longer than most trees and has enjoyed a revival as a street tree because of its rugged constitution. Be aware that this species has genders and be sure to plant a male—the females produce fruit that is malodorous.

Growing
Ginkgo prefers **full sun.** The soil should be **fertile** and **well drained,** but this tree adapts to most soils. It also tolerates urban conditions and cold weather. Little or no pruning is necessary.

Tips

Though its growth is slow until it becomes established, ginkgo eventually becomes a large tree that is best suited as a specimen in parks and large gardens. It can also be used as a street tree. If you buy an unnamed plant, be sure it has been propagated by grafting. Seed-grown trees may prove to be female, and the stinky fruit is not something you want littering your lawn, driveway or sidewalk.

Recommended

G. biloba is variable in habit. It grows 50–100' tall, with an equal or greater spread. The leaves can turn an attractive shade of yellow in fall, after a few cool nights. Female plants are generally avoided because the fruit has an unpleasant odor. Several cultivars are available. **'Autumn Gold'** is a broadly conical male cultivar. It grows 50' tall and spreads 30'. The fall color is bright golden yellow. **'Magyar'** has upright, stiff branches and survives in difficult situations, making it a good choice for urban streets. This male selection grows to 50' tall and 20–40' wide. **'Princeton Sentry'** is a narrow, upright male cultivar 40–80' tall and 10–25' in spread.

Problems & Pests

This tree seems to have outlived most of the pests that might have afflicted it. A leaf spot may affect ginkgo, but it doesn't cause any real trouble.

This tree sheds nearly all of its golden fall leaves within a single day, making raking a snap.

G. biloba

Ginkgo appears to have been saved from extinction by its long-time use in Asian temple gardens. Today this 'living fossil' grows almost entirely in horticultural settings.

Ginkgo's unique leaves resemble those of maidenhair fern (inset).

Golden Rain Tree

Koelreuteria

Features: habit, foliage, flowers **Habit:** rounded, spreading, deciduous tree
Height: 25–40' **Spread:** 6–40' or more **Planting:** B & B; spring **Zones:** 6–8
(marginally hardy in Zone 5)

GOLDEN RAIN TREE IS ONE OF THE FEW TREES WITH YELLOW
flowers, and one of the only trees to flower in mid-summer. It is a good
choice as a street tree, or as a shade tree near a home where space is limited.
Golden rain tree shows good adaptability to different soil types. It is not
reliably hardy in northern parts of Illinois but should do well downstate.
The fruit of this tree is unique—conspicuous, lime green, lantern-like capsules that become papery and brown
in late summer to fall.

*Koelreuteria is native to the Orient.
The genus is named for Joseph
Koelreuter, an 18th-century German
professor of natural history.*

Growing

Golden rain tree prefers **full sun**. The soil should be **average to fertile, moist** and **well drained**. This tree tolerates heat, drought, wind and polluted air. It is also pH adaptable.

Tips

Golden rain tree makes an excellent shade or specimen tree for small properties. Its ability to adapt to a wide range of soils makes it useful in many situations. The fruit can be messy but will not stain a patio or deck if the tree is planted to shade these areas.

K. paniculata (both photos)

Prune minimally. Remove dead and broken branches in mid- to late winter.

Recommended

K. paniculata is an attractive, rounded, spreading tree that grows 30–40' tall, with an equal or greater width. It bears long clusters of small yellow flowers in mid-summer, followed by red-tinged, green, capsular fruit. The leaves are attractive and somewhat lacy in appearance. In some years, fall color can be a bright yellow. **'Fastigiata'** is an upright, columnar tree that reaches 25' in height, with a spread of no more than 6'. It bears fewer flowers than the species. **'September'** has a spreading habit and bears many flowers in late summer and early fall. It is hardy only to Zone 6.

Problems & Pests

Rare problems with canker, leaf spot, root rot and wilt can occur.

Hawthorn

Crataegus

Features: late-spring or early-summer flowers, fruit, foliage, thorny branches
Habit: rounded, deciduous tree, often with a zigzagged, layered branch pattern
Height: 15–40' **Spread:** 12–40'
Planting: B & B, container; early spring
Zones: 3–8

HAWTHORNS ARE KNOWN FOR the 'thorny' part of their common name. Aside from being decidedly well armed, hawthorns are similar to crabapples and share many of their features, including strong flowering in spring, persistent, brightly colored fruit and good fall color. The berries, or haws, persist through fall because birds typically wait to feed on them until a frost softens the fruit. If you'd prefer a cultivar that does not have thorns, look for *C. crus-galli* 'Inermis.'

The thorniness of these plants can be an asset if you wish to block access with an impenetrable hedge, or repel burglars with a barrier underneath windows.

Growing

Hawthorns grow equally well in **full sun** or **partial shade**. They adapt to any **well-drained** soil and tolerate urban conditions.

Hawthorns should be pruned much like crabapples. Cut out crossing interior limbs and dead inner wood in late winter to early spring, while plants are dormant. Prune to keep branches away from pedestrian walkways. Hawthorn hedges can be pruned after flowering, in fall or in late winter to spring. Remove any diseased growth immediately. It is prudent to wear leather gloves and safety goggles when pruning hawthorns.

C. laevigata 'Paul's Scarlet' (above)

Tips

Hawthorns can be grown as specimen plants or hedges in urban sites and exposed locations.

These trees are small enough to include in most gardens. With the long, sharp thorns, however, a hawthorn might not be a good selection if there are children about.

C. crus-galli (center), *C. laevigata* (below)

Recommended

C. crus-galli (cockspur hawthorn) grows 20–30' tall and 20–35' wide. It features stout, curved thorns, horizontal branching and a large, spreading crown that flattens with age. This Illinois native is resistant to cedar-apple rust on the foliage and has moderate resistance to cedar-quince rust on the fruit. It produces floriferous clusters of foul-smelling white flowers in late spring to early summer. The rounded fruit is dark red and persists into winter.

The glossy, dark green, spoon-shaped leaves turn bright red in fall. **'Inermis'** (var. *inermis*) is a thornless selection with good disease resistance. (Zones 4–7)

C. laevigata 'Paul's Scarlet' (below)

C. laevigata (*C. oxyacantha;* English hawthorn) is a low-branching, rounded tree with zigzagged layers of thorny branches. It grows 15–25' tall and spreads 12–25'. White or pink late-spring flowers are followed by bright red fruit in late summer. Many cultivars are available. **'Paul's Scarlet'** ('Paulii,' 'Coccinea Plena') has many showy, deep pink double flowers. This cultivar is popular but very susceptible to blight. (Zones 4–8)

C. mollis (downy hawthorn, red haw) is a rounded Illinois native tree of variable thorniness. It grows 15–25' tall and wide and is moderately prone to cedar-apple rust on the foliage. Woolly clusters of foul-smelling white flowers bloom in mid- to late spring, followed by pear-shaped red fruit that is enjoyed by birds. The young leaves and twigs are covered in soft, white hairs. The large, mid-green, serrated leaves turn yellow to bronze-red in fall. (Zones 3–6)

C. punctata (dotted hawthorn) grows 20–30' tall and wide or slightly wider, with a rounded to spreading crown that flattens with age. This Illinois native is highly prone to cedar-apple rust on the foliage when this disease is present in an area. It has softly hairy, dark green leaves and short, stout thorns. The abundant, malodorous white flowers have pink stamens, giving the flowers a pinkish tinge. The flowers appear in clusters in late spring. The fruit is rounded to slightly pear shaped and dark red with pale speckles. (Zones 4–7)

C. viridis (green hawthorn) is a rounded, thorny tree with a dense habit. This Illinois native grows 20–40' tall, with an equal or slightly lesser spread. White flowers appear in late spring, followed by bright red fruit in fall. The glossy green leaves can turn red or purple in fall. The foliage is slightly susceptible to rust. **'Winter King'** has an attractive rounded to vase-shaped habit. The red fruit is larger and persists longer than that of the species. (Zones 4–7)

Problems & Pests

Borers, caterpillars, leaf miners, scale insects, skeletonizers, canker, fire blight, fungal leaf spot, powdery mildew, rust and scab are possible problems. Stress-free hawthorns will be less susceptible.

C. laevigata (above), 'Paul's Scarlet' (below)

The genus name Crataegus *comes from the Greek* kratos, *'strength,' a reference to the hard, fine-grained wood.*

Hemlock

Tsuga

Features: foliage, habit, cones **Habit:** pyramidal or columnar, evergreen tree
Height: 5–80' **Spread:** 5–35' **Planting:** B & B, container; spring or fall
Zones: 3–8

LOVELY SOFT-NEEDLED FOLIAGE AND CINNAMON RED BARK GIVE
a distinctive air to the many shape and size combinations of hemlock. And
while this drought-intolerant tree and its cultivars may not be the perfect
choice for a windbreak in exposed locations, they work well as specimens in
the mixed landscape and make excellent hedges. When shaping hemlock for
hedges, remove protruding shoots rather than shearing the branch tips.

*Don't cut these evergreen boughs for use
as holiday decorations. The needles drop
quickly once the branches are cut.*

Growing

Hemlock usually grows well in any light from **full sun to heavy shade**. The soil should be **humus rich, moist** and **well drained**. This tree is drought sensitive and grows best in cool, moist conditions. It is also sensitive to air pollution and salt, so keep it away from roads.

Hemlock trees need little pruning, though they respond well to it. The cultivars can be pruned to control their growth as required. Trim hemlock hedges in summer.

Tips

With its delicate needles, hemlock is among the most beautiful evergreens to use as a specimen tree. It can also be shaped to form a hedge. The smaller cultivars may be included in shrub or mixed borders. The many dwarf forms are useful in small gardens.

Recommended

T. canadensis (eastern hemlock) is a graceful, narrowly pyramidal tree that grows 40–80' tall and spreads 25–35'. It is native to the eastern U.S., not including Illinois. Many cultivars are available, including groundcovers and dwarf forms. '**Jeddeloh**' is a rounded, mound-forming, slow-growing cultivar 5' tall and 6' in spread. '**Pendula**' is a small, upright, weeping form that grows about 5' tall and wide.

Problems & Pests

Stress-free trees have few problems. Possible problems may be caused by aphids, mites, scale insects, weevils, woolly adelgids, gray mold, needle blight, rust and snow blight.

T. canadensis

'Jeddeloh'

Holly
Inkberry, Winterberry
Ilex

Features: glossy, sometimes spiny leaves; fruit, habit **Habit:** erect or spreading, evergreen or deciduous shrub or tree **Height:** 3–50' **Spread:** 3–40'
Planting: B & B, container; spring or fall **Zones:** 3–9

THE WONDERFUL COMBINATION OF GLOSSY EVERGREEN FOLIAGE and lovely berries puts these shrubs near the top of many gardeners' wish lists. That hollies need to be sheltered from drying winter winds and sun doesn't deter us. That we should amend soils and keep them evenly moist during summer heat spells doesn't dampen our enthusiasm. That it is necessary to grow both male and female plants to assure fruiting isn't a turnoff, either. Some species are deciduous and may be a better choice for northern areas.

Growing

These plants prefer **full sun** but tolerate partial shade. The soil should be of **average to rich fertility, acidic, humus rich** and **moist. Shelter** plants from winter wind to help prevent the leaves from drying out. Apply a summer mulch to keep the roots cool and moist.

Hollies grown as shrubs require very little pruning. Simply remove any damaged growth in spring. Hollies grown as hedges can be trimmed in summer.

Tips

Hollies can be used in groups, in woodland gardens and in shrub and mixed borders. They can also be shaped into hedges.

Inkberry looks much like boxwood and has similar uses in the landscape. Use it as a low hedge or in a mass planting. It adapts to regular shearing and forms a fuller, more

I. glabra 'Nigra'

A vase of cut winterberry branches is a perfect way to brighten a room during the long, gray winter months.

I. verticillata 'Red Sprite'

I. verticillata (above), 'Sparkleberry' (below)

The showy, scarlet berries look tempting, especially to children, but are not edible.

appealing plant when cut back hard on a regular basis.

All hollies have male and female flowers on separate plants, and both must be present for the females to set fruit. Pollination is based on proximity—one male plant within 10' of any compatible female plant should be sufficient.

Recommended

I. glabra (inkberry) is a rounded shrub with glossy, deep green, ever-green foliage and dark purple fruit. It grows 6–10' tall and spreads 8–10'. **'Compacta'** is a female cultivar with a dense branching habit. It usually grows 3–6' tall and 6–8' wide but can become larger. **'Densa'** is an upright cultivar that holds its foliage well right to the plant base. It grows up to 6' tall and wide. **'Nigra'** is a dwarf female cultivar with dark, glossy leaves that develop a purple hue in winter. This shrub grows up to 36" in height, with an equal spread. **'Shamrock'** has bright green foliage and an upright habit. It grows 3–4' tall and wide. (Zones 5b–9)

I. x meserveae (blue holly, meserve holly) is a hybrid group of erect or spreading, dense, evergreen shrubs. They grow 10–15' tall, with an equal spread, and bear glossy red or some-times yellow fruit that persists into winter. Tolerant of pruning, they make formidable hedges or barriers. Many cultivars have been developed, often available in male and female pairs. The males and females can be mixed and matched. **'Blue Boy'** and **'Blue Girl'** grow about 10' tall, with an equal spread. 'Blue Girl' bears abundant red berries. Both are quite cold hardy. 'Blue Prince' and 'Blue Princess' have large leaves, and 'Blue Princess' bears fruit prolifically. These cultivars grow 10–12' tall, with an equal spread. CHINA BOY ('Mesdob') has dark green foliage. It grows 8–15' tall and 8–10' wide and is quite cold hardy. It is the pollinator for CHINA GIRL ('Mesog'), a smaller shrub with blue-green foliage and red berries. It usually grows 5–8' tall and wide but may reach 10' in height and spread. GOLDEN GIRL ('Mesgolg') is a loose, pyramidal plant and is one of the few hollies with yellow fruit. It grows 8–15' tall, spreads 6–10' and has dark green foliage. (Zones 5–8)

I. opaca (American holly) is an excellent evergreen tree holly with dark green, minimally toothed, leathery leaves and red fruit. It can grow 40–50' tall and spread 20–40' but is often smaller in garden settings. This Illinois native often has a

I. x *meserveae* GOLDEN GIRL

I. glabra 'Densa'

I. x meserveae cultivar
I. opaca

neatly pyramidal form when young, becoming more open at maturity. Leaves and fruit vary among the many cultivars. 'Miss Helen' has dark green leaves and glossy red fruit that persists through autumn; it will reach 25' in height and 12–20' in spread. 'Old Heavy Berry' is a vigorous plant with prolific crops of bright red fruit. (Zones 5–9)

I. serrata (Japanese winterberry) is a bushy, deciduous shrub that generally grows 6–8' tall and wide but can reach 15' tall and 10' wide in ideal conditions. It has finely serrated, dull green foliage and abundant white to pink flowers. The rounded red fruit ripens early and persists well into winter. Some varieties have yellow or white fruit. This species is a good choice for creating bonsai specimens. (Zones 5–7)

I. serrata x *I. verticillata* **hybrids** are vigorous, fast-growing, deciduous shrubs with plentiful fruit. 'Bonfire' is a mounding female shrub with a spreading habit. It grows 8–10' tall and wide or slightly wider and produces abundant red fruit that ripens before the foliage falls, bending the branches with the weight of the fruit. 'Sparkleberry' is a female shrub growing 8–12' tall and 8–10' wide. It has toothed, dark green foliage that often persists into early winter. The shiny red fruit is produced in abundance and persists through the winter. 'Apollo' is a good male counterpart for 'Bonfire' and 'Sparkleberry.' It grows 8–10' tall and 6–10' wide, with ascending branches and red-tinged new foliage. (Zones 4–9)

I. verticillata (winterberry, winterberry holly) is a deciduous Illinois native grown for its explosion of red fruit that persists into winter. It is good for naturalizing in moist sites in the garden. It grows 6–8' tall, sometimes taller, with an equal spread. **'Afterglow'** is a rounded shrub 5–8' tall and slightly wider than tall. It has small, shiny green leaves that develop bright orange and yellow fall color when the shrub is young and greenish yellow fall color when mature. It has orange to red-orange fruit and is hardy to Zone 4. **'Aurantiaca'** (forma *aurantiaca*) bears reddish orange fruit that doesn't persist as long as that of some other winterberries. **'Jim Dandy'** is a compact male cultivar, useful for pollinating. It grows up to 6' tall and 5–6' wide. **'Red Sprite'** is a dwarf cultivar that grows 3–4' tall and wide and bears bright red fruit. **'Southern Gentleman'** is a popular male pollinator but is not as compact as 'Jim Dandy,' growing up to 9' tall and 7–9' wide. **'Winter Gold'** features gold fruit. This multi-stemmed shrub grows 6–8' tall, with an equal spread. **'Winter Red'** has profuse, very persistent, rounded, bright red fruit and shiny dark green foliage. It forms a rounded, multi-stemmed shrub 6–9' tall and wide. (Zones 3–9)

Problems & Pests

Aphids may attack young shoots. Leaf miners and scale insects can present problems, as can root rot in poorly drained soils.

I. x *meserveae* 'Blue Princess'

Even with the most hardy selections of blue holly, a sheltered, well-drained site is critical for success.

I. opaca

Honeylocust
Gleditsia

Features: summer and fall foliage, habit **Habit:** rounded, spreading, deciduous tree **Height:** 20–100' **Spread:** 15–70' **Planting:** B & B, container; spring or fall **Zones:** 4–8

HONEYLOCUST IS A TALL, AIRY TREE BEARING FINE-TEXTURED deciduous foliage. It casts a lighter, more dappled shade than other shade trees. The foliage does not need special fall cleanup as it resists raking, instead typically blowing to the nearest windbreak. The pods and small twig debris make the tree somewhat messy, but its good points outweigh the bad, and it makes a fine choice for almost any sufficiently large and open area.

Growing

Honeylocust prefers **full sun**. The soil should ideally be **fertile** and **well drained,** though this tough tree adapts to most soil types, including alkaline, acidic or salty soils. Honeylocust also tolerates floods and drought.

Prune young plants to establish a good branching pattern. Mature trees often require removal of dead interior wood.

Tips

Use honeylocust as a specimen tree. Though it is often used as a street tree, this species is a poor choice for narrow streets because the vigorous roots can break up pavement and sidewalks.

Recommended

G. triacanthos var. *inermis* (thornless honeylocust) is a spreading, rounded tree up to 100' tall and up to 70' in spread. The fall color is a warm golden yellow. The flowers are inconspicuous, but the long, pealike pods that develop in late summer persist into fall and sometimes still dangle from the branches after the leaves have fallen. This variety is thornless and many cultivars have been developed from it, often smaller and better suited for the home garden. The cultivars listed here generally do not bear fruit. 'Elegantissima' is a dense, slow-growing, shrubby plant 20–25' tall and 15' wide, with graceful, mid-green foliage. 'Moraine' grows in a broad vase shape 40–60' tall and 50–70' wide. It has golden yellow fall coloring. SKYLINE ('Skycole') is an upright cultivar that has denser

'Sunburst'

foliage than the species. It grows 45–60' tall, with a spread of 35–45', and has good resistance to honeylocust plant bug. 'Sunburst' is fast growing and broad spreading. It grows 30–40' tall and 25–30' wide. The foliage emerges bright yellow in spring and matures to light green over the summer.

Problems & Pests

Aphids, borers, caterpillars, honeylocust plant bug, mites, webworm, canker, heart rot, leaf spot, powdery mildew and tar spot can cause problems. Honeylocust aphids can cause serious damage if they become abundant, although most years they do not multiply fast enough to be of concern.

The species, G. triacanthos, *is heavily armored with branched thorns up to 6" long.*

Honeysuckle
Lonicera

Features: flowers, habit, fruit **Habit:** rounded, upright shrub or twining climber; deciduous or semi-evergreen **Height:** 6–20' **Spread:** 6–20' **Planting:** container or bare-root in spring; B & B in fall **Zones:** 4–8

HONEYSUCKLES CAN BE NEATLY DIVIDED INTO VINES AND SHRUBS. Climbing types typically feature intricate, fragrant flowers of multiple colors. They bloom over a long period and can set fruit toward autumn. Shrub honeysuckles received a bad name a generation ago when *L. tatarica* was used as a hedging material; it was overplanted and became susceptible to insects that disfigured the plants. But you will still see many shrub honeysuckles in older residential neighborhoods. For wonderful spring fragrance in a shrub form, try winter honeysuckle *(L. fragrantissima).*

Growing

Honeysuckles grow well in **full sun** or **partial shade**. The soil should be **average to fertile** and **well drained**. Climbing honeysuckles prefer a **moist, humus-rich** soil.

Shrub honeysuckles benefit from annual thinning, otherwise known as renewal pruning, after flowering is complete. Trim hedges twice a year to keep them neat, usually once in early summer and then again in mid- to late summer. Trim back climbing honeysuckles in spring.

Tips

Shrub honeysuckles can be used in mixed borders, in naturalized gardens and as hedges. Most are large and take up a lot of space when mature.

Climbing honeysuckles can be trained to grow up a trellis, fence, arbor or other structure. They can spread as widely as they climb to fill the space provided.

Recommended

L. x *brownii* (scarlet trumpet honeysuckle, Brown's honeysuckle) is a twining, deciduous climber that bears red or orange flowers in summer. The vine can grow 10–20' tall, and it is hardy in Zones 5–8. **'Dropmore Scarlet'** is a cultivar of this hybrid. It is one of the cold-hardiest climbing honeysuckles, hardy to Zone 4. It bears bright red flowers most of the summer.

Honeysuckle flowers are often scented and attract hummingbirds as well as bees and other pollinating insects.

L. x heckrottii

Plant honeysuckle in a pot and let it climb up a front stair railing.

L. x brownii 'Dropmore Scarlet'

L. fragrantissima (winter honey-suckle, sweet breath of spring) forms a large, bushy, deciduous or semi-evergreen shrub. It grows 6–10' high, with an equal spread. Over a long period in early or mid-spring, it bears small, lemon-scented, creamy white flowers. (Zones 4–8)

L. x heckrottii (goldflame honey-suckle) is a twining, deciduous to semi-evergreen vine with attractive blue-green foliage. It grows 10–20' tall and bears fragrant, pink and yel-low flowers profusely in spring and sporadically into fall. (Zones 4–8)

L. periclymenum (common honey-suckle, woodbine) is a twining, deciduous vine that grows 10–20' tall. It bears fragrant, red- or purple-flushed, white or yellow flowers over a long period in summer and fall. **'Belgica'** (early Dutch honeysuckle) has red-streaked, creamy white flow-ers. **'Harlequin'** has reddish purple stems, and its leaves are variegated

L. sempervirens
L. periclymenum 'Harlequin'

green, pink and cream. The flowers are white or yellow with pale mauve outer petals. (Zones 4–8)

L. sempervirens (trumpet honeysuckle, coral honeysuckle) is a twining, deciduous climber that is native to Illinois. It grows 10–20' tall and bears orange or red flowers in late spring and early summer. Many cultivars are available, with flowers in yellow, red or scarlet. '**Sulphurea**' bears yellow flowers. *L. sempervirens* is also a parent of many hybrids, including *L.* x *brownii*. (Zones 5–8)

Problems & Pests

Occasional problems with aphids, leaf miners, leaf rollers, scale insects, blight and powdery mildew can occur.

L. x *brownii* 'Dropmore Scarlet'

Choosing the right honeysuckle, planting it in the proper site and pruning regularly make all the difference in enjoying these plants.

L. sempervirens 'Sulphurea'

Hornbeam

Carpinus

Features: habit, fall color **Habit:** pyramidal, deciduous tree **Height:** 10–70'
Spread: 10–50' **Planting:** B & B, container; spring **Zones:** 3–9

AMERICAN HORNBEAM *(C. CAROLINIANA)* IS A NATIVE TREE THAT
often grows in the understory along the edges of woodlands. It needs good
drainage, but with that condition met, it makes a great choice for a home
landscape. Its growth is slow and refined (rarely getting out of bounds), and
it has interesting, sinewy-looking bark that resembles muscles—thus one
common name, musclewood. The fall color is outstanding, from yellow to
reddish purple. The European version *(C. betulus)* is more common in the
trade and is good for screening or hedging.

*These slow-growing understory trees can be
planted underneath very large older trees to
create a pleasing visual balance.*

Growing

Hornbeams like to receive **full sun** or **partial shade**. The soil should be **average to fertile** and **well drained**. American hornbeam prefers **moist** soil conditions and grows well near ponds and streams.

Pruning is rarely required, though it is tolerated. Remove damaged, diseased and awkward branches as needed. Trim hedges in late summer.

Tips

These small to medium-sized trees can be used as specimens or shade trees in smaller gardens or can be pruned to form hedges. The narrow, upright cultivars are often used to create barriers and windbreaks.

Recommended

C. betulus (European hornbeam) is a pyramidal to rounded tree. It grows 40–70' tall and spreads 30–50'. The foliage turns bright yellow or orange in fall. **'Columnaris'** is a narrow, slow-growing cultivar. It reaches 30' in height and spreads 20'. **'Fastigiata'** is an upright cultivar that is narrow when young but broadens as it matures. It grows 50' tall and 40' wide. (Zones 4–8)

C. caroliniana (American hornbeam, ironwood, musclewood, bluebeech) is a small, slow-growing tree, tolerant of shade and city conditions. It grows 10–30' tall, with an equal spread. The foliage turns yellow to red or purple in fall. (Zones 3–9)

As the alternative name ironwood suggests, American hornbeam has dense, heavy, strong wood.

C. caroliniana

Problems & Pests

Borers are becoming a more prevalent problem. Rare problems with canker, dieback, powdery mildew and rot can occur.

C. betulus 'Fastigiata'

Horsechestnut
Buckeye
Aesculus

Features: late-spring or summer flowers, foliage, spiny fruit **Habit:** rounded
or spreading, deciduous tree or shrub **Height:** 8–80' **Spread:** 8–70'
Planting: B & B, container; spring or fall **Zones:** 3–9

ONE OF THE MOST MEMORABLE PLANTINGS OF HORSECHESTNUT
in Illinois can be seen at Cantigny Gardens in Wheaton. An allée of these
stately trees leads the eye from the palatial Colonel Robert R. McCormick
home south to what was once the stable area and now is a magnificent golf
course. In spring, the trees are frosted with neatly upright flower tresses.
Later in the season, the fruits drop and can be split open to reveal an
extremely hard-shelled, two-toned nut—a most
prized possession of my boyhood. In addition to
the tree forms, this genus includes wonderful
shrubs. Bottlebrush buckeye has long, narrow
spikes of flowers that bloom in July.

Growing

Horsechestnuts and buckeyes grow well in
full sun or **partial shade**. The soil should be
fertile, moist and **well drained**. These trees
dislike excessive drought.

Little pruning is required. Remove wayward branches in winter or early spring.

Tips

The tree-sized *Aesculus* species and hybrids are best suited to large gardens as specimen and shade trees. Their roots can break up sidewalks and patios if planted too close. These trees give heavy shade, excellent for cooling buildings but difficult to grow grass beneath. Use a shade-loving groundcover instead of grass under these trees.

The smaller, shrubbier buckeyes are useful in a space-restricted setting, where they can be used as specimens, in shrub or mixed borders or in mass plantings to fill unused corners or to cover hard-to-mow banks.

All parts of *Aesculus* plants, especially the seeds, are toxic. People have been poisoned when they confused the nuts of these trees with edible sweet chestnuts (from *Castanea* species).

Recommended

A. x *arnoldiana* 'Autumn Splendor' is a tree with an oval to rounded crown. It grows 30–40' tall, with an equal spread. The foliage is scorch resistant and remains dark green all summer, turning brilliant purple-red in fall. This hybrid blooms in spring, producing erect clusters of yellow flowers with orange and red markings. The fruit is round, spiked and yellow-brown. (Zones 4–8)

A. x *carnea* (red horsechestnut) is a dense, rounded to spreading tree that grows 30–70' tall, with a spread of 30–50'. It is smaller than common

A. glabra

A. x *carnea* 'Briotii'

A. x carnea

The seeds of these plants are used in many floral displays and dried holiday arrangements.

A. hippocastanum

horsechestnut but needs more regular water in summer. Spikes of dark pink flowers are borne in late spring and early summer. 'Briotii' has large, lobed leaves and stunning red flowers in spring. It grows 25–40' tall, with an equal spread. This cultivar is hardy in Zones 5–9. 'O'Neill' grows slowly to 35' in height and 25' in spread. It bears bright red flowers. (Zones 4–8)

A. glabra (Ohio buckeye) forms a rounded tree with a dense canopy. It grows 20–40' tall, with an equal spread. The flowers are not very showy and the fruit is not as spiny as that of other buckeyes. This species is susceptible to scorch and will look best when grown in damp, naturalized conditions, such as next to a stream or pond. This species is native to Illinois. (Zones 3–7)

A. hippocastanum (common horsechestnut) is a large, rounded tree that branches right to the ground if grown in an open setting. It grows 50–80' tall and spreads 40–70'. The flowers, borne in spikes up to 12" long, appear in late spring; they are white with yellow or pink marks. 'Baumannii' bears spikes of white double flowers and produces no fruit. (Zones 3–7)

A. parviflora (bottlebrush buckeye) is a spreading, mound-forming, suckering shrub 8–12' tall and 8–15' wide. The plant is covered with spikes of white flowers in early to mid-July. This species is not susceptible to the pest and disease problems that plague its larger cousins. (Zones 4–9)

A. pavia (red buckeye) is a low-growing to rounded, shrubby tree that is native to southern Illinois. It grows 15–20' tall, with an equal spread. The flowers are cherry red, blooming in late spring to early summer. The foliage ranks among the most handsome of the buckeyes. This species needs consistent moisture. (Zones 4–8)

Problems & Pests

Horsechestnuts are most susceptible to disease when under stress. Scale insects, anthracnose, canker, leaf scorch, leaf spot, powdery mildew and rust can all cause problems.

Horsechestnut and buckeye flowers attract hummingbirds to the garden. Though the seeds are poisonous to people, squirrels enjoy them with no apparent harm.

A. *hippocastanum* fall foliage (above) & capsules (below)

Hydrangea

Hydrangea

Features: flowers, habit; also fall foliage of some species **Habit:** deciduous mounding shrub, woody climber or spreading shrub or small tree **Height:** 2–80' **Spread:** 2–20' **Planting:** container; spring or fall **Zones:** 3–9

HYDRANGEAS CAN BE CONFUSING TO THE AVERAGE GARDENER FOR a number of reasons: there are so many of them; most species are classified as subshrubs although they may die back to the ground every winter like perennials; and one of the most popular types is really a rather strong-willed vine. Huge blooms and an extended blooming period are two reasons modern gardeners have pushed these old-time favorites back into the horticultural limelight. Oakleaf hydrangea stands out with its bold and interesting structure, but the hydrangeas are winners all.

Growing

Hydrangeas grow well in **full sun** or **partial shade**. *H. arborescens* tolerates heavy shade. Shade or partial shade will reduce leaf and flower scorch in the hotter regions. The soil should be of **average to high fertility, humus rich, moist** and **well drained**. These plants perform best in cool, moist conditions, although established oakleaf hydrangea will tolerate some drought if the roots are kept well mulched.

H. macrophylla responds to the level of aluminum ions in the soil, and this level in turn depends on pH. In acidic soil the flowers tend to be blue, while the same plant grown in an alkaline soil will tend to have pink flowers. Most cultivars develop their best color in one or the other soil type.

Pruning requirements vary from species to species. See the Recommended section for specific suggestions.

Tips

Hydrangeas come in many forms and have many uses in the landscape. Include them in shrub or mixed borders, use them as specimens or informal barriers, or plant them in groups or containers. Climbing varieties can be trained up trees, walls, fences, pergolas and arbors. They will also grow over rocks and can be used as groundcovers.

A hydrangea inflorescence (flower cluster) consists of inconspicuous fertile flowers and/or showy sterile flowers. *Mophead* (or *hortensia*) inflorescences consist almost entirely of showy sterile flowers

H. paniculata cultivar (above)

H. macrophylla 'Nikko Blue'
H. paniculata 'Limelight'

H. quercifolia 'Snow Queen' in fall color

Considered the Cadillac of vines, climbing hydrangea is beautiful, especially when grown up a tall, high-limbed tree.

H. quercifolia

clustered together to form a globular, snowball-like shape. *Lacecap* inflorescences consist of a combination of sterile and fertile flowers. The showy sterile flowers form a loose ring around the smaller fertile ones, giving this flatter inflorescence a delicate, lacy appearance. Both types are well worth growing.

Recommended

H. anomala subsp. *petiolaris* (*H. petiolaris;* climbing hydrangea) is considered by some gardeners to be the most elegant climbing plant available. It grows 50–80' tall, clinging to any rough surface by means of little rootlets that sprout from the stems. Though this plant is shade tolerant, it will produce the best flowers when exposed to some direct sun each day. The leaves are a dark, glossy green and sometimes show yellow fall color. For more than a month in summer, the vine is covered with white lacecap flower clusters, and the entire plant appears to be veiled in a lacy mist. This hydrangea can be pruned after flowering, if required, to restrict its growth. (Zones 4–9)

H. arborescens (smooth hydrangea, wild hydrangea) is native to Illinois. It forms a rounded shrub 3–5' tall and wide. It is often grown as a perennial, with new growth forming from the base each year. This plant flowers on new growth and will look most attractive if cut right back to the ground in fall. The flowers of the species are not very showy, but the cultivars have large, showy blossoms. **'Annabelle'** bears large, ball-like mophead clusters of white flowers from early to mid-summer. A single inflorescence may be up to 12" in diameter. This cultivar is more compact than the species and is useful for brightening up a shady wall or corner of the garden. It's common for this plant to collapse under its own weight, especially after a rain. **'Grandiflora'** (hills of snow hydrangea) bears its white flowers in 6" diameter, mophead clusters, blooming about 10–14 days earlier than 'Annabelle.' The individual sterile flowers are larger than those of 'Annabelle,' but the clusters are smaller. **'Radiata'** (subsp. *radiata*) bears white lacecap flower clusters from early to mid-summer and has silvery white leaf undersides. **WHITE DOME** ('Darsdom') bears very large lacecap flower clusters from early to mid-summer. The bold leaves are dark green and the stems are strong. (Zones 3–9)

H. macrophylla (bigleaf hydrangea) is a rounded or mounding shrub that flowers from mid- to late summer. It grows 3–5' tall and spreads up to 6'. Flower buds form on the previous season's growth, and a severe winter or late-spring frost can kill this species back to the point where no flowering occurs. Prune flowering shoots back to the first strong buds once flowering is finished or early the following spring. On mature, established plants, you can remove one-third of the oldest growth yearly or as needed to encourage vigorous new growth. The many cultivars can have mophead or lacecap clusters with flowers in shades of pink, red, blue or purple. **'All Summer Beauty'** bears dark blue mophead clusters on the previous and sometimes the

H. anomala subsp. *petiolaris* (above)

H. macrophylla
H. arborescens WHITE DOME

H. macrophylla

Mophead flowers can be used in fresh or dried arrangements. For long-lasting fresh flowers, water the hydrangea deeply the evening before cutting to help keep the petals from wilting. For drying, wait until the blooms begin to change color in late summer before cutting.

H. serrata 'Blue Bird'

current season's growth, making this cultivar useful where other bigleaf hydrangeas are frequently killed back in winter. 'Alpenglow' bears dark red mophead clusters. 'Dooley' bears blue or pink mophead clusters. Flowers are produced all along the shoots, so if the buds at or close to the stem ends are killed by frost, the buds farther along the stems still produce flowers. ENDLESS SUMMER bears deep pink mophead flower clusters over a long season on current and prior-year growth. It survives cold winters and late-spring frosts well. 'Nikko Blue' bears many large, blue to deep lavender mophead clusters. 'Variegata' features leaves with creamy white mottled margins and bears light purple lacecap flower clusters. (Zones 5–9)

H. paniculata (panicled hydrangea) is a spreading to upright large shrub or small tree. It grows 10–22' tall, spreads to 8' and bears white flowers from late summer to early fall. Full sun is required for the best blooms. This species requires little pruning. When young it can be pruned to encourage a shrub-like or tree-like habit. The entire shrub can be cut to within 12" of the ground each fall to encourage vigorous new growth the following summer. 'Grandiflora' (peegee hydrangea) is a spreading large shrub or small tree 15–25' tall and 10–20' in spread. The mostly sterile flowers are borne in mophead clusters up to 18" long. 'Limelight' bears upright mophead clusters of light chartreuse flowers. 'Little Lamb' bears smaller mophead flower clusters than the species; its delicate white flowers mature to pink in fall. 'Pink Diamond' bears large lacecap clusters of white flowers that turn an attractive deep pink in fall. 'Unique' bears large, upright mophead clusters of white flowers that turn pink in fall. (Zones 4–8)

H. quercifolia (oakleaf hydrangea) is a mound-forming shrub that is native to the southeastern U.S. It grows 4–8' tall, with an equal spread, and features attractive, cinnamon brown, exfoliating bark. The large leaves are lobed like an oak's and often turn bronze or bright red in fall. Conical clusters of sterile and fertile flowers are borne from midsummer to fall. Pruning can be done after flowering. Remove spent flowers and cut out some of the older growth to encourage young replacement growth. 'Pee Wee' and 'Sikes Dwarf' are compact dwarf cultivars that grow half the size of the species. 'Snowflake' features double flowers in clusters 12–15" long. The flowers open white and fade to pink with age. The clusters are so heavy they cause the stems to arch toward the ground. This cultivar prefers partial shade. 'Snow Queen' bears large, upright flower clusters. The foliage turns a deep, blood red color in fall. (Zones 4–8)

H. macrophylla

H. serrata (sawtooth hydrangea) is a shrub with a compact, upright habit. It grows 4–5' tall, with an equal spread. The pink or blue, usually lacecap flowers are produced in summer and fall. See *H. macrophylla* for pruning guidelines. 'Blue Billow' is a lacecap type with large blue flowers aging to pink. 'Blue Bird' bears blue or light pink lacecap flower clusters. The leaves turn coppery red in fall. 'Preziosa' bears small, pink mophead flower clusters. (Zones 5–7)

Problems & Pests
Occasional problems include slugs, gray mold, leaf spot, powdery mildew, ringspot virus and rust. Hot sun and excessive wind will dry out the petals and turn them brown.

H. arborescens 'Annabelle'

Juniper
Juniperus

Features: foliage, variety of colors, sizes and habits **Habit:** evergreen; conical or columnar tree, rounded or spreading shrub, or prostrate groundcover **Height:** 4"–70'
Spread: 1–48' **Planting:** B & B, container; spring or fall **Zones:** 2–9

FEW SHRUBS ARE AS ADMIRED, OR AS CURSED, AS THE JUNIPERS. They are valued for their hardiness, adaptability to soil and light conditions, year-round color and tolerance of pruning. They are detested for becoming 'living meatballs' in countless foundation plantings, where they are used merely for screening and not for their ornamental impact. Try combining junipers with other shrubs, or use a number of juniper types together for contrast between the prostrate groundcovers and the more upright tree shapes.

Junipers come in all shapes and sizes and can suit almost any garden. Grow them in the sun to avoid open, straggly growth.

Growing

Junipers prefer **full sun** but tolerate light shade. Ideally the soil should be of **average fertility** and **well drained,** but these plants tolerate most conditions.

Though these evergreens rarely need pruning, they tolerate it well. They can be used for topiary and can be trimmed in summer as required to maintain their shape or limit their size.

Tips

With the wide variety of junipers available, there are endless uses for them in the garden. They make prickly barriers and hedges, and they can be used in borders, as specimens or in groups. The larger species make good windbreaks, while the low-growing species work well in rock gardens and as groundcovers.

The prickly foliage gives some gardeners a rash.

Recommended

J. chinensis (Chinese juniper) is a conical tree that grows 50–70' tall and spreads 15–20'. It is very rarely grown in favor of its many cultivars. The cultivars lend themselves to use in smaller gardens. **'Fairview'** is a narrow, pyramidal plant that grows 15–25' tall and 48' wide. The silvery blue 'berries' provide good winter interest. **'Fruitlandii'** is a vigorous spreader with bright green, dense foliage. It grows about 36" tall and 6' wide. **'Hetzii'** is an upright, spreading cultivar that grows 5–10' tall, with an equal spread. It has attractive blue-green needles. **'Hetzii Columnaris'** forms an attractive,

J. chinensis

The blue 'berries' (actually fleshy cones) are used to season meat dishes and to give gin its distinctive flavor. They also make a nice addition to potpourri.

J. horizontalis

J. sabina 'Buffalo'
J. horizontalis with *Thuja* behind

narrow pyramid about 20' tall and 5–8' wide. **'Hetzii Glauca'** has ascending branches and silver-blue foliage. It grows 10' tall, with a spread of up to 15'. **'Iowa'** is an upright shrub with blue-green needles. It reaches 8–15' in height and 4–8' in spread. **'Mountbatten'** has a conical habit and large 'berries.' It reaches 20' in height and 15' in spread. **'Old Gold'** is a spreading cultivar with yellow foliage on new spring growth. It grows 24–36" tall and spreads 3–4'. **'Pfitzeriana'** is a wide-branching, broadly pyramidal selection growing 6–10' tall and 10–15' wide. It has dull gray-green foliage and pendulous branch tips. **'Pfitzeriana Compacta'** is a dwarf form that grows about 4' tall, with an equal or greater spread. **Var.** *sargentii* **'Glauca'** (blue Sargent juniper) is a low-growing, spreading variety with bluish foliage. It grows only 12–24" tall but can spread 5–6'. **'Saybrook Gold'** is a low, spreading cultivar with bright gold needles that take on a bronze hue in winter. It grows 24–36" tall, with a spread of about 6'. **'Sea Green'** has arching branches in a fountain pattern and strong green color through the winter. It grows 6' tall and up to 8' wide. (Zones 3–9)

J. conferta (shore juniper) is a stellar groundcover for dry, sandy soils. It grows 12–18" tall and spreads 6–9'. The species and many cultivars are hardy in Zones 6–9 and therefore aren't hardy in northern areas of Illinois. **'Blue Pacific'** has excellent blue-green foliage and compact growth, rarely growing higher than 12". The spread is 6–9'. **'Emerald Sea'** is the most hardy cultivar, to Zone 5.

It is similar to 'Blue Pacific' but has a looser habit and grows taller.

J. horizontalis (creeping juniper) is a prostrate, creeping groundcover that is native to Illinois and boreal regions across North America. It grows 12–24" tall and spreads up to 8'. The foliage is blue-green, with a purple hue in winter. This juniper looks attractive cascading down rock walls. It is relatively short-lived in the landscape because it is susceptible to diseases. **'Bar Harbor'** grows 12" tall and spreads 6–10'. The foliage turns a distinct purple in winter. **'Wiltonii'** ('Blue Rug') is very low growing, with trailing branches and silvery blue foliage. It grows 4–6" tall and spreads 6–8'. (Zones 3–9)

J. procumbens (Japanese garden juniper) is a wide-spreading, stiff-branched, low shrub 12–36" tall and 6–15' wide. **'Nana'** is a dwarf, compact, mat-forming shrub. It grows 12–24" tall and spreads 6–12'. (Zones 4–9)

J. conferta 'Emerald Sea'

J. horizontalis 'Wiltonii'

J. chinensis behind lower cultivar
J. squamata

J. sabina (Savin juniper) is a variable, spreading to erect shrub. It grows 4–15' tall and may spread 5–20'. Many popular cultivars are available. **'Broadmoor'** is a low spreader with erect branchlets. It grows 24–36" tall and spreads up to 10'. **'Buffalo'** has bright green, feathery foliage that holds its color well in winter. It grows 12" tall and spreads about 8'. CALGARY CARPET ('Monna') is a low, spreading plant about 12" tall and 4–5' in spread. (Zones 3–7)

J. scopulorum (Rocky Mountain juniper) is a rounded or spreading tree or shrub that grows 30–50' tall and spreads 3–20'. It is highly prone to fungal blight in Illinois. The cultivars are less susceptible. **'Skyrocket'** is a very narrow, columnar tree with gray-green needles. It grows up to 20' tall but spreads only 12–24". **'Tolleson's Weeping'** has arching branches and pendulous, silvery blue, string-like foliage. It grows about 20' tall and spreads 10'. It is sometimes grafted to create a small, weeping standard tree. This cultivar can be used in a large planter. (Zones 3–7)

J. squamata (singleseed juniper) forms a prostrate or low, spreading shrub or a small, upright tree. It grows up to 30' tall and spreads 3–25'. It is rarely grown in favor of the cultivars. **'Blue Carpet'** forms a low groundcover with blue-gray needles. It grows 8–12" high and spreads 4–5'. **'Blue Star'** is a compact, rounded shrub with silvery blue needles. It grows 12–36" tall and spreads about 3–4'. (Zones 4–7)

J. virginiana (eastern redcedar) is a durable tree of variable form, from upright to wide spreading. It usually grows 40–50' tall but can grow taller, and it spreads 8–20'. This species is native to Illinois and most of eastern and central North America. 'Canaertii' is a pyramidal tree that grows to 35' tall and 20' wide. It has dark green foliage and bluish white fruit. 'Glauca' is a narrow, upright cultivar with silvery blue new foliage that matures to silvery green in summer. It grows up to 25' tall and 6–10' wide. 'Grey Owl' has threadlike branchlets of blue foliage, which contrasts with the yellow twigs. It has a spreading habit and reaches 10' tall and wide. 'Silver Spreader' is a low, wide-spreading cultivar with silvery foliage. It grows up to 36" tall and spreads 2–4'. (Zones 2–9)

Problems & Pests

Although junipers are tough plants, occasional problems may be caused by aphids, bagworm, bark beetles, caterpillars, leaf miners, mites, scale insects, canker, cedar-apple rust and twig blight.

J. virginiana

Juniper was used traditionally to purify homes affected by sickness and death.

J. horizontalis with lower cultivar beneath

Katsura-Tree

Cercidiphyllum

Features: summer and fall foliage, habit **Habit:** rounded or spreading, often multi-stemmed, deciduous tree **Height:** 10–70' **Spread:** 10–70' or more **Planting:** B & B, container; spring **Zones:** 4–8

KATSURA-TREE IS A TRUE STANDOUT AMONG LARGE SHADE TREES. Its foliage is purplish when it emerges in spring, maturing to a bluish green in summer and in fall changing to mostly yellows, with some apricot hues in more acidic soils. The scallop-edged, heart-shaped leaves are similar to those of redbud, and the two trees share part of their genus names. Katsura-tree is drought sensitive, so watering is recommended during dry periods, especially when the trees are young. Pests and diseases rarely present problems.

C. japonicum *is the largest native deciduous tree in Japan and China, growing as tall as 130' in the wild.*

Growing

Katsura-tree grows equally well in **full sun** or **partial shade**. The soil should be **fertile, humus rich, neutral to acidic, moist** and **well drained**. This tree will become established more quickly if watered regularly during dry spells for the first year or two.

Pruning is unnecessary. Damaged branches can be removed as needed.

Tips

Katsura-tree is useful as a specimen or shade tree. The species is sizable and is best used in large landscapes. The cultivars can be wide spreading but are more appropriate than the species for smaller gardens.

This tree is native to eastern Asia, and the delicate foliage blends well into Japanese-style gardens.

Recommended

C. japonicum grows 40–70' tall, with an equal or sometimes greater spread. It is a slow-growing tree that takes a long time to exceed 40'. The heart-shaped, blue-green leaves turn yellow and orange in fall and develop a spicy scent. **'Pendula'** is one of the most elegant weeping trees available. It is usually grafted to a standard and grows 10–25' tall, with an equal or greater spread. Mounding, cascading branches sweep the ground, giving the entire tree the appearance of a waterfall tumbling over rocks. **'Red Fox'** ('Rotfuchs') grows to 15–18' tall and 10–15' wide. Its foliage is vivid purple-red when young, turning to bronze-green in summer.

C. japonicum
'Pendula'

Kentucky Coffee Tree
Gymnocladus

Features: summer and fall foliage, fruit, bark, habit **Habit:** upright to spreading, deciduous tree **Height:** up to 50–75' **Spread:** 20–50' **Planting:** B & B; spring or fall **Zones:** 3–8

ONE CULTIVAR OF KENTUCKY COFFEE TREE, 'J.C. MCDANIEL,' IS a male (fruitless) plant with an upright-spreading branching habit. It was named for a professor and plant breeder from the University of Illinois horticulture department, so you know it's tough enough to survive in our state. The common name relates to Kentucky settlers who used the beans as a coffee substitute—not something that is recommended today as the beans and their pods have been determined to be toxic in large quantities. Good bark, interesting compound leaves and blue-green foliage are among this tree's fine attributes.

This reliable tree rarely suffers from pest or disease problems.

Growing

Kentucky coffee tree grows best in **full sun**. It prefers **fertile, moist, well-drained** soil but adapts to a range of conditions. This tree tolerates alkaline soil, drought and urban conditions.

Pruning is rarely required. Remove dead, diseased or damaged growth as needed, and do any necessary formative pruning in fall or spring.

Tips

Kentucky coffee tree makes an attractive specimen tree for spacious landscapes. It is ideal for parks, golf courses and large home gardens.

This tree often doesn't leaf out until the middle of May.

Recommended

G. dioicus is a spreading tree with compound leaves up to 36" long, each consisting of many dark green to blue-green leaflets. This Illinois native grows 60–75' tall, with a spread of 40–50', and bears large clusters of white flowers in late spring or early summer. Leathery pods follow the flowers and ripen to reddish brown. The leaves turn yellow in fall. The ridged bark adds interest to the landscape in winter. '**Espresso**' develops a compact, oval form up to 50' tall and 25–30' wide. '**J.C. McDaniel**' (PRAIRIE TITAN) was introduced at the University of Illinois in Champaign. It is a male clone with an upright, spreading habit, blue-green foliage that turns yellow in fall and a wonderful winter form. It grows 10–15' tall and 6–8' wide in 10 years. Its mature size is 50–70' tall and 20–40' wide.

G. dioicus (both photos)

Kerria
Japanese Kerria
Kerria

Features: mid- to late-spring flowers, habit **Habit:** mounding or arching, suckering, deciduous shrub **Height:** 3–7' **Spread:** 3–8' **Planting:** B & B, container; spring or fall **Zones:** 4–9

KERRIA ADAPTS TO AREAS WHERE GARDENERS OFTEN HOPE FOR help—in shade. Equally adept as an understory, rambling shrub in a woodland garden or as a pruned specimen in a shrub border, kerria adds bright yellow flowers to the spring bloom. It also contributes yellow fall foliage and distinctive yellow-green to bright green, arching stems that keep their color through the winter. 'Pleniflora' grows looser and taller than the species and has interesting ball-shaped, fully double blooms.

Growing
Kerria prefers **partial shade** but adapts to other light levels. The soil should be of **average fertility** and **well drained**. Fewer flowers will appear on a plant grown in soil that is too fertile.

Prune after the bloom. Cut flowering shoots back to young side shoots or strong buds, or right to the ground. The entire plant can be cut back to the ground after flowering if it becomes overgrown and needs rejuvenating.

Tips

Kerria is useful in group plantings, woodland gardens and shrub or mixed borders.

Most flowers emerge in spring, but some may appear sporadically in summer.

'Albaflora' (above)

Recommended

K. japonica grows 3–6' tall and spreads 3–8'. It has yellow single flowers. **'Albaflora'** ('Albiflora,' Albescens') bears light yellow to white flowers. **'Aurea-variegata'** has gold-edged foliage. **'Golden Guinea'** bears large single blooms over a long period. **'Picta'** has grayish blue-green foliage with creamy margins. **'Pleniflora'** ('Flora Pleno') has double flowers. It grows 6–7' tall, with an equal spread, and its habit is more upright than that of the species.

'Picta'

Problems & Pests

Canker, leaf and twig blight, leaf spot and root rot may occur but are not serious.

Kerria flowers can resemble old-fashioned yellow roses, and this plant is indeed a member of the rose family.

K. japonica

Larch

Larix

Features: summer and fall foliage, cones, habit **Habit:** pyramidal, deciduous conifer
Height: 30–100' **Spread:** 12–40' **Planting:** B & B, container; early spring
Zones: 1–7

EVERGREEN OR DECIDUOUS? MANY PEOPLE
would guess that larches belong in the former
category because of their cones and needle
foliage. Most conifers (cone-bearing trees),
such as pine and spruce, are evergreen, and
larches are certainly conifers. But larches
belong in the small group of deciduous
conifers. Their needles turn yellow in fall
before dropping for winter, leaving the
tree's bare frame and cones showing.
Larches are large trees (reaching more
than 50'), with slightly drooping branches.
They are typically and effectively used as
specimens.

Growing

Larches grow best in **full sun**. The soil
should be of **average fertility, moist**
and **well drained**. Though they tolerate
most conditions, larch trees generally
require good drainage. *L. laricina* is an
exception; it tolerates wet soils because
it naturally grows in bogs.

Pruning is rarely required.

*Larches are good trees for attracting
birds to the garden.*

Tips

Larches make interesting specimen trees. They are among the few coniferous, needled trees that lose their foliage each year. In fall the needles turn golden yellow before dropping, and in winter the cones stand out on the bare branches.

Recommended

L. decidua (European larch) is a large, narrow, pyramidal tree. It grows 70–100' tall and spreads 12–30'. 'Pendula' has a weeping habit and is usually grafted to a standard. Specimens vary greatly from the bizarre to the elegant. (Zones 3–6)

L. kaempferi (Japanese larch) grows 50–100' tall and spreads 15–40'. It has pendulous branchlets, but its growth is less formal than that of *L. decidua*. The summer color of the needles is also bluer than that of *L. decidua*. Fall color is excellent. 'Diane' (contorted larch) has contorted and twisted branches and twisted, bright, light green foliage. It is an interesting selection, especially in winter, when its misshapen form stands out. (Zones 4–7)

L. laricina (tamarack, eastern larch) is an open, pyramidal tree with drooping branchlets. It grows 30–80' tall and spreads 15–30'. This species is native to Illinois and much of boreal North America. (Zones 1–6)

Problems & Pests

Problems may be caused by aphids, case bearers, caterpillars, sawflies, needle blight and rust. Canker can be a problem for *L. decidua*.

L. laricina

Be prepared to reassure your neighbors that your larch is not dying when it loses its needles in fall.

L. decidua 'Pendula'

Lilac

Syringa

Features: mid-spring to early-summer flowers, habit **Habit:** rounded or suckering, deciduous shrub or small tree **Height:** 3–30' **Spread:** 3–30' **Planting:** B & B, container; late winter or early spring **Zones:** 2–8

LILACS ARE EASY TO TAKE FOR GRANTED—EVERY HOME LANDSCAPE seems to have one, and many of us have strong memories of the lilacs we grew up with. These shrubs are also generally easy to grow. While new cultivars of the common French lilac continue to be introduced (with some exciting variations in bloom color), it is the dwarfs and tree lilacs that have captured the public's fancy in recent years. If you ever want to get your fill of lilacs in one place, journey to Lombard, which is just west of Chicago, during their Lilac Festival—Lilacia Park in the center of town is awash in the fragrant blooms.

Growing

Lilacs grow best in **full sun**. The soil should be **fertile, humus rich** and **well drained**. These plants tolerate open, windy locations, and the improved air circulation helps keep powdery mildew at bay.

Many lilacs benefit from renewal pruning. On established *S. vulgaris*, *S. x hyacinthiflora* and *S. laciniata,* remove one-third of the oldest growth each year after the bloom to make way for vigorous young growth and to prevent the plants from becoming leggy, unattractive and overgrown. *S. meyeri, S. microphylla,* *S.* 'Josee,' *S. patula* and *S. reticulata* need only minimal pruning each year after the plants bloom to remove dead, damaged, diseased

Not all lilac varieties are equally fragrant, so choose your lilac carefully if this feature is important to you.

S. x *hyacinthiflora* 'Evangeline'

S. meyeri

S. vulgaris 'Sensation'

Don't limit your view of lilacs to the common French lilac seen in your grandmother's garden. You have hundreds of beautiful plants to choose from.

S. meyeri 'Palibin'

and wayward growth. All lilacs listed here, except *S. reticulata* when grown as a single-trunked tree, respond well to occasional hard pruning when plants are dormant. This can be done all at once but is best spread over two years. On mature plants, remove the thickest stalks at the base after the plants become dormant for the season—borers tend to tunnel into these woody havens and can kill the entire bush.

Deadhead lilacs as much as possible to keep plants neat. Remove the flower clusters as soon as they are spent to give the plant plenty of time to produce next season's flowers.

Tips
Include lilacs in shrub or mixed borders or use them to create informal hedges. Japanese tree lilac can be used as a specimen or small shade tree.

Recommended
S. x *hyacinthiflora* (hyacinth-flowered lilac, early-flowering lilac) is an upright hybrid that becomes spreading as it matures. It can grow up to 15' tall, with an equal spread. Clusters of fragrant flowers appear in mid- to late spring. The following cultivars are resistant to powdery mildew and bacterial blight. **'Anabel'** is an early-blooming cultivar with pink flowers. It grows 6–9' tall and wide. **'Evangeline'** bears light purple double flowers. This nonsuckering cultivar grows 8–10' tall and wide. **'Excel'** bears lavender flowers and grows 8–10'. **'Pocahontas'** bears very fragrant reddish purple flowers. It grows 10–12' tall and wide. (Zones 3–7)

S. 'Josee' is a dwarf hybrid that grows 4–6' tall, with an equal spread. It bears clusters of lavender pink blooms in late spring and sporadically until the first frost. (Zones 2–8)

S. laciniata (cutleaf lilac) is a dense, rounded shrub 6' tall and 6–10' wide. The blue-green foliage is deeply cut, with each leaf having three to nine lobes. In mid- to late spring, small, open clusters of fragrant, light mauve flowers are borne where the leaves meet the stem. The flowers arise from deep purple buds. This species tolerates heat and resists mildew. (Zones 4–8)

S. meyeri (Meyer lilac, dwarf Korean lilac) is a compact, rounded shrub that grows 3–8' tall and 3–12' wide.

S. meyeri TINKERBELLE

The wonderfully fragrant flowers of S. vulgaris *have inspired the development of some 800–900 cultivars.*

S. reticulata 'Ivory Silk' in very early bloom

S. reticulata 'Ivory Silk'
S. vulgaris

It produces fragrant pink or lavender flowers in late spring and early summer and sometimes again in fall. It does not sucker profusely. The **Fairy Tale Series** is a new group of hybrids developed from crosses between *S. meyeri* and other lilacs. The hybrids reach 5–6' in height, with an equal spread. In this series, FAIRY DUST ('Baildust') bears fragrant, dusty pink flowers. TINKER-BELLE ('Bailbelle') bears fragrant, bright pink flowers that open from dark pink buds. Both hybrids may continue to bloom sporadically over the summer. **'Palibin'** bears clusters of fragrant mauve pink flowers. (Zones 3–7)

S. microphylla (littleleaf lilac) is an upright, broad-spreading shrub that grows 6' tall and spreads 9–12'. It bears fragrant, lilac pink flowers in early summer and sometimes again in fall. This is a very neat shrub with small, tidy leaves and attractive, airy clusters of flowers. **'Superba'** grows 7' tall and up to 12' wide. Its deep red flower buds open to rich pink blooms. This cultivar is quite resistant to powdery mildew. (Zones 4–7)

S. patula (Manchurian lilac) is a hardy lilac from Korea and northern China. It grows 5–10' tall, spreads 3–8' and bears small clusters of fragrant, lilac-colored flowers. This species produces very few suckers. **'Miss Kim'** is similar to the species in shape and size but is denser in habit. The dark green leaves turn burgundy in fall. (Zones 3–8)

S. reticulata (Japanese tree lilac) is a rounded large shrub or small tree that grows 20–30' tall and wide.

It bears fragrant cream-colored flowers in early summer and does not produce many suckers. This species and its cultivars are resistant to powdery mildew, scale insects and borers. 'Ivory Silk' has a narrower habit. It grows 20–25' tall and spreads 6–10'. (Zones 3–7)

S. vulgaris (French lilac, common lilac) is the plant most people think of when they think of lilacs. It grows 8–22' tall, spreads 6–22' and bears fragrant, lilac-colored flowers in late spring and early summer. This suckering, spreading shrub has an irregular habit, but consistent maintenance pruning will keep it neat and in good condition. Many cultivars are available, of which the following are but a few examples.

S. vulgaris with paler-flowered hybrid

'Alba' has white single flowers. 'Belle de Nancy' has pink double flowers. 'Charles Joly' has magenta double flowers. 'Mme. Lemoine' has large, white double flowers. 'President Lincoln' features very fragrant, blue single flowers. 'Sensation' bears white-margined, purple flowers. 'Wonderblue' ('Little Boy Blue') grows 4–5' tall and wide and bears clusters of fragrant, single, sky blue flowers. (Zones 3–8)

Lilacs are frost-loving shrubs that don't flower at all in the warm southern U.S.

S. vulgaris 'Alba'

Problems & Pests

Borers, caterpillars, root-knot nematodes, scale insects, leaf spot, powdery mildew and stem blight are all possible troublemakers for lilacs. Lilac decline, a systemic disease spread by leafhoppers, is characterized by witches'-brooms (branch mutations), chlorosis (leaf yellowing) and a lessened quality of blooms. A plant afflicted with this disease slowly loses energy and dies.

Linden

Tilia

Features: habit, foliage **Habit:** dense, pyramidal to rounded, deciduous tree
Height: 35–80' **Spread:** 20–45' **Planting:** B & B, bare-root, container; spring
or fall **Zones:** 2–8

LINDENS BOAST MANY OUTSTANDING ATTRIBUTES THAT MAKE
them fine choices for the home landscape. They cast moderate shade from
a pyramidal form that opens with age. The bark contrasts nicely with the
dark green leaves, which often have silvery undersides. Lindens bear fragrant
yellow flowers in early summer and feature wonderful golden yellow autumn
coloring. As a bonus, they'll even withstand pollution.

*Lindens are desirable shade
and street trees because of their
picturesque shape, moderately fast
growth and wide adaptability.*

Growing

Lindens grow best in **full sun**. The soil should be **average to fertile, moist** and **well drained**. These trees adapt to most pH levels but prefer an **alkaline** soil. *T. cordata* tolerates pollution and urban conditions better than the other lindens listed here.

Little pruning is required. Remove dead, damaged, diseased or awkward growth as needed. On multistemmed specimens, all but the strongest stems should be pruned.

Tips

Lindens are useful and attractive street trees, shade trees and specimen trees. Their tolerance of pollution and their moderate size make lindens ideal for city gardens.

The flower clusters of all lindens are attached to long, lance-shaped bracts.

Recommended

T. americana (basswood, American linden) grows 60–80' tall and spreads about half this wide. Fragrant flowers appear in early to mid-summer. This tree is very cold hardy (Zones 2–8) and is native to most of the eastern half of the U.S. It is rarely used in gardens. The smaller '**Redmond**' is more commonly grown. It has a pyramidal habit, dark green foliage and fragrant summer flowers. This recommended cultivar of the Morton Arboretum grows 35–50' tall and 20–30' wide. It is hardy in Zones 3–7. 'Redmond' may also be found attributed to *T. x euchlora*.

T. americana (both photos)

Basswood has lightweight wood that is prized for use by carvers.

T. cordata (littleleaf linden) is a dense, pyramidal tree that may become rounded with age. It grows 60–70' tall, spreads 30–45' and bears small flowers with narrow yellow-green bracts in summer. **'Baileyi'** (SHAMROCK) has an open-topped habit and reaches 40' in height and 30' in width. **'Greenspire'** is a compact cultivar 40–50' tall and 20–25' in spread. **'June Bride'** has a pyramidal growth habit, glossy green foliage and yellow June flowers. It grows 50' tall and 25' wide. (Zones 3–7)

T. x *flavescens* (*T.* 'Flavescens') is a hybrid of *T. americana* and *T. cordata*. It grows 50–65' tall and 25–40' wide, with a straight trunk and a pyramidal to rounded crown. Drooping clusters of fragrant, pale yellow flowers are produced in summer. This hybrid is resistant to linden mite. (Zones 3–7)

T. cordata (above)

T. tomentosa (silver linden) has a broad pyramidal or rounded habit. It can be grown as a multi-stemmed tree. This species grows 50–70' tall, spreads 25–45' and bears small, fragrant flowers in summer. The glossy green leaves have fuzzy, silvery undersides. **STERLING SILVER** ('Sterling') is a broad pyramidal tree that grows about 50' tall and 25' wide. The leaves are intensely silver on the undersides. This cultivar is resistant to Japanese beetle. (Zones 4–7)

Problems & Pests

Occasional problems can occur with aphids, borers, caterpillars, Japanese beetle, leaf miners, mites, anthracnose, canker, leaf spot and powdery mildew.

Given enough space, lindens will branch all the way to the ground.

T. cordata (both photos)

Magnolia

Magnolia

Features: flowers, fruit, foliage, habit, bark **Habit:** upright to spreading, deciduous shrub or tree **Height:** 8–40' **Spread:** 8–30' or more **Planting:** B & B, container; winter or early spring **Zones:** 3–9

AFTER A LONG ILLINOIS WINTER, THE SIGHT OF THE FIRST STAR magnolia flowers is sure to lift spirits and send us searching for other signs of early color. We know, too, that the larger, more languid blooms of the saucer magnolias can't be far behind. And if the pinkish or purplish flowers are too commonplace in your neighborhood, seek out one of the wonderful new yellow-flowered cultivars.

Despite their often fuzzy coats, magnolia flower buds are frost sensitive.

Growing

Magnolias grow well in **full sun** or **partial shade**. The soil should be **fertile, humus rich, acidic, moist** and **well drained**. A summer mulch will help keep the roots cool and the soil moist. *M. virginiana* tolerates wet soil and shade.

Very little pruning is needed. When plants are young, thin out a few branches to encourage an attractive habit. Avoid transplanting, but if necessary, transplant in early spring.

Tips

Magnolias are used as specimen trees, and the smaller species can also be used in borders.

Avoid planting magnolias where the morning sun will encourage the blooms to open too early in the season. The sensitive blossoms can be damaged by cold, wind and rain.

De Vos/Kosar hybrid 'Ann'

M. x soulangiana

M. x loebneri 'Merrill'

Recommended

M. x 'Butterflies' is an upright tree that grows about 15' tall and spreads about 11'. In mid-spring, it bears yellow, cup-shaped flowers with red stamens. (Zones 5–9)

M. De Vos/Kosar hybrids are crosses of *M. liliiflora* 'Nigra' and *M. stellata* 'Rosea.' They grow 8–10' tall and 10' wide. These hybrids are less likely to suffer frost damage because they flower later than many other magnolias. **'Ann'** bears purple-red flowers. **'Betty'** has flowers with many white petals that are dark purple on the outsides. **'Susan'** bears large, purple-red flowers. (Zones 5–9)

M. x 'Elizabeth' bears soft yellow, mid-spring blooms. This well-proportioned, pyramidal tree grows 35–40' high and nearly as wide. (Zones 5–9)

M. liliiflora (*M. quinquepeta*; lily magnolia) forms a large, rounded shrub 8–12' tall and wide. The outsides of the petals are purple and open to reveal white insides. The flowers are borne in mid- to late spring. This species can look scruffy by the end of the season and is more famous as one of the parents of *M. x soulangiana*. (Zones 5–9)

M. x loebneri (Loebner magnolia) was developed from a cross between *M. kobus* and *M. stellata*. This rounded, spreading tree grows 15–30' tall, with an equal or greater spread. It is one of the earliest magnolias to bloom, bearing white or pink flowers in early to mid-spring. This hybrid and many of its cultivars are hardy in Zones 5–9. **'Leonard Messel'** bears flowers that are white on the inside and pink on the outside, with a darker pink or purple stripe down the center of each petal. **'Merrill'** bears abundant white flowers. It is fast growing and cold hardy to Zone 3.

M. **x** *soulangiana* (*M.* x *soulangeana;* saucer magnolia) forms a rounded, spreading shrub or tree. It grows 20–30' tall, with an equal spread. Pink, purple or white flowers emerge in mid- to late spring. **'Alexandrina'** is an upright tree. Its flower petals are pink on the outside and white on the inside. **'Brozzonii'** has white flowers with a pinkish purple tinge on the base of the petals. (Zones 5–9)

M. stellata (star magnolia) is a compact, bushy or spreading shrub or small tree. It grows 10–20' tall and spreads 10–15'. Many-petaled, fragrant white flowers appear in early to mid-spring. The species and many cultivars are hardy in Zones 4–9. **'Centennial'** is a vigorous, upright cultivar that is cold hardy to Zone 3. Its white double flowers have 28 to 32 petals each. **'Royal Star'** is a vigorous cultivar with pink buds that open to white double flowers.

M. virginiana (sweetbay magnolia, swamp magnolia) is a spreading, open shrub or small, multi-stemmed tree. It grows 10–20' tall, with an equal spread, and bears very fragrant, creamy white flowers in late spring or early summer. (Zones 5–9)

Problems & Pests
Possible problems affecting magnolias include scale insects, snails, thrips, treehoppers, weevils, canker, dieback, leaf spot, powdery mildew and *Verticillium* wilt.

M. stellata 'Royal Star'

Just one stunning magnolia flower display every few years will make up for any losses from frost damage in other years.

M. stellata

Maple
Acer

Features: foliage, bark, fruit, fall color, habit, flowers **Habit:** small, multi-stemmed tree or large shrub; deciduous **Height:** 6–80' **Spread:** 6–70' **Planting:** B & B, container; preferably spring **Zones:** 2–9

WHAT WOULD CHILDHOOD BE LIKE WITHOUT MAPLE TREES? There are the whirlybird seedpods that can be tossed into the wind over and over, and there's the autumnal ritual of raking the many-hued leaves into large piles into which one may jump. As adults, we can readily appreciate maples for their dense, shade-producing foliage, their neat appearance in a landscape and their near-supernatural coloration in autumn. Small wonder that so many species of maple are selected to grace our home landscapes, parkways and parks. They are hardy, problem-resistant, reliable growers.

Growing

Generally maples do well in **full sun** or **light shade**, though their preference varies from species to species. The soil should be **fertile, moist,** high in **organic matter** and **well drained.**

If maples are allowed to grow naturally, you simply need to remove dead, damaged or diseased branches at any time. Begin pruning maples to be grown as hedges or bonsai when the plants are very young. All pruning should take place when maples are fully leafed out, in early to mid-summer.

A. japonicum

Maples offer a wealth of diversity, with sizes to suit every garden. Many of these trees or large shrubs beautify the garden all year long.

Tips

Maples can be used as specimen trees or as large elements in shrub or mixed borders. Some species work well as hedges, some are useful as understory plants bordering wooded areas, and others can be grown in containers on patios or terraces. Few Japanese gardens are without the attractive smaller maples. Almost all maples can be used to create bonsai specimens.

Recommended

A. campestre (hedge maple) forms a dense, rounded tree 25–35' tall, with an equal spread. Its low-branching habit and tolerance of heavy pruning make it popular as a hedge plant. The foliage is often killed by frost before it turns color, but in a warm fall it may turn an attractive yellow. (Zones 4–8)

A. x *freemanii* (Freeman maple) varies in habit and fall coloration. It can grow 75–80' tall and 45–50' wide. **AUTUMN BLAZE** ('Jeffersred')

A. x *freemanii* 'Morgan'

A. saccharum *is the main source of sap used to make the famous, delicious maple syrup, but other maples can also be tapped for their sweet sap.*

A. *miyabei* STATE STREET

is more drought tolerant than *A.* x *freemanii* and has a consistently strong orange-red fall color. It grows 50–60' tall and 40–50' in spread. '**Marmo**,' a Chicagoland Grows introduction, has an excellent uniform habit and inconsistent red and yellow fall color that lasts for several weeks. It grows 45–70' tall and 35–40' wide. '**Morgan**' is a fast-growing tree with an open habit and bright orange to red fall color. (Zones 4–7)

A. ginnala (Amur maple) can withstand temperatures as low as –50° F. It adapts to many soil types and a wide pH range. This species grows 15–25' tall, with an equal or greater spread. It can be grown as a large, multi-stemmed shrub or can be pruned to form a small tree. It is often used in cold climates in place of *A. palmatum* or *A. japonicum* for

Japanese-style gardens. The fall foliage is often a brilliant crimson, developing best in full sun, but Amur maple will also grow well in light shade. (Zones 2–8)

A. griseum (paperbark maple) grows very slowly to 20–35' tall, with a width half or equal to the height. It adapts to many conditions. This maple is popular because of its orange-brown bark that peels and curls away from the trunk in papery strips. It is difficult to propagate, so it can be expensive and sometimes hard to find. (Zones 5–8)

A. japonicum (fullmoon maple, Japanese maple) is an open, spreading tree or large shrub. It grows 20–30' tall, with an equal or greater spread. This species is more cold hardy than *A. palmatum,* with a few specimens surviving in sheltered Zone 4 gardens. The leaves turn stunning shades of yellow, orange and red in fall. 'Aconitifolium' has deeply lobed leaves that turn deep red in fall. (Zones 5–7)

A. miyabei is a medium-sized specimen tree with a broad pyramidal habit. STATE STREET ('Morton') is a Chicagoland Grows introduction that grows 60' tall and 50' wide. This cultivar is more cold hardy than *A. campestre* and more heat and drought tolerant than *A. platanoides.* It keeps its green foliage until late in fall then turns golden yellow for a brief period before the leaves drop. (Zones 4–7)

A. palmatum (Japanese maple) is considered by many gardeners to be one of the most lovely and versatile

A. platanoides samaras

Maple fruits, called samaras, have wings that act like miniature helicopter rotors and help in seed dispersal.

A. saccharum (center), *A. palmatum* cultivar (below)

A. saccharum

Maple wood is hard and dense. It is used for fine furniture construction and for some musical instruments.

A. miyabei STATE STREET

trees available. Though many cultivars and varieties are quite small, the species generally grows 15–25' tall, with an equal or greater spread. With enough space it may even reach 50'. Because it leafs out early in spring, this tree can be badly damaged or killed by a late-spring frost.

Two distinct groups of cultivars have been developed from *A. palmatum.* Types without dissected leaves, derived from *A. p.* var. *atropurpureum,* are grown for their purple foliage, though many lose their purple coloring as summer progresses. Two that keep their color are 'Bloodgood' and 'Moonfire,' both of which grow to about 15' tall and wide. Types with dissected leaves, derived from *A. p.* var. *dissectum,* have foliage so deeply lobed and divided that it appears fern-like or even thread-like. The leaves can be green, as in the cultivar 'Waterfall,' or red, as in 'Red Filigree Lace' and 'Crimson Queen.' 'Ornatum' has dissected leaves with silvery variegations. These trees are generally small, growing to 6–10' tall and wide. (Zones 5–8)

A. platanoides (Norway maple) is a rounded or oval tree 40–50' tall or taller, with an equal or slightly lesser spread. It has very dense growth, so grass may not grow well beneath it. Its fall color can be good unless an early frost hits before the color develops. This maple is a tough city tree, but don't use it near natural wooded areas; the seedlings are prolific and can outcompete many native plants. 'Crimson King' is a very common cultivar with dark purple foliage. 'Deborah' is easy to grow and has a strong central leader. It has wavy-margined, leathery, dark green to bronze-green foliage that is purple-red when young and orange-yellow in fall. **'Drummondii'** (harlequin maple) has light green foliage with wide creamy margins. Any growth that doesn't develop the variegated foliage should be pruned out. EMERALD LUSTRE ('Pond') is a vigorous, well-branched selection that has excellent cold hardiness. The dark green foliage is red tinged when young and brilliant yellow in fall. It will provide shade earlier than the other *A. platanoides* selections. (Zones 4–8)

A. rubrum (red maple) is native to Illinois. This species is pyramidal when young, becoming more rounded as it matures. It grows 40–70' tall, with a variable spread of 20–70'. Single- and multi-stemmed specimens are available. The cold tolerance of red maple varies depending on where the tree has been grown. Locally bred trees will adapt best to the local climate. Fall color varies from tree to tree, some developing no fall color and others developing bright yellow, orange or red foliage. Choose named cultivars for the best fall color. **'Bowhall'** is an upright pyramidal form 40–50' tall and 10–15' wide. The foliage turns orange-red in late fall. OCTOBER GLORY has brilliant fall leaves, starting out orange and gradually turning dark red. The color turns late in fall and an early frost can spoil it. RED SUNSET ('Franksred') boasts deep orange to red color that appears early in fall. It has good cold tolerance. (Zones 4–8)

A. griseum

A. platanoides 'Crimson King'

A. *palmatum* var. *dissectum*

A. *saccharinum* leaves showing silvery undersides

A. saccharinum (silver maple) is a fast-growing, large, rounded tree with drooping branches. It grows 50–80' tall and spreads 30–50'. This species is a poor choice close to buildings and on small properties because it has weak wood and tends to drop a lot of debris. On a rural or large property this fast-growing Illinois native can be quite impressive, particularly when a light breeze stirs the leaves and reveals their silvery undersides. 'Skinneri' (forma *laciniatum*) is a pyramidal selection with a central leader and deeply cut foliage. (Zones 3–9)

A. saccharum (sugar maple) is considered by many to be the most impressive and majestic of all the maples. It has a rounded pyramidal outline, grows 60–80' tall and spreads 40–50'. Its brilliant fall color ranges from yellow to red. This large species is native to Illinois. It does not tolerate restricted, polluted,

urban conditions but makes a spectacular addition to parks, golf courses and other large properties. **'Endowment'** is a fast-growing columnar cultivar with scarlet fall color. **GREEN MOUNTAIN** has dark green foliage and tolerates drought and small growing spaces. The fall color may be yellow, orange or scarlet. **'Majesty'** ('Flax Hill Majesty') is a densely branched cultivar with an upright oval habit. The fall color is scarlet. (Zones 3–8)

Problems & Pests
Aphids, borers, caterpillars, leafhoppers, scale insects, anthracnose, canker, leaf spot and *Verticillium* wilt can affect maples. Chlorosis (leaf yellowing) caused by nutrient deficiency can occur in alkaline soils. Leaf scorch can be prevented by watering young trees during hot, dry spells.

A. x freemanii 'Marmo'

The smaller maples, such as
A. japonicum, A. palmatum
and A. griseum, *make ideal specimens for the home garden.*

A. platanoides

Mountain-Ash

Sorbus

Features: form, flowers, foliage, fruit **Habit:** rounded to broadly pyramidal, single or multi-stemmed, deciduous tree **Height:** 20–50' **Spread:** 20–30' **Planting:** B & B, container; spring or fall **Zones:** 2–8

MOUNTAIN-ASH TREES ARE BELOVED FOR THEIR FOUR-SEASON interest—white flowers in spring, clean green foliage in summer, berries and strong color in fall and gray bark for winter interest. Unfortunately, they are also susceptible to a number of insect and disease conditions that can kill them at a relatively early age. Trees subjected to urban pollution, drought and poor soil will most likely be targets for borers, fire blight, crown gall and canker, among other problems. Those grown well, in stress-free conditions, will make fine, small specimen trees that generate a plethora of orange-red berries.

Growing

Mountain-ashes grow well in **full sun, partial shade** or **light shade** and in **average to fertile, humus-rich, moist, well-drained** soil. They prefer **neutral to slightly acidic** soil but tolerate slightly alkaline soil. *S. aucuparia* tolerates pollution and urban conditions better than other mountain-ashes.

These trees need very little pruning. Remove damaged, diseased and awkward growth as needed.

Tips

Use mountain-ashes as specimen trees in small gardens or in woodland and natural gardens, where they attract a variety of wildlife to the garden. Birds enjoy the fruit.

Recommended

S. alnifolia (Korean mountain-ash) is a broad, pyramidal to rounded tree 35–50' tall and 20–30' wide. Young trees are more erect, broadening with age. This species has dark green, serrated leaves that turn golden yellow in fall. Unlike those of most mountain-ashes, the leaves are not divided into leaflets. Clusters of white flowers are produced in mid-spring, followed by persistent orange-red fruit. This species is the least susceptible mountain-ash to borers. (Zones 4–8)

Mountain-ash fruit is edible but should be eaten in moderation. Gathered after the first frost, it makes an excellent jelly.

S. aucuparia (European mountain-ash) is a tree 20–35' tall and 20–30' wide, with a rounded crown. The mid- to dark green, divided leaves turn red to orange in fall. Dense clusters of white flowers appear in late spring. 'Asplenifolia' has finely divided leaflets. 'Xanthocarpa' has orange-yellow fruit. (Zones 2–7)

Problems & Pests

Mountain-ashes are susceptible to fire blight, which may eventually be fatal. Be prepared to replace these trees after 10–15 years. Other problems include aphids, borers, sawflies, scale insects, anthracnose, canker, crown gall, powdery mildew and rust.

Ninebark

Physocarpus

Features: flowers, fruit, bark, foliage **Habit:** upright, sometimes suckering, deciduous shrub **Height:** 5–10' **Spread:** 5–15' **Planting:** container; spring or fall **Zones:** 2–8

NINEBARK HASN'T RECEIVED THE PUBLICITY OF SOME OTHER woody plants, but that situation is beginning to change. DIABOLO was named shrub of the year by the Illinois Nurserymen's Association in 2003, and SUMMER WINE, a cross between DIABOLO and *P. opulifolius* 'Nanus,' is another heralded introduction. If you are familiar with the sprawling, coarse species of ninebark, check out these more refined cultivars, which often have colorful foliage. You may not actually find nine layers, but the peeling, flecked bark of ninebark does add interest to the winter landscape.

Growing

Ninebark grows well in **full sun** or **partial shade**. The best leaf coloring develops in a sunny location. The soil should be **fertile, moist** and **well drained**. This shrub adapts to alkaline soil.

Little pruning is required, but you can remove one-third of the old stems each year after flowering is finished to encourage vigorous new growth.

'Nugget'

Ninebark is an easy-growing shrub that adapts to most garden conditions.

Tips

Ninebark works well in a shrub or mixed border, or as part of a woodland or naturalistic garden.

Recommended

P. opulifolius (common ninebark) is native to Illinois. This suckering shrub has long, arching branches and exfoliating bark. It grows 5–10' tall and spreads 6–15'. Light pink flowers in early summer are followed by fruit that ripens to reddish green. **'Dart's Gold'** grows 5' in height and spread. It has bright gold leaves that hold their color well in summer. **DIABOLO** ('Monlo') has attractive purple foliage and grows 8–10' in height and spread. **'Nugget'** is a compact plant with bright yellow foliage that matures to lime green over the summer. This cultivar grows 6' tall, with an equal spread. **SUMMER WINE** ('Seward') is a neat, compact plant 5–6' in height and width. It has dark crimson foliage and pinkish white, midsummer flowers.

Problems & Pests

Occasional problems with leaf spot and powdery mildew may occur.

P. opulifolius

DIABOLO (below)

Oak

Quercus

Features: summer and fall foliage, bark, habit, acorns **Habit:** large, rounded, spreading, deciduous tree **Height:** 40–100' **Spread:** 10–100' **Planting:** B & B, container; spring or fall **Zones:** 2–9

OAKS DEFINE THE CONCEPT OF MAJESTY, WITH FORM, FOLIAGE, bark and fall color that are hard to beat. The problem we have as an urban-suburban population is our propensity to undertake construction near these wonderful trees. Oaks are completely intolerant of disruption or compaction of their rootzones and often die within five or six years of such disturbance. But keep work areas well back from oaks, and you'll enjoy magnificent specimens long into the future.

Growing

Oaks grow well in **full sun** or **partial shade**. *Q. muehlenbergii* needs full sun. The soil should be **fertile, moist** and **well drained**. Most oaks prefer slightly acidic soils but will adapt to alkaline conditions. *Q. palustris* does not tolerate alkaline soils.

Do not disturb the ground around the base of an oak; these trees are very sensitive to changes in grade.

No pruning is needed. These trees can be difficult to establish. Most should be transplanted only when young; exceptions are *Q. bicolor*, *Q. palustris* and *Q. robur*, which can better tolerate transplanting as older trees.

Q. macrocarpa

Oaks are important commercial trees. Their wood is used for furniture, flooring, veneers, boat building and wine and whiskey casks.

Tips

Oaks are large trees best suited to be grown as specimens or in groves in parks and large gardens. *Q. imbricaria* responds well to pruning and is sometimes used as a hedging plant.

The acorns are generally not edible. Acorns of certain oak species are edible but usually must be processed first to leach out the bitter tannins.

Recommended

Q. alba (white oak) is a rounded, spreading tree with peeling bark. This Illinois native species grows 50–100' tall, with an equal spread. The leaves turn purple-red in fall. (Zones 3–9)

Q. bicolor (swamp white oak) is also native to our state. This broad, spreading tree has peeling bark. It grows 50–70' tall, with an equal or

Q. bicolor

Q. alba

Oaks have been held sacred by many cultures throughout history. The ancient Greeks believed these trees were the first ones created, and the Roman poet Virgil said that they gave birth to the human race.

Q. palustris

greater spread. The leaves turn orange or red in fall. (Zones 3–8)

Q. imbricaria (shingle oak, laurel oak) is a broad, spreading tree with smooth bark. It grows 50–70' tall, with an equal spread. The leaves of this Illinois native turn yellowish brown or sometimes reddish orange in fall. (Zones 4–8)

Q. macrocarpa (bur oak, mossycup oak) is a large, broad tree with furrowed bark. It is also native to Illinois. This species grows 50–80' tall, with an equal spread. The leaves turn shades of yellow in fall. (Zones 2–8)

Q. muehlenbergii (chinkapin oak, yellow chestnut oak) is an open, rounded Illinois native with scaly, flaky bark. It grows 40–50' tall and 50–70' wide. The foliage somewhat resembles that of holly. The leaves turn yellow, orange-brown or brown in fall. (Zones 5–7)

Q. palustris (pin oak, swamp oak) is a fast-growing, pyramidal to columnar tree with smooth bark. This Illinois native tree grows 60–70' tall and 25–40' wide. The foliage develops a good red to reddish brown color in fall. This species is typically not recommended in the Chicago area because it does not tolerate alkaline soils. (Zones 4–8)

Q. prinus (chestnut oak, basket oak) is a dense tree with a rounded habit and deeply furrowed bark. It grows 60–70' tall, with an equal spread. The leaves turn yellow-orange to yellow-brown in fall. The sweet acorns attract wildlife to the garden. (Zones 4–8)

Q. REGAL PRINCE (*Q.* x *warei* 'Long') is a cross between *Q. bicolor* and *Q. robur* 'Fastigiata.' It grows 40–60' tall and 20–30' wide, forming an upright oval shape. The leaves are a glossy dark green with silvery undersides and are mildew resistant. Fall color is a rusty red-orange. (Zones 4–8)

Q. imbricaria (above)

Q. robur (English oak) is a rounded, spreading tree, growing 40–60' tall and 50–60' wide. The fall color is golden yellow and the bark is deeply furrowed. '**Concordia**' is a slightly smaller, rounded plant with golden yellow new leaves that turn green with age. Narrow, columnar cultivars suitable for restricted spaces are also available; most grow 60' tall but spread only 10–15.' They include '**Fastigiata**,' a columnar selection with ascending branches, and '**Skyrocket**,' which is similar to 'Fastigiata' and very mildew resistant. (Zones 3–8)

Q. rubra (center), *Q. prinus* (below)

Q. rubra (northern red oak) is a rounded, spreading, fast-growing tree that grows 60–75' tall, with an equal spread. The bark of this Illinois native is generally smooth but can be somewhat furrowed. The fall color ranges from yellow to red-brown. The roots are shallow. This oak develops chlorosis in highly alkaline soils. (Zones 4–9)

Problems & Pests
The many possible problems are rarely serious: borers, gypsy moth caterpillars, leaf miners, leaf rollers, leaf skeletonizers, scale insects, canker, leaf gall, leaf spot, powdery mildew, rust, twig blight and wilt.

Pear

Pyrus

Features: early to mid-spring flowers, fruit, habit, bark, fall foliage **Habit:** columnar to broadly pyramidal, deciduous tree **Height:** 35–50' **Spread:** 15–30'
Planting: B & B, container; early spring **Zones:** 5–8

PEAR TREES ARE VERY ATTRACTIVE, BUT IN MANY COMMUNITIES they seem to be relegated to plantings beneath power lines. They flower reliably with a dazzling display of white in spring, followed by good green foliage and relatively strong fall color. And then there is the all-important advantage: carefully chosen cultivars top out slightly under the height of the wires. Few situations generate argument as heated as when a mature shade tree has half or more of its growth amputated at the behest of an electrical utility.

The scientific name honors J. Callery, a French missionary to China who brought this pear species to the Western world.

Growing

Pear grows best in **full sun**. The soil should be **fertile** and **well drained**, but this tree adapts to most soil conditions and tolerates drought and pollution.

Very little pruning is needed. Remove awkward, crossing and damaged branches in early spring.

CHANTICLEER (both photos)

Tips

Pear makes an excellent specimen tree. It can be quite messy when the fruit ripens, so plant away from parked cars, patios and decks and be prepared for some cleanup around the tree. The fruit of this ornamental pear species and its cultivars is not considered edible.

Pear trees, like apples, can be trained to form espalier specimens against a wall or fence.

Recommended

P. calleryana (Callery pear) is a thorny, irregular, conical tree rarely grown in favor of the cultivars. 'Aristocrat' is a fast-growing, broadly pyramidal, thornless tree growing 40–50' tall and 20–30' wide. It has shiny dark green foliage that is tinged purple when young, becoming a brilliant deep red in fall. The flowers are white, and the fruit is red to yellow. 'Autumn Blaze' has an irregular, open crown and horizontal branching. It grows 40' tall and 25–30' wide, and its fall color is bright red to purple. **CHANTICLEER** ('Glen's Form,' 'Select,' 'Cleveland Select,' 'Stone Hill') has a narrow, pyramidal form. It grows 35–40' tall and spreads 15–20'. It blooms profusely in spring, and its leaves turn red in fall. It is fairly resistant to fire blight. Many other cultivars are also available, but they are beginning to show susceptibility to fire blight.

Problems & Pests

Occasional trouble is possible with aphids, caterpillars, leaf rollers, scale insects, fire blight, powdery mildew and scab.

Pine

Pinus

Features: foliage, bark, cones, habit **Habit:** upright, columnar or spreading, evergreen tree **Height:** 2–120' **Spread:** 2–50' **Planting:** B & B, container; spring or fall **Zones:** 2–8

PINES ARE SUCH A DIVERSE GROUP OF PLANTS, IT IS DIFFICULT TO know the best way to recommend them: are they specimens, candidates for hedges or general landscape plants? The answer, of course, is all of the above. Much of the debate surrounding pines does not concern the beauty of the many species but rather proper care in the first year to keep them alive (see general planting instructions in this book's introduction) and their susceptibility to pests such as sawflies. Diagnosing a pine problem is never easy. If you have a concern, contact the University of Illinois Extension. Otherwise, simply enjoy these low-maintenance trees.

Growing

Pine trees grow best in **full sun**. They adapt to most **well-drained** soils. *P. flexilis* tolerates partial shade and needs moist, well-drained soil. Pines are not heavy feeders, but soil of **moderate fertility** is recommended.

Generally, little or no pruning is required. Hedges can be trimmed in mid- to late May. Pinch up to one-half the length of the 'candles,' the fully extended but still soft new growth, to shape the pine or to regulate growth.

Tips

Pines can be used as specimen trees, hedges or windbreaks. Smaller cultivars can be included in shrub or mixed borders to provide texture and interest year-round.

Austrian pine (*P. nigra*) was long recommended as the pine most tolerant of urban conditions. Over the years, it has proven to be susceptible to diplodia tip blight. If grown, it should be given good air circulation to help prevent the disease.

Recommended

P. aristata (bristlecone pine) is a fairly small, slow-growing pine with a conical or shrubby habit. It grows 8–30' tall and spreads 6–20'. It is not pollution tolerant but survives in poor, dry, rocky soil. The needles may dry out in areas exposed to winter winds. (Zones 4–8)

P. banksiana (jack pine) has a rounded to conical habit when young and becomes irregular and sometimes unruly as it matures. It

P. aristata

Most pine seeds are edible, though many are too small to bother with. Commercially available 'pine nuts' come from P. pinea *and other species.*

P. cembra

P. mugo
P. flexilis

grows 30–50' tall, with a variable but lesser spread. This tree is native to northeastern Illinois. It is useful in northern Illinois gardens but is often considered too scruffy for areas where less hardy, more attractive species thrive. (Zones 2–8)

P. cembra (Swiss stone pine) has a dense, columnar habit. It grows 25–40' tall and spreads 10–15'. This slow-growing pine is resistant to white pine blister rust. (Zones 3–7)

P. flexilis (limber pine) is a broad, pyramidal tree growing 50' tall and spreading 15–35'. This species has flexible branches and tolerates wind. 'Vanderwolf's Pyramid' has blue-green needles. It is an upright grower, to 40' tall and 20' wide. (Zones 3–7)

P. mugo (mugo pine) is a low, rounded, spreading shrub or tree. It grows 10–20' tall and spreads 15–20'. **Var. *pumilio*** (var. *pumilo*) is a dense variety that forms a mound 2–8' tall and wide. Its slow growth and small size make it a good choice for planters and rock gardens. (Zones 2–7)

P. parviflora (Japanese white pine) grows slowly to 20–50' tall and wide. It is conical or columnar when young and matures to a spreading, irregular, flat-topped crown. This species has been used to create bonsai. 'Brevifolia' has a narrow, columnar habit with distinctly horizontal branches. It will reach 8–10' in height and 4' in width in 15 years. (Zones 4–8)

P. strobus (eastern white pine) is native to Illinois. It is a slender, conical tree 50–120' tall and 20–40' in spread, with soft, plumy needles. It is sometimes grown as a hedge. Young trees can be killed by white pine blister rust, but mature trees are resistant. 'Compacta' is a dense, rounded cultivar that grows slowly to reach 6' in height and width. It is wider than tall when young. 'Fastigiata' is an attractive, narrow, columnar form that grows up to 70' tall and one-third as wide. 'Pendula' has long, ground-sweeping branches. It must be trained to form an upright leader when young to give it some height and shape; otherwise, it can be grown as a groundcover or left to spill over the top of a rock wall or slope. It develops an unusual soft, shaggy, droopy appearance as it matures. (Zones 3–8)

P. sylvestris (Scots pine) grows 30–70' tall and spreads 20–40'. It is rounded or conical when young and develops an irregular, flat-topped, spreading habit when mature. Trees of this species vary in size, habit and needle color and length. Young Scots pine are popular as Christmas trees. 'Watereri' is a rounded to broadly pyramidal tree that grows 10–12' tall and wide or slightly wider. It may reach 25' in height and width with age. This cultivar's needles are blue-gray. (Zones 2–7)

Pines are easy to distinguish from other needled evergreens. Pine needles are borne in bundles of two, three or five, while spruce, fir and hemlock needles are borne singly.

P. wallichiana
P. aristata

P. wallichiana (Himalayan pine, Bhutan pine, blue pine) is a graceful tree that generally grows 30–50' tall and 20–30' wide. In ideal conditions it can reach 120' or more in height and 40' in spread. It is upright and conical when young and develops a wide-spreading, domed crown and slightly pendulous branches with age. It has long, silvery blue-green needles that droop as they age.
PRAIRIE GIANT ('Morton') is a very hardy selection from the Morton Arboretum. It forms a loose, broadly pyramidal specimen that spreads with age. It grows 15–20' tall and 8–10' wide in 10 years and produces long, pendulous cones. (Zones 5–7)

'Methuselah,' a bristlecone pine that grows high in the White Mountains of California, is more than 4700 years old—the world's oldest known living thing.

P. sylvestris
P. strobus 'Compacta'

Problems & Pests

Borers, caterpillars, leaf miners, mealybugs, sawflies, scale insects, blight, blister rust, cone rust, pitch canker and tar spot can all cause problems. The European pine-shoot moth attacks pines with needles in clusters of two or three.

P. mugo var. *pumilio*

P. parviflora

Potentilla
Shrubby Cinquefoil
Potentilla

Features: flowers, foliage, habit **Habit:** mounding, deciduous shrub **Height:** 18"–4'
Spread: 2–6' **Planting:** bare-root, container; spring or fall **Zones:** 2–8

POTENTILLA IS FOUND WHERE FEW OTHER SHRUBS DARE TO GROW. Its hardiness is legendary. Reaching a flowering peak in late spring, this shrub continues to bloom at a lesser rate until frost. Another reason for potentilla's popularity is its slow growth rate. It remains rounded and manageable with virtually no maintenance. If you have seen one too many yellow potentillas in an urban island planting within a sea of concrete, consider the cultivar 'Abbotswood,' with white flowers, or 'Princess,' with pink flowers. Other cultivars stretch the color palette to oranges and near reds.

The plant we call potentilla is now known as Dasiphora floribunda *in the scientific community. Botanists have changed the scientific name a number of times, and former incarnations include* Dasiphora fruticosa, Pentaphylloides floribunda, Pentaphylloides fruticosa, Potentilla floribunda, Potentilla fruticosa *subsp.* floribunda *and* Potentilla fruticosa *var.* tenuifolia.

Growing

Potentilla prefers **full sun** but tolerates partial or light shade. The soil should ideally be of **poor to average fertility** and **well drained**, but this plant tolerates most conditions, including sandy or clay soil and wet conditions. It does not tolerate drought. Too much fertilizer or too rich a soil will encourage weak, floppy, disease-prone growth.

If you wish to shape your potentilla, do so in late winter. Either cut back all of the stems by one-third, or do selective renewal pruning by removing one or two of the oldest stems annually.

Tips

Potentilla is useful in a shrub or mixed border. The smaller cultivars can be included in rock gardens and on rock walls. On slopes that are steep or awkward to mow, potentilla can prevent soil erosion and reduce

'Abbotswood'

Potentilla tolerates excess lime in the soil and handles extreme cold very well. Try this small shrub as a low-maintenance alternative to turfgrass.

'Pink Beauty'

'Abbotswood'
P. fruticosa

the time spent maintaining a lawn. Potentilla can even be used to create a low, informal hedge.

If your potentilla's flowers fade in bright sun or in hot weather, try moving the plant to a more sheltered location. A cooler location that still gets lots of sun or a spot with some shade from the hot afternoon sun may be all your plant needs to keep its color. Colors should revive in fall as the weather cools. Plants with yellow or white flowers are the least negatively affected by heat and sun.

Recommended

P. fruticosa is native to Illinois. This yellow-flowered shrub is the parent of many, many cultivars, of which the following are a few popular and interesting ones. **'Abbotswood'** is one of the best white-flowered cultivars. It grows 30–36" tall and spreads up to 4'. **'Goldfinger'** has large yellow flowers and a mounding habit. It grows up to 40" tall, with an equal spread. **'Gold Star'** has large yellow flowers and a spreading habit. It grows 24–36" tall and spreads 3–4'. **'Jackmannii'** has good dark green foliage and yellow flowers; it finishes blooming earlier than 'Goldfinger.' It grows 3–4' tall and 3–5' wide. **'McKay's White'** bears creamy white flowers, but it doesn't develop seedheads. It grows 24–36" tall, with an equal spread. **'Pink Beauty'** bears pink semi-double flowers that stand up well in the heat and sun of summer. It grows 24–36" tall, with an equal spread. **'Primrose Beauty'** has gray-green foliage and primrose yellow blossoms that pale with age. It grows to 4' tall and 6' wide. **'Princess'** ('Pink Princess') has light pink flowers that fade to white in hot weather. It grows about 36" tall, with an equal spread. **'Snowbird'** bears large, white semi-double flowers. This robust, somewhat spreading plant grows about 32" tall and spreads up to 4'. **'Tangerine'** has orange flowers that bleach to yellow if the plant is exposed to too much direct sunlight, so place it in partial or light shade. This cultivar grows 18–24" tall and spreads 3–4'.

Problems & Pests
Though infrequent, problems with spider mites, fungal leaf spot and mildew are possible.

A tea of potentilla leaves is pleasant and has been thought to relieve coughs and fevers.

'McKay's White'
'Tangerine'

Privet

Ligustrum

Features: adaptability, fast growth, dense growth **Habit:** upright or arching, deciduous shrub **Height:** 6–15' **Spread:** 6–15' **Planting:** bare-root; spring or fall **Zones:** 3–7

WHILE NOT ORNAMENTALLY OVERWHELMING, PRIVETS DO SERVE their purpose—as low-cost, fast-growing, narrow shrubs most often used for hedges or screening. They can be sculpted into various shapes. Although deciduous, privets have dense growth that allows them to be used as barrier plants even in winter. Many species bloom in early summer, with fragrance as a bonus, and form persistent berries in autumn.

Growing

Privets grow equally well in **full sun** or **partial shade**. These shrubs adapt to any **well-drained** soil. They tolerate polluted, urban conditions and winter salt from roads and walkways.

Privets are perhaps the most commonly used hedging plants in our garden landscapes.

Privet hedges can be pruned twice each summer. Plants grown in borders or as specimens should be kept neat by removing up to one-third of the mature growth each year after blooming is finished.

L. amurense (both photos)

Tips

Privets are commonly grown as hedges because they are fast growing, adaptable and inexpensive. Left unpruned, a privet becomes a large shrub with arching branches. This form looks quite attractive, especially when in bloom.

Privet berries are poisonous. Wear gloves when pruning; the foliage may cause skin irritation.

Recommended

L. amurense (Amur privet) is a large, multi-stemmed shrub that is usually pruned to form a dense hedge. It grows 12–15' tall and spreads 8–15'. It bears small white flowers in early to mid-summer, followed by small berries that ripen to black. The dark green foliage may turn a dark bronzy purple in fall, but the color is not exceptional. (Zones 3–7)

L. vulgare 'Cheyenne' is a hardy, fast-growing, rounded, multi-stemmed shrub that grows 6–12' tall and 6–10' wide. This cultivar produces fragrant clusters of white flowers in early to mid-summer, followed by small black fruit. The shiny, dark green foliage persists into fall and takes on a purple tinge, but it is not showy. The species is hardy in Zones 4–7, but the cultivar is even hardier, to Zone 3.

Problems & Pests

Occasional problems can occur with aphids, Japanese beetle, leaf miners, scale insects, canker, leaf spot, powdery mildew and root rot.

The original seeds for 'Cheyenne' were collected in 1934 by Dr. Edgar Anderson of the Arnold Arboretum, in a dry, cold area of the Balkans near Sarajevo.

Redbud

Cercis

Features: spring flowers, fall foliage **Habit:** rounded or spreading, multi-stemmed, deciduous tree or shrub **Height:** 20–30' **Spread:** 25–35' **Planting:** B & B, container; spring or fall **Zones:** 4–9

WITH ITS ROSY PINK CLOUD OF BLOOMS IN EARLY SPRING, REDBUD is a favorite in almost any home landscape setting. Lovely heart-shaped leaves emerge after the flowery introduction. While many gardeners plant redbud as a specimen, it grows as an understory tree in the forest and looks more natural if planted to the north of a larger deciduous tree. Northern Illinois is close to the northern edge of the range for the native *C. canadensis*, so you may have trouble establishing a young tree if winters are severe. Providing it a sheltered location will help.

Growing

Redbud grows well in **full sun, partial shade** or **light shade**. The soil should be a **fertile, deep loam** that is **moist** and **well drained**.

Pruning is rarely required. The growth of young plants can be thinned to encourage an open habit at maturity. Awkward branches can be removed after the bloom. This plant has tender roots and does not like being transplanted.

Tips

Redbud can be used as a specimen tree, in a shrub or mixed border or in a woodland garden.

Recommended

C. canadensis (eastern redbud) is a spreading, multi-stemmed tree that bears red, purple or pink flowers in mid-spring, before the leaves emerge. The young foliage is bronze, fading to green over the summer and turning bright yellow in fall. 'Alba' (var. *alba*) has white flowers. 'Forest Pansy' has purple or pink flowers and dark reddish purple foliage that fades to green over the summer. The best foliage color is produced when this cultivar is cut back hard in early spring, but plants cut back this way will not produce flowers that year. 'Silver Cloud' has foliage irregularly variegated with creamy white spots. It doesn't bear as many flowers as the species. 'Forest Pansy' and 'Silver Cloud' are hardy in only the southern half of Illinois.

Select a redbud from a locally grown source. Plants grown from seeds produced far to the south are not hardy in northern regions.

C. canadensis (both photos)

Problems & Pests

Caterpillars, leafhoppers, scale insects, weevils, blight, canker, dieback, downy mildew, leaf spot and *Verticillium* wilt are potential problems for redbud.

Rhododendron
Azalea
Rhododendron

Features: late-winter to early-summer flowers, foliage, habit **Habit:** upright, mounding, rounded, evergreen or deciduous shrub **Height:** 1–10' **Spread:** 3–10'
Planting: B & B, container; spring or fall **Zones:** 3–8

IT'S HARDLY SURPRISING THAT RHODODENDRONS ARE EXTREMELY popular in Illinois. They are at their flowering peak on exactly the same weekend that we descend like locusts on garden centers in search of anything with color. Instead of an impulse purchase, plant selection should be the result of careful consideration of where the plant will go. The soil may need appropriate amendment to give the transplants a chance to survive. Even if you hear claims that a series of rhododendrons will thrive in neutral soil, acidify such soil anyway with composted pine bark or pine needles. In general, small-leaved rhododendrons are less particular about soil conditions than large-leaved species are.

Growing

Rhododendrons prefer **partial shade** or **light shade.** The deciduous azaleas typically perform best in **full sun** or **light shade,** while the evergreen azaleas tend to appreciate **partial shade.** A location **sheltered** from strong winds is preferable. The soil should be **fertile, humus rich, acidic, moist** and **well drained.** These plants are sensitive to high pH, salinity and winter injury. They need regular watering during periods of drought.

Shallow planting with a good mulch is essential, as is excellent drainage. In heavy soils, elevate the crown 1" above soil level when planting to ensure surface drainage of excess water. Don't dig near rhododendrons and azaleas; their root systems are shallow and resent being disturbed.

Dead and damaged growth can be removed in mid-spring. Spent flower clusters should be removed if possible. Grasp the base of the cluster between your thumb and forefinger and twist to remove the entire

R. catawbiense 'Cilpinense'

cluster. Be careful not to damage the new buds that form directly beneath the inflorescences.

Tips

These plants grow and look better when planted in groups. Use them in shrub or mixed borders, in woodland

Northern Lights hybrid

R. mucronulatum

gardens or in sheltered rock gardens. Take care to give them a suitable home with protection from the wind and full sun. In a protected location they should not need burlap covering in winter.

Rhododendrons and azaleas are grouped in the genus *Rhododendron*. Although hybridizing is blurring the distinction, in general rhododendrons are robust, evergreen shrubs whose flowers have 10 stamens. Azaleas tend to be smaller, evergreen or deciduous shrubs whose smaller flowers have 5 stamens.

Recommended

R. catawbiense (Catawba rhododendron, mountain rosebay) is a large, rounded, evergreen species native to the southeastern U.S. It grows 6–10' tall, with an equal spread. Clusters of reddish purple flowers appear in late spring. **'Album'** has light purple buds and white flowers. **'Cilpinense'** has white flowers flushed with pink. **'English Roseum'** has light pink flowers and is heat tolerant. **'Nova Zembla'** has purple-hued red flowers. It is also heat tolerant. (Zones 4–8)

R. **Kurume hybrids** are evergreen azaleas developed in Japan. These hybrids are slow growing and are popular for creating bonsai specimens. They bear small but plentiful flowers in a wide range of colors. **'Blaauw's Pink'** bears salmon pink flowers in late spring and early summer. This cultivar grows 3–5' tall, with an equal spread. (Zones 5–8)

R. mucronulatum (Korean rhododendron) is a rounded to upright, deciduous shrub that grows 1–8' in height and spreads 3–8'. It features pinkish purple flowers that appear in early spring. 'Cornell Pink' bears bright pink flowers. (Zones 4–8)

R. Northern Lights hybrids are broad, rounded, deciduous azaleas. They grow about 5' tall, spread about 36" and bloom in mid- to late spring. They are very cold hardy and are excellent choices for gardens in the north of Illinois. 'Apricot Surprise' has yellow-orange flowers. 'Golden Lights' has fragrant, yellow flowers. 'Orchid Lights' is a bushy, compact plant with light purple flowers. 'Rosy Lights' has fragrant, dark pink flowers. 'Spicy Lights' has fragrant, light orange-red flowers. 'White Lights' has fragrant, white flowers. (Zones 3–7)

R. PJM hybrids are compact, rounded, dwarf, evergreen rhododendrons. They grow 3–6' tall, with an equal spread. Flowers in a range of colors are produced in early to mid-spring. These hybrids are weevil resistant. 'Aglo' bears pink flowers with reddish throats. 'Olga Mezitt' bears peachy pink flowers. The leaves turn red in fall and winter. 'Regal' spreads a little wider than its height and bears pink flowers. 'Victor' is compact and slow growing, with pink flowers. (Zones 4–8)

Problems & Pests

Rhododendrons and azaleas suffer few problems if planted in good conditions with well-drained soil. When plants are stressed, however, aphids, black vine weevil, caterpillars, Japanese beetle, lace bugs, leafhoppers, scale insects, leaf gall, petal blight, powdery mildew, root rot and rust can cause problems.

R. catawbiense 'Nova Zembla' (above)

PJM hybrid 'Aglo'

Northern Lights hybrid 'Golden Lights'

Rose-of-Sharon
Hardy Hibiscus
Hibiscus

Features: mid-summer to fall flowers **Habit:** bushy, upright, deciduous shrub
Height: 8–12' **Spread:** 6–10' **Planting:** B & B, container; spring or fall
Zones: 5–9

THE PROS GIVE VERY CLEAR INSTRUCTIONS ON THE USE OF THIS upright shrub: grow it as an informal hedge, or use it in a combined shrub border. The reason for the limited options? The plant doesn't offer enough interest when not in flower. But that doesn't stop gardeners in my neighborhood from using it extensively as a specimen—I'm just guessing, but they probably bought it in full flower and wanted to show it off when they arrived home. And they can't really be blamed. Rose-of-Sharon shines in late summer when it brings several interesting colors to the heat-stricken days of July and August. Look for the newer cultivars, which elevate this shrub into the realm of horticultural eye candy.

Rose-of-Sharon attracts birds and butterflies and repels deer.

Growing

Rose-of-Sharon prefers **full sun**. This plant tolerates partial shade but becomes leggy and produces fewer flowers. The soil should be **humus rich, moist** and **well drained**.

Pinch young rose-of-Sharon plants to encourage bushy growth. Train them to take a tree form by selectively pruning out all but the strongest single stem and removing the side branches up to the height where you want the plant to bush out. The flowers form on the current year's growth; prune back tip growth in late winter or early spring for larger but fewer flowers.

Some cultivars are heavy seeders and can produce unwanted seedlings. To avoid this problem, shear off and dispose of the seedheads right after blooming finishes.

'Red Heart'

A well-tended rose-of-Sharon is one of the most beautiful and prolific blooming shrubs for the late-season garden.

'Blue Bird'

BLUE SATIN

Grow rose-of-Sharon as a bushy shrub or train it into a small patio tree.

'Diana'

Tips

Rose-of-Sharon is best used in shrub or mixed borders. The leaves emerge late in spring and drop early in fall. Plant along with evergreen shrubs to make up for the short period of green.

This plant develops unsightly legs as it matures. Plant low, bushy perennials or shrubs around the base to hide the bare stems.

Recommended

H. syriacus forms an erect, multi-stemmed shrub that bears dark pink flowers from mid-summer to fall. It can be trained as a small, single-stemmed tree. Many cultivars are available. **'Aphrodite'** bears rose pink flowers with dark red centers. **'Blue Bird'** bears large blue flowers with red centers. **BLUE SATIN** ('Marina') is a vigorous plant that bears rich blue flowers. **BLUSH SATIN** ('Mathilde') bears light pink flowers with red centers. **'Diana'** bears large white flowers. **'Freedom'** bears reddish pink semi-double flowers. **'Helene'** has white flowers with red or pink petal bases. **'Lady Stanley'** bears light pink double flowers with darker pink centers and veins. **LAVENDER CHIFFON** ('Notwood-one') features lavender flowers, each with a second ring of small lacy petals in the center. **'Purpurea Variegata'** is grown for its attractive cream-margined leaves. The purple flowers don't open fully. **'Red Heart'** bears white flowers with red centers. **ROSE SATIN** ('Minrosa') bears pink flowers with red centers. **VIOLET SATIN** ('Floru') bears reddish violet flowers. The plants are vigorous and bloom for a long time in summer and fall. **WHITE CHIFFON** ('Notwoodtwo') bears white flowers, each with a small second ring of lacy petals in the center. **'Woodbridge'** bears pink flowers with deeper pink centers.

Problems & Pests

Rose-of-Sharon can be afflicted with aphids, caterpillars, mealybugs, mites, scale insects, bacterial blight, fungal leaf spot, root and stem rot, rust, *Verticillium* wilt and viruses.

'Lady Stanley'

'Woodbridge'

Sassafras

Sassafras

Features: aromatic summer and fall foliage, habit, bark **Habit:** irregular to pyramidal, suckering, deciduous tree **Height:** 30–80' **Spread:** 25–50' **Planting:** B & B, container; spring **Zones:** 4–8

AH, ROOT BEER. THE FLAVORING ORIGINALLY CAME FROM THE roots of this woodland tree, which has also contributed a wide range of herbal remedies and teas. All parts of the plant are aromatic. The most distinctive feature of the foliage is the varied leaf shapes on the same plant. Some leaves have two lobes, making them rather resemble mittens; others have three lobes; and still others have none.

Growing

Sassafras will grow well in **full sun,
partial shade** or **light shade**. The soil
should be of **average fertility, acidic,
humus rich, moist** and **well drained**.
This tree develops a deep taproot
and should be planted when it is
young to avoid disturbing the root.

Sassafras needs little to no pruning.
If you would like a single-stemmed
specimen, remove the suckers. If
suckers are left in place, a dense
colony will form.

Tips

Sassafras can be used as a specimen
in a woodland garden, near a water
feature or along a roadside. It is
attractive in naturalized plantings,
but it isn't a strong competitor and
may eventually be overcome by
other plants.

Recommended

S. albidum is a medium to large,
irregular, suckering tree that is
native to Illinois. The aromatic
leaves may be unlobed or have two
or three lobes, with different leaf
types present on the same plant.
The leaves turn bright red in fall.
Male and female flowers are borne
on separate plants in spring. Female
plants bear fruit that ripens to dark
blue. The fruit is a favorite food of
birds, and the seeds they disperse
can sprout to become numerous
seedlings. The red fruit stalks
(pedicels) persist on the tree after
the fruit disappears, and they are
somewhat showy.

*Sassafras leaves are popular for
children's crafts and leaf collections
because of their variable shapes.*

Problems & Pests

Possible problems with Japanese
beetle, scale insects, weevils, canker,
leaf spot, mildew and rot can occur
but are uncommon.

*Safrole is a toxic compound in
oil of sassafras. Root beer is now
made with synthetic flavorings or
with oil of sassafras that has had
the safrole removed.*

Serviceberry
Saskatoon, Juneberry, Shadberry
Amelanchier

Features: spring or early-summer flowers, edible fruit, fall color, habit, bark
Habit: single- or multi-stemmed, deciduous large shrub or small tree
Height: 3–30' **Spread:** 3–30' **Planting:** B & B, container; spring or fall
Zones: 3–9

WHETHER AS SHRUBS OR SMALL TREES, SERVICEBERRIES GENERALLY grow with an open habit that gives the feeling of a naturalized plant. They put on a good show of white flowers in spring, and most develop blueberry-sized dark fruit that attracts a wide range of birds. Fall color is another attribute—most serviceberries have foliage that turns a warm yellow to red. Tree forms provide good winter interest in their branching patterns.

Serviceberry fruit can be used in place of blueberries in any recipe, having a similar but generally sweeter flavor.

Growing

Serviceberries grow well in **full sun** or **light shade**. The soil should be **fertile, humus rich, moist** and **well drained**. *A. canadensis* tolerates boggy soil conditions.

Young plants, particularly multi-stemmed ones, can be pruned after flowering is finished to encourage healthy growth and an attractive habit. Only the strongest, healthiest stems should be allowed to remain. Dead, damaged, diseased and awkward branches can be removed as needed.

A. alnifolia 'Regent' (above)

Tips

Serviceberries make beautiful specimen plants or even shade trees in small gardens. Spring flowers, edible fruit, attractive fall color and an often artistic branching habit make these excellent ornamental trees all year long. The shrubbier forms can be grown along the edges of a woodland garden or in a border. In the wild, serviceberries are sometimes found growing near water sources, and they can make beautiful pondside or streamside plants.

A. laevis (center), *A. canadensis* (below)

Recommended

A. alnifolia (saskatoon serviceberry, alder-leaved serviceberry) is a large, rounded, suckering shrub 3–12' tall, with an equal spread. It bears clusters of white flowers in late spring, followed by dark purple edible fruit in summer. The foliage turns shades of yellow, orange and red in fall. 'Regent' is a compact plant with attractive flowers, delicious fruit and good fall color. It grows 4–6' tall, with an equal spread. (Zones 3–8)

A. canadensis

*The alternative common name
shadberry may have come about
because the spring flowers appear
about the time shadfish spawn.*

A. arborea

A. arborea (common serviceberry,
Juneberry) is native to Illinois. This
small single- or multi-stemmed tree
grows 15–25' tall and spreads 15–30'.
Clusters of fragrant white flowers are
borne in spring. The edible fruit
ripens to reddish purple in summer.
The foliage turns in fall to shades
ranging from yellow to red.
(Zones 4–9)

A. canadensis (shadblow serviceberry) forms a large, upright, suckering shrub. It grows 6–20' tall and
spreads 5–15'. White spring flowers
are followed by edible dark purple
fruit in summer. The foliage turns
orange and red in fall. **'Prince
William'** is an upright cultivar that
grows about 8' tall and spreads about
6'. The new leaves emerge a reddish
color, turning dark green in summer
and then orange to scarlet in fall.
RAINBOW PILLAR ('Glenform')
forms a compact, columnar shrub
that grows 8–15' tall and 5' wide. It
has strong fall color and is hardy to
Zone 4. (Zones 3–8)

A.* x *grandiflora (apple serviceberry)
is a small, spreading, often multi-
stemmed tree. It grows 20–30' tall,
with an equal spread. The new foliage
is often a bronze color, turning green
in summer and bright orange or red
in fall. White spring flowers are followed by edible purple fruit in summer. The parent hybrid and some
cultivars are hardy in Zones 4–8.
'Autumn Brilliance' is a fast-growing
cultivar that reaches 25' in height and
about 20' in spread. The leaves turn
brilliant red in fall. This cultivar is
hardy to Zone 3. **'Ballerina'** has
bright red fall color. **'Forest Prince'**
and **'Princess Diana'** may be either

single- or multi-stemmed. They flower prolifically in spring, and the foliage turns brilliant red in fall. They are also hardy to Zone 3. **'Robin Hill'** has pink buds that open to white flowers. It has an upright habit, spreading half as much as the species.

A. laevis (Allegheny serviceberry) is a native Illinoisan tree that has a spreading habit. It grows about 25' tall, with an equal spread. The new leaves are reddish, turning green in summer. Fall color is scarlet. White mid-spring flowers are followed by sweet, dark blue fruit. **'Cumulus'** has an upright, oval habit. It reaches 15–25' in height and 15–20' in spread. This cultivar has white spring flowers and red-orange fall color. (Zones 4–8)

Problems & Pests
Problems with borers, leaf miners, fire blight, leaf spot, powdery mildew and rust can occur but are generally not serious.

A. x grandiflora 'Robin Hill'

A. x grandiflora 'Princess Diana'

Smokebush

Cotinus

Features: summer floral display, summer and fall foliage **Habit:** bushy, rounded, spreading, deciduous tree or shrub **Height:** 8–15' **Spread:** 8–15' **Planting:** container; spring or fall **Zones:** 4–8

THE 'SMOKE' IS A WONDERFUL ILLUSION. SMOKEBUSH PRODUCES inconspicuous yellow flowers in early summer. When those flower stalks mature, long, feather-like hairs emerge and change to pink or purple, giving the effect of puffs of smoke. New cultivars have dark foliage, providing contrast in a mixed border. Some cultivars also have a dense habit and a neater appearance. Others are more open, giving a naturalistic look.

Growing

Smokebush grows well in **full sun** or **partial shade**. It prefers soil to be of **average fertility, moist** and **well drained**. Established plants adapt to dry, sandy soils. Smokebush is very tolerant of alkaline, gravelly soil.

Long, lanky growth develops from pruning cuts. Plants grown for their foliage are often pruned to the ground each spring, encouraging lush, colorful growth. Alternatively, to avoid lanky growth, shear or prune young plants lightly, then leave them to develop and mature more naturally.

Tips

Smokebush can be used in a shrub or mixed border, as a single specimen or in groups. It is a good choice for a rocky hillside planting.

Recommended

C. coggygria grows 10–15' tall and wide. It develops large, puffy plumes of flowers that start out green and turn pinky gray in summer. The green foliage turns red, orange and yellow in fall. **'Daydream'** develops many pink plumes. The habit is more dense than that of the species. **'Flame'** has bluish green foliage that turns bright orange-red in fall. The flowers are purple-pink. **'Nordine'** ('Nordine Red') is the hardiest of the purple-leaved cultivars. It has pink flowers, showy red fruit and plum purple foliage that turns yellowy orange in fall. **'Royal Purple'** (purple smokebush) has purplish red flowers and dark purple foliage that turns reddish purple in fall. **'Velvet Cloak,'** which grows 10–12' tall and wide, also has deep purple

C. coggygria (above), 'Royal Purple' (below)

foliage with a reddish purple fall color. Its flowers are purple. **'Young Lady'** has abundant smoky pink flowers and green foliage. It grows 8–10' tall and wide.

Problems & Pests

Verticillium wilt is a serious problem that excellent drainage will help prevent. Powdery mildew is also possible, especially on the purple-leaved forms.

Spirea

Spiraea

Features: summer flowers, habit **Habit:** round, bushy, deciduous shrub
Height: 2–10' **Spread:** 2–12' **Planting:** bare-root, container; spring or fall
Zones: 3–9

SPIREAS ARE OLD-FASHIONED SHRUBS THAT BECAME ALL THE RAGE
when dwarf, colorful types were introduced. They are now beginning to
achieve cutting-edge status again as groundcover species join the mix. The
venerable bridal wreath spireas *(S. x vanhouttei* and *S. trilobata)* are still on
the market, but the *S. japonica* cultivars that grow only 2–4' in height and
spread are more readily available at garden centers. When selecting plants,
watch the bloom periods—some flower incredibly early. *S. japonica* cultivars
wait until early summer to flower, then rebloom if pruned.

Growing

Spireas prefer **full sun**. The soil should be **fertile, moist** and **well drained**.

Pruning is necessary to keep spireas tidy and graceful. The tight, shrubby types require less pruning than the larger, more open forms, which may require heavy renewal pruning in spring.

The appropriate pruning method depends on the flowering time for any given species. Those that bloom in spring and early summer usually form their flowers the previous year. These plants should be pruned immediately after flowering is complete. Cut out one-third of the old stems to encourage new, young growth.

Plants that flower later in summer or in fall usually form flowers during the current year. Cut these plants to within 12" of the ground in early spring, as the buds begin to swell, to encourage lots of new growth and flowers later in the season.

Tips

Spireas are used in shrub or mixed borders, in rock gardens and as informal screens and hedges.

Recommended

S. betulifolia (birchleaf spirea) is a dense, mound-forming shrub that grows 2–4' in height and spread. It bears clusters of small white flowers in early to mid-summer. The foliage turns golden yellow and bronze in fall and provides a long-lasting colorful display. 'Tor' has purple fall foliage. (Zones 3–9)

S. thunbergii 'Mount Fuji'

Under a magnifying glass, the flowers of these rose family members indeed resemble tiny roses.

S. betulifolia 'Tor' in fall color

S. nipponica
S. japonica 'Shirobori'

S. japonica (Japanese spirea) forms a clump of erect stems 4–6' tall and up to 5' wide. Pink or white flowers are borne in mid- and late summer. There are many cultivars and hybrids of this species; check to see what is available at your local nursery. '**Gold Flame**' grows 24–36" tall and 2–4' wide. The new foliage emerges red and matures to yellow-green, with red, orange and yellow fall color. '**Limemound**' grows about 36" tall and 6' wide. The stems are red and the foliage is yellow with good fall color. '**Neon Flash**' bears vivid pink flowers. It grows up to 36" tall and wide. '**Shirobori**' ('Shirobana') grows 24" tall and wide. Both pink and white flowers appear on the same plant. (Zones 3–9)

S. nipponica (Nippon spirea) is an upright shrub with arching branches. It grows 3–8' tall, with an equal spread. White blossoms appear in mid-summer. '**Snowmound**' (snowmound Nippon spirea) is more frequently grown than the species. The spreading, arching branches are covered with flowers in early summer. This cultivar grows 3–5' tall, with an equal spread. (Zones 4–8)

S. thunbergii (Thunberg spirea) is a dense, arching shrub. It grows 3–5' tall and spreads 3–6'. Small clusters of white flowers appear along the stems in spring, before the leaves emerge. '**Mount Fuji**' has small, narrow leaves, each with a white stripe down the center. '**Ogon**' has narrow yellow leaves that turn bronzy in fall. (Zones 4–8)

S. trilobata (dwarf bridal wreath spirea, dwarf Vanhoutte spirea) is

Spireas come in sizes, forms, flower colors and summer and fall leaf colors to suit almost every sunny area.

S. x *cinerea* is covered with white blooms before the foliage emerges in early spring. It grows in a rounded form, 4–5' tall and wide. '**Grefsheim**' has a mounding habit. (Zones 4–7)

a dense, bushy shrub with arching branches. It grows 4–5' tall and wide. White flowers are borne in clusters in early summer. '**Swan Lake**' is a smaller plant with arching branches. It grows 3–4' tall and wide or slightly wider and bears abundant white flowers along its branches. (Zones 3–8)

S. x *vanhouttei* (bridal wreath spirea, Vanhoutte spirea) is a dense, bushy shrub with arching branches. It grows 6–10' tall and spreads 10–12'. White flowers are borne in clusters in early summer. (Zones 3–8)

S. japonica cultivar (above)

Problems & Pests

Aphids, dieback, fire blight, leaf spot and powdery mildew can cause occasional problems.

These ornamental shrubs are popular because they adapt to a variety of situations and require only minimal care once established.

S. japonica 'Neon Flash'

S. x *vanhouttei*

Spruce

Picea

Features: foliage, cones, habit **Habit:** conical or columnar, evergreen tree or shrub
Height: 3–80' **Spread:** 2–20' **Planting:** B & B, container; spring or fall **Zones:** 2–8

RENOWNED FOR THEIR EXCELLENT TALL, CONICAL GROWTH
habits, trees of the genus *Picea* add an element of formality to the garden.
The vertical lines are strong and must be considered in the overall home
landscape—too often they overpower their space. Known too for their sticky
trunks and resinous branch tips, spruces are often sold as the Christmas trees
with superior fragrance. Dwarf, slow-growing cultivars, such as dwarf
Alberta spruce, are used for plant sculpture and bonsai.

*Stradivarius used spruce to make
his renowned violins.*

Growing

Spruce trees grow best in **full sun**. Dwarf Alberta spruce prefers **light shade** and a **sheltered** location. The soil should be **deep, well drained** and **neutral to acidic**. Spruces tolerate alkaline soils.

Pruning is rarely needed.

Spruces are best grown from small, young stock because they dislike being transplanted when larger or more mature.

Tips

Spruce trees are used as specimens and windscreens. The dwarf and slow-growing cultivars can also be used in shrub or mixed borders or even in containers.

Oil-based pesticides such as dormant oil can take the blue out of your blue-needled spruce.

Recommended

P. abies (Norway spruce) is a fast-growing, pyramidal tree with dark green needles. It grows 70–80' tall and spreads about 20'. This species is wind tolerant. **'Cupressina'** is a narrowly conical plant that works well for screening. It grows 30–40' tall and 10–15' wide. **'Nidiformis'** (nest spruce) is a slow-growing, low, compact, mounding form. It grows about 3–4' tall and spreads 3–5'. **'Pendula'** has a variable growth habit. It can be staked to a desired height to create a weeping form, or it can be left to sprawl along the ground and over objects. It spreads 10–15'. (Zones 2–8)

P. abies 'Nidiformis'

Spruce is the traditional Christmas tree in Europe.

P. abies 'Pendula'

P. glauca 'Conica'

Spruce trees frequently produce branch mutations, or 'witches'-brooms,' which can be propagated to form new cultivars of various sizes, shapes and colors.

P. pungens var. glauca 'Mission Blue'

P. glauca (white spruce) is native to many northern states. This conical tree with blue-green needles grows 40–60' tall and 10–20' in spread. It can grow up to 160' tall in the wild. **'Conica'** (dwarf Alberta spruce, dwarf white spruce) is a dense, conical, bushy shrub that grows 6–8' tall and spreads 24–36". This cultivar works well in planters. **'Densata'** (var. *densata;* Black Hills spruce) grows in a narrow, dense shape, 20–40' tall and 10–20' wide. It has blue-green foliage. (Zones 2–6)

P. omorika (Serbian spruce) is a slow-growing, narrow, spire-like tree with upward-arching branches and drooping branchlets. Two white stripes run the length of each needle. This tree grows 30–50' tall and spreads 10–15'. It is best planted in spring. (Zones 4–8)

P. pungens (Colorado spruce) is a
conical or columnar tree with stiff,
blue-green needles and dense
growth. This drought-tolerant,
hardy tree grows 30–60' tall, with a
spread of 10–20'. **Var.** *glauca* (Colorado blue spruce) is similar to the
species, but with blue-gray needles.
The following cultivars have been
developed from this variety, and
some are smaller. **'Fat Albert'** is a
dense, cone-shaped tree with
ascending branches and steel blue
needles. It typically grows 10–15'
tall and 7–10' wide but can grow to
40' tall and 15' wide in perfect conditions. **'Hoopsii'** grows up to 60'
tall and 20' wide. It has a dense,
pyramidal form and even more
blue-white foliage than var. *glauca.*
'Mission Blue' is a broad-based,
dense form up to 40' tall and 20–25'
wide, featuring bold blue foliage.
'Montgomery' has silvery blue-gray
foliage. It is rounded when young,
eventually developing a leader and
becoming broadly pyramidal with
age. It grows 3–5' tall and wide.
(Zones 2–8)

Problems & Pests
Possible problems include aphids,
caterpillars, gall insects, nematodes,
sawflies, scale insects, spider mites,
needle cast, rust and wood rot.

*Because spruces can maintain their
lower branches right to the ground
as they mature, they make excellent
screens, windbreaks and graceful
specimens.*

P. abies
P. glauca

P. pungens var. glauca cultivar (below)

Stewartia

Stewartia

Features: mid-summer flowers, summer and fall foliage, exfoliating bark
Habit: broad, conical or rounded, deciduous tree **Height:** 20–80' **Spread:** 15–40'
Planting: B & B, container; spring **Zones:** 5–7

STEWARTIAS BOAST TRUE FOUR-SEASON APPEAL, BUT AT A PRICE.
They have exacting requirements: most need an acidic soil, and they need to be
sited out of full sun but not in dense shade. These plants have fine green foliage.
The flowers—3" camellia-like blooms—appear above the leaves in June and
July for about six weeks. Fall coloration is varied, and the bark, a mottled combination of brown, gray, creamy yellow and orange, adds winter interest. Use
stewartias as specimens—they are far too special to put off to the side.

*Stewartias are rarely affected
by pests or diseases.*

Growing

Stewartias grow well in **light shade**. The soil should be of **average to high fertility, humus rich, neutral to acidic, moist** and **well drained**. These plants need **shelter** from strong winds. Pruning is rarely required.

These plants do not transplant easily. Do not transplant a stewartia taller than 4–5'.

Tips

Stewartias are used as specimen trees and in group plantings. They make good companions for rhododendrons because they enjoy similar conditions.

It can take several years for the flaking bark to develop. Branches that have a diameter of less than 2" don't exfoliate.

Recommended

S. koreana (Korean stewartia) is a pyramidal to oval tree 20–30' tall and 15–25' wide. It can grow to 50' in height in ideal conditions. It has zigzagged branches and dense, dark green foliage that turns a wonderful orange-red in fall. Large, camellia-like, white flowers with yellow stamens are produced in summer. The bark exfoliates to reveal a patchwork of color.

S. monadelpha (tall stewartia) can grow shrubby and multi-stemmed or narrowly conical and single-stemmed. It generally grows 20–30' tall, with an equal spread, but can reach 80' in height in ideal conditions. The mid-summer white flowers are hidden by the leaves, but the

S. koreana

bright red fall color and the exfoliating bark are worthy features.

S. pseudocamellia (Japanese stewartia) is a broad, columnar or pyramidal tree. It grows 20–40' tall, with an equal spread. Attractive white flowers with showy yellow stamens appear in mid-summer. The leaves turn shades of yellow, orange and red in fall. The bark is scaly and exfoliating, leaving the trunk mottled with gray, orange, pink and red-brown. This species may survive in Zone 4 in a sheltered spot.

S. monadelpha

St. Johnswort
St. John's Wort
Hypericum

Features: tidy habit, attractive foliage, summer to fall flowers **Habit:** deciduous, semi-evergreen or evergreen, rounded shrub **Height:** 2–4' **Spread:** 2–5'
Planting: container; spring **Zones:** 4–9

JUST WHEN ILLINOIS REACHES THAT TOASTY PHASE OF SUMMER, you will start to notice neat, rounded shrubs with yellow flowers all around town. St. Johnsworts bloom right in the height of summer and continue blooming for many weeks. Because these shrubs are so hardy, you will see them in some of the most impossible locations—parking lot islands come to mind. These plants are not to everyone's taste, but they can be a godsend for places in the garden where little else will grow.

Growing

St. Johnsworts grow best in **full sun** but can tolerate partial shade. **Well-drained** soil of **average fertility** is preferred, but these plants adapt to most soil conditions except wet soils. They tolerate drought and heavy, rocky or alkaline soils.

Many medicinal and magical properties have been attributed to St. Johnsworts. The flowers have been used to produce yellow or red dyes.

Flowers form on new wood, so do any pruning in spring. Little pruning is required, though plants can be cut back to within 6–12" of the ground if they need renewing.

Tips

St. Johnsworts make good additions to mixed or shrub borders. The late-summer flowers can brighten up plantings that are looking tired or faded in the heat of summer. These durable shrubs are also useful for areas where the soil is poor and watering is difficult.

H. frondosum 'Sunburst'
Hypericum cultivar

Recommended

H. frondosum (golden St. Johnswort) forms a rounded, upright mound. This deciduous species grows 2–4' tall and wide. Bright yellow flowers are borne in mid- and late summer. The long, dense stamens give each flower a fuzzy, bushy appearance. 'Sunburst' is a more compact cultivar, up to 36" tall and wide, with blue-green foliage. The flowers are larger and are produced longer into fall than those of the species. (Zones 5–8)

H. 'Gemo' is a dense, mounded, deciduous shrub that grows 3–4' in height and spread. It has willow-like leaves and bears small, bright yellow flowers in summer. The fall color is yellow. (Zones 4–8)

H. kalmianum (Kalm's St. Johnswort) is native to Illinois. This bushy evergreen shrub grows 24–36" tall and wide. Yellow flowers are borne from mid- to late summer. Winter interest is provided by gnarled branches with reddish peeling bark. 'Ames' is a compact, more

hardy cultivar with many plentiful small, yellow flowers. (Zones 4–8)

H. x 'Sungold' is a rounded, deciduous to semi-evergreen shrub 24–36" tall and up to 5' wide. It has clean, blue-green, leathery foliage, golden yellow flowers that bloom in mid- to late summer, and excellent russet fall color. This cultivar may survive given shelter in Zone 5. (Zones 6–9)

Problems & Pests

Occasional problems may occur with scale insects, thrips, leaf spot and rust.

Sumac

Rhus

Features: summer and fall foliage, summer flowers, late-summer to fall fruit, habit **Habit:** bushy, suckering, colony-forming, deciduous shrub **Height:** 2–25'
Spread: equal to or greater than height **Planting:** container; spring or fall
Zones: 2–9

THE START OF FALL IS ANNOUNCED EACH YEAR WHEN THE BROAD leaf fronds of sumacs take on their characteristic orange-red hues. The flat crown and horizontally oriented foliage of these small trees make their change-of-color announcement look like nature's roadside sign. All of the species recommended here are native to Illinois. They work well in a natural-istic setting because their striking shape may look out of place in a refined garden bed. Try some of the cultivars if you'd like a sumac with more compact growth.

Growing

Sumacs develop the best fall color in **full sun** but tolerate partial shade. The soil should ideally be of **average fertility, moist** and **well drained.** Once established, sumacs are very drought tolerant.

These plants can become invasive. Remove suckers that come up where you don't want them. Cut out some of the oldest growth each year and allow some suckers to grow in to replace it. If the colony is growing in or near your lawn, you can mow down any young plants that pop up out of bounds.

Tips

Sumacs can be used to form a specimen group in a shrub or mixed border, in a woodland garden or on a sloping bank. Both male and female plants are needed for fruit to form.

When pulling up suckers, be sure to wear gloves to avoid getting the unusual, onion-like odor all over your hands.

R. typhina

The fruit is edible. For a refreshing beverage that tastes much like pink lemonade, soak the ripe fruit in cold water overnight and then strain and sweeten to taste.

R. aromatica 'Gro-Low'

R. typhina
R. typhina 'Dissecta'

Recommended

R. aromatica (fragrant sumac) forms a low mound of suckering stems 2–6' tall and 5–10' wide. Clusters of inconspicuous yellow flowers appear in spring, followed in late summer by fuzzy fruit that ripens to red. The aromatic foliage turns red or purple in fall. This species tolerates hot, dry, exposed conditions. It can be used to prevent erosion on hills too steep for mowing. **'Green Globe'** is a rounded, dense shrub that grows 6' in height and spread. **'Gro-Low'** ('Grow-low') is a groundcover growing about 24" tall and spreading up to 8'. (Zones 3–9)

R. copallina (shining sumac, flame-leaf sumac) has exotic, shiny foliage with 'wings' on the leaf stalks between the leaflets. Greenish yellow flowers appear in mid-summer. In fall the foliage turns crimson. Fuzzy red fruit appears in mid-fall. This species grows 12' tall and wide. Use it as a spreading shrub in a mass planting. **PRAIRIE FLAME** (var. *latifolia* 'Morton') has a compact habit, glossy foliage, yellowish white August flowers and brilliant red-orange fall color. It grows 5–7' in height and width. (Zones 4–9)

R. glabra (smooth sumac) grows 8–12' tall, with an equal or greater spread, and forms a bushy, suckering colony. Green summer flower spikes are followed, on female plants, by fuzzy, red fruit. The foliage turns brilliant shades of orange, red and purple in fall. (Zones 2–8)

R. typhina (*R. hirta*; staghorn sumac) is a suckering, colony-forming shrub whose branches are covered with velvety fuzz. This species grows 15–25' tall and spreads 25' or more. Fuzzy, yellow, early-summer blooms are followed by hairy, red fruit. The leaves turn stunning shades of yellow, orange and red in fall. '**Dissecta**' has finely cut leaves that give the plant a lacy, graceful appearance. This cultivar is more compact than the species, growing 6' in height and spreading 10'. '**Laciniata**' has finely cut, lace-like leaves and lace-like bracts. (Zones 3–8)

Problems & Pests

Caterpillars, scale insects, canker, dieback, leaf spot, powdery mildew, wood rot and *Verticillium* wilt can afflict sumacs.

Poison-sumac (Toxicodendron vernix, *formerly* Rhus vernix) *can be difficult to distinguish from other sumacs. Its sap may cause severe skin reactions. To identify poison-sumac, crush a fresh leaf on white paper. The juice stains of poison-sumac will turn black over about 24 hours.*

R. glabra

R. aromatica

Summersweet Clethra

Sweet Pepperbush, Sweetspire

Clethra

Features: fragrant summer flowers, habit, fall foliage **Habit:** rounded, suckering, deciduous shrub **Height:** 2–8' **Spread:** 2–8' **Planting:** B & B, container; spring **Zones:** 3–9

SUMMERSWEET CLETHRA, AS ITS common name suggests, bears wonderfully fragrant flowers in summer. The white or pink flowers are borne in clusters that appear from July through August. In fall, the foliage turns yellow. This upright shrub works best in a shrub border or in a mixed planting with perennials. It thrives in partial shade.

Try one of the new dwarf cultivars at the front of a border, to better enjoy the lovely fragrance.

Growing

Summersweet clethra grows the best in **light or partial shade**. The soil should be **fertile, humus rich, acidic** and **moist**. This plant tolerates poorly drained, organic soils.

Deadhead if possible to keep the shrub neat. Minimal pruning is best. One to three old, unproductive stems can be removed every second or third year if the growth seems congested. Dwarf cultivars typically require little if any pruning.

Tips

Although not aggressive, this shrub tends to sucker, forming a colony of stems. Use it in a border or in a woodland garden. The light shade along the edge of a woodland is an ideal location.

Recommended

C. alnifolia is a large, rounded, upright, colony-forming shrub. It grows 3–8' tall, spreads 3–6' and bears attractive spikes of white, highly fragrant flowers in mid- to late summer. The foliage turns yellow in fall. **'Hummingbird'** is a compact plant that grows 24–40" tall, with a spread similar to that of the species. **'Paniculata'** produces large flowers with intense fragrance. It grows 5–8' tall and wide. **'Pink Spires'** ('Rosea') bears pink flowers. It grows up to 8' tall and wide. **'Ruby Spice'** bears deep pink, fade-resistant flowers. **'September Beauty'** bears large white flowers later in the season than the other cultivars and the species. **'Sixteen Candles'** is a dense dwarf cultivar 24–30" tall and 24–42" wide.

'Ruby Spice'

Problems & Pests

This plant is generally trouble free, though some fungal infections, such as root rot, can occur.

Summersweet clethra is useful in damp, shaded gardens, where the late-season flowers are much appreciated.

'Hummingbird'

Sweetgum
Liquidambar

Features: habit, fall color, spiny fruit, corky bark **Habit:** pyramidal to rounded, deciduous tree **Height:** 50–75' **Spread:** 40–50' or more **Planting:** B & B; spring **Zones:** 5–9

ALWAYS A CONTENDER FOR THE BEST FALL COLOR AWARD, THIS tree has distinctive, star-shaped leaves that exhibit an autumn riot of yellow, orange, red and purple. Sweetgum is not often seen in parts of the state that have alkaline soil conditions, except where gardeners have taken the trouble to amend the soil. The corky bark provides winter interest. Look for the CHEROKEE or 'Rotundiloba' cultivars if you want a sweetgum with few of the spiny fruit capsules.

Growing

Sweetgum grows well in **full sun** or **partial shade,** but it develops the best color in full sun. The soil should be of **average fertility,** slightly **acidic, moist** and **well drained.** This tree needs lots of room for its roots to develop. The foliage may develop late after very cold winters.

Little pruning is required. Remove dead, damaged, diseased or awkward branches in spring or early summer.

Tips

Sweetgum is attractive as a shade tree, street tree or specimen tree, or as part of a woodland garden. The spiny fruit makes it inappropriate near patios, decks and walkways.

Recommended

L. styraciflua is native to Illinois. This neat, symmetrical, pyramidal or rounded tree grows 60–75' tall and 40–50' wide. Spiny fruits drop off the tree over the winter and often into the following summer. Corky ridges may develop on young bark but disappear as the tree ages. CHEROKEE ('Ward') has fruits that typically fall before they become scaly capsules. This cultivar is very hardy and has strong corky bark, even on mature trees. It grows more than 50' tall and wide. '**Moraine**' is a fast-growing, cold-hardy cultivar, hardy to the warmer parts of Zone 4. It boasts brilliant red fall color. '**Rotundiloba**' is not as cold hardy as the species. Its leaf lobes have rounded tips. It does not bear any fruit, and this admirable feature alone makes it worth growing in

L. styraciflua (above), cultivar (below)

Zone 6 gardens. '**Variegata**' grows 50–60' tall, with a slightly lesser spread. It has dark green leaves that are mottled with creamy yellow.

Problems & Pests

Occasional problems can occur with borers, caterpillars, scale insects, leaf spot and rot. Iron chlorosis (leaf yellowing) can be a problem in too alkaline a soil.

Sweetgum's name comes from its fragrant, gummy resin, which has been used as chewing gum, as incense and in a balm.

Sweetspire
Itea

Features: habit, fragrant flowers, fall color **Habit:** upright to arching, deciduous shrub **Height:** 2–10' **Spread:** 3–10' or more **Planting:** container; spring **Zones:** 5–9

A STRAGGLY SHRUB IN THE WILD, SWEETSPIRE HAS BEEN REFINED through development of new cultivars and now offers neat, compact additions to the shrub border. This shrub is particularly valued for the early-summer fragrance that wafts from showy, elongated flower clusters. Vibrant fall color is another good reason to use sweetspire. As Tim Wood of Spring Meadow Nursery said of LITTLE HENRY, 'If burning bush has good fall color, then this plant is a wildfire.' Cultivars may outgrow their size predictions but can be kept in check by pruning after they flower.

Growing
Sweetspire grows well in all light conditions from **full sun to full shade.** Plants grown in full sun develop the best fall color. The habit will be more arching in sun and more upright in shade. The soil should be **fertile** and **moist,** though sweetspire is fairly adaptable.

One-third of the older growth can be removed to the ground each year once flowering ends. Do not prune in early spring or you will lose the current season's flower buds.

Tips

Sweetspire is an excellent shrub for low-lying and moist areas of the garden. It grows well near streams and water features. It is also a fine choice for plantings near decks, patios and pathways, where the scent of the fragrant flowers can be enjoyed.

Recommended

I. virginica (Virginia sweetspire) is an upright to arching, suckering shrub that is native to Illinois. It usually grows 3–5' tall but can grow up to 10' tall, with an equal or greater spread. Spikes of fragrant white flowers appear in early summer, and the leaves turn purple and red in fall. **'Henry's Garnet'** bears many long, white flower spikes and consistently develops dark reddish purple fall color. It grows 3–4' tall, with an equal or greater spread. **LITTLE HENRY** ('Sprich') is a compact cultivar 24–36" tall and 36" wide, with a low, mound-forming habit. It bears bright white flower spikes and develops bright red fall color. **SCARLET BEAUTY** ('Morton') is a large, upright Chicagoland Grows selection. It grows 4–5' tall and wide and has bright scarlet fall foliage.

Problems & Pests

Sweetspire may suffer infrequent problems with aphids or leaf spot. Chlorosis (leaf yellowing) may occur in highly alkaline soils or during drought.

LITTLE HENRY (above), 'Henry's Garnet' (below)

The colorful fall leaves usually persist on the plant until freezing weather sets in. They may last all winter in a very mild year.

Tulip Tree
Tulip Poplar
Liriodendron

Features: early-summer flowers, foliage, fruit, habit **Habit:** large, rounded, oval, deciduous tree **Height:** 70–100' **Spread:** 33–50' **Planting:** B & B, container; spring **Zones:** 4–9

THIS STATELY NATIVE TREE HAS, AS ITS COMMON NAME SUGGESTS, tulip-like flowers of greenish yellow and orange. The uniquely shaped leaves are also rather like tulip blossoms in outline. In the wild, tulip tree has reached 200' and was once the king of many forests that were cleared for civilization. Too big for the small landscape or a parkway, it is a very worthy choice for park-like settings.

The genus name, Liriodendron, *comes from the Greek and means 'lily tree.'*

Growing

Tulip tree grows well in **full sun** or **partial shade.** The soil should be **average to rich,** slightly **acidic** and **moist.** This tree needs plenty of room for its roots to grow. It does not tolerate drought.

Little pruning is required.

Tips

This beautiful, massive tree needs lots of room to grow. Parks, golf courses and large gardens can host this tree as a specimen or in a group planting, but its susceptibility to drought and need for root space make it a poor choice as a specimen, shade or street tree on smaller properties.

Recommended

L. tulipifera is native to the eastern U.S. It is known more for its unusually shaped leaves than for its tulip-like flowers because the blooms are often borne high in the tree and go unnoticed until the falling petals litter the ground. The foliage turns golden yellow in fall. The fruit is a cone-shaped cluster of long-winged nutlets, green at first and maturing to pale brown. The leaves of '**Aureomarginata**' (MAJESTIC BEAUTY, 'Aureomarginatum') have yellow-green margins.

Problems & Pests

Aphids and sooty mold can be common. Borers, leaf miners, scale insects, leaf spot and powdery mildew may also afflict tulip tree. Drought stress can cause some of the leaves to drop early.

L. tulipifera (both photos)

Viburnum

Viburnum

Features: flowers, summer and fall foliage, fruit, habit **Habit:** bushy or spreading, deciduous shrub **Height:** 2–20' **Spread:** 2–15' **Planting:** bare-root, B & B, container; spring or fall **Zones:** 2–9

IF YOU HAVE ROOM FOR JUST ONE SHRUB IN THE HOME LANDSCAPE, make it a viburnum. These attractive shrubs come in many shapes and sizes. Almost all are hardy and easy to care for, with multi-season interest. Many have fragrant blooms and striking foliage, and the showy fruit comes in colors ranging from bright yellow to bright pink, rich red and deep blue. American cranberrybush (*V. trilobum*), an Illinois native, has large leaves, rich fall color and clusters of vibrant red berries that last from late summer to winter.

Growing

Viburnums grow well in **full sun, partial shade** or **light shade**. The soil should be of **average fertility, moist** and **well drained**. Viburnums tolerate both alkaline and acidic soils.

Little pruning is needed. Remove awkward, dead, damaged or diseased branches as needed.

Tips

Viburnums can be used in borders and woodland gardens. They are a good choice for plantings near patios, decks and swimming pools.

Most viburnums need to be cross-pollinated to fruit well, so try to grow more than one plant or variety of a given species.

Viburnum fruit varies in its palatability. The tart fruit of *V. trilobum* is popular for making jellies, pies and wine. It can be sweetened somewhat by freezing or by gathering after the first frost or two.

Recommended

V. x *burkwoodii* (Burkwood viburnum) is a rounded shrub that is evergreen in warm climates, but not in Illinois. It grows 6–10' tall and spreads 5–8'. Clusters of pinkish white flowers appear in mid- to late spring and are followed by red fruit that ripens to black. '**Mohawk**' grows 7' tall and wide. The red-marked white flowers have an excellent spicy clove fragrance. Dark red buds appear several weeks before the flowers open. This cultivar has glossy green foliage that turns orange-red in fall. (Zones 4–8)

V. dilatatum 'Michael Dodge'

Viburnums look lovely in the shade of evergreen trees. Their richly textured foliage complements shrubs and perennials that bloom in late spring.

V. sargentii 'Onondaga'

V. opulus

Viburnums are generally easy to grow and adapt to most soils.

V. nudum 'Winterthur'

V. carlesii (Korean spice viburnum) is a dense, bushy, rounded shrub that grows 3–8' tall, with an equal spread. Spherical clusters of white or pink, spicy-scented flowers appear in mid- to late spring. The fruit is red, ripening to black. The foliage may turn red in fall. 'Aurora' has dark green foliage that is light green and copper tinged when young and dull red in fall. The flower buds are red, opening to reveal pink flowers that fade to white with age. 'Cayuga' is a disease-resistant hybrid that grows 4–5' tall, with an equal spread. It bears large flower clusters with pink buds that contrast with the fragrant white flowers. 'Compactum' is a dwarf selection growing 3–5' tall and wide. (Zones 5–8)

V. dentatum (arrowwood) is an upright, arching shrub that grows 6–15' tall, with an equal spread. Clusters of white flowers appear in

late spring or early summer, followed by dark blue fruit in fall. This shrub is hardy and durable and adapts to almost any soil conditions. AUTUMN JAZZ ('Ralph Senior') has creamy white flowers followed by blue-black fruit in fall. The fall foliage features many shades of yellow through red. This Chicagoland Grows selection reaches 10–15' in height and spread. BLUE MUFFIN ('Christom') is a compact cultivar that flowers prolifically and bears clusters of bright blue fruit. It grows 5–7' tall, with an equal spread. CHICAGO LUSTRE ('Synnestvedt'), another Chicagoland Grows selection, has glossy, dark green foliage. NORTHERN BURGUNDY ('Morton') is a Chicagoland Grows selection that grows 10–12' tall and 6–8' wide. It has burgundy fall color and a dense growth pattern. (Zones 2–8)

V. plicatum f. *tomentosum* 'Mariesii'

Many species of birds are attracted to viburnums for the edible fruit and the shelter they provide.

V. dilatatum (linden viburnum) is an open, upright shrub. It grows 8–10' tall and spreads 6–10'. Clusters of white late-spring or early-summer flowers are followed by bright red berries in fall. The foliage turns

V. trilobum

V. opulus
V. plicatum

bronze, red or burgundy in fall. This species and some cultivars are generally hardy in only the southern half of Illinois (Zones 5–7). **CARDINAL CANDY** ('Henneke') bears plentiful flowers and fruit and is hardy to Zone 4. It grows 5–6' tall, with an equal spread. **'Michael Dodge'** bears yellow fruit that contrasts with the bright red fall foliage.

V. x *juddii* features dark, leathery foliage and a rounded habit. It reaches 6–8' in height and width. The slightly fragrant May flowers are pink in bud, opening to white. The red fruit turns black, providing a contrast with the red fall foliage. (Zones 4–8)

V. lantana (wayfaringtree) is a large, multi-stemmed shrub or small tree 10–20' tall and 10–15' wide. Clusters of white flowers are borne in late spring and early summer, followed by green fruit that ripens to orange and red before finally turning black in fall. **'Mohican'** is a compact cultivar that grows 8–12' tall and wide. The fruit of the cultivar stays red longer than that of the species. (Zones 3–8)

V. nudum (smooth witherod, possumhaw) is a bushy, spreading shrub that is native to Illinois. It grows 12–15' tall and spreads about 6'. Clusters of white flowers appear in early summer, followed by pink fruit that ripens to blue and then black. The pink and blue fruit are present at the same time, creating a striking contrast. **'Winterthur'** flowers and fruits prolifically, and the foliage turns bright red in fall. (Zones 5–9)

V. opulus (*V. opulus* var. *opulus*; European cranberrybush, guelderrose) is a rounded, spreading shrub that grows 8–15' tall and spreads 8–12'. The white flower clusters consist of an outer ring of showy sterile flowers encircling inner fertile flowers, giving the plant a lacy look when in bloom in late spring. The fall foliage and bitter, inedible fruit are both red. 'Nanum' ('Compactum') is dense and slow growing, reaching 2–5' in height and spread. 'Roseum' ('Sterilis'; European snowball bush) bears large clusters of white flowers but does not form fruit. (Zones 3–8)

V. plicatum (Japanese snowball viburnum) is hardy in the southern half of Illinois. It is a bushy, upright shrub with arching stems, reaching 10–15' in height and 12–15' in spread. Ball-like clusters of white flowers appear in late spring, followed by bright red,

V. rufidulum EMERALD CHARM

ovoid fruit that turns black as it ripens. The fall color is reddish purple. 'Chyverton' has a horizontal habit, growing 3–5' tall and up to 12' wide. It has large white blooms. 'Mary Milton' bears pink flowers and has bright red fall foliage. Forma *tomentosum* (doublefile viburnum) has graceful, horizontal branching that gives the shrub a layered effect. It grows 8–10' tall

V. opulus

V. plicatum f. *tomentosum* 'Molly Schroeder'

The long, straight stems of
V. dentatum *have been used to*
make arrow shafts, leading to
the common name arrowwood.

V. opulus 'Roseum'

and spreads 8–12'. The leaves have fuzzy undersides. Clusters of inconspicuous fertile flowers surrounded by showy sterile flowers blanket the branches. Several cultivars have been developed from this variety. **'Lanarth'** has very showy clusters of flowers with large, white sterile florets. **'Mariesii'** has more distinctly layered branches than the parent variety. **'Molly Schroeder'** bears lacy clusters of pink flowers. It blooms in spring and again in fall. **'Shasta'** grows to 6' tall and wide and bears plentiful white flowers in May. The showy sterile flowers are scattered throughout each cluster in addition to forming an outer ring. **'Summer Snowflake'** ('Fujisanensis') bears clusters of white flowers from late spring until fall. This compact cultivar grows about 6' tall, with a similar spread. (Zones 5–8)

V. prunifolium (blackhaw viburnum) is native to Illinois. It features reddish purple fall color and a

horizontally branched, tree-like form 12–15' tall and 8–12' wide. It grows in sun or shade and tolerates dry soil. The May blooms are white and the fruit is pink before turning to black. (Zones 3–9)

V. rufidulum EMERALD CHARM ('Morton') has white spring flowers and waxy, dark blue, ovoid fruit. The glossy foliage turns burgundy in fall. This cultivar grows 10–12' tall and 8–10' wide. (Zones 5–9)

V. dentatum BLUE MUFFIN
V. carlesii

V. sargentii (Sargent viburnum) is a large, bushy shrub that grows 10–15' tall, with an equal spread. The white early-spring blossoms consist of clusters of inconspicuous fertile flowers surrounded by showy sterile flowers. Red fruit follows in summer and early fall. The fall color is yellow, orange and red. 'Onondaga' has purple stems and red to pink fertile flowers ringed with showy, pinkish white sterile flowers. The purplegreen foliage turns red in fall. (Zones 3–7)

V. trilobum (*V. opulus* var. *americanum;* American cranberrybush, highbush cranberry) is a dense, rounded shrub that is native to much of central North America, including Illinois. It grows 8–15' tall, with a spread of 8–12'. White clusters of showy sterile and inconspicuous fertile flowers appear in early summer, followed by edible red fruit. The fall color is red. This species is resistant to aphids. 'Bailey Compact' is a compact plant 5–6' tall and wide, with bright red fall foliage. 'Compactum' is also smaller and more dense than the species, growing 5–6' tall and wide. 'Hahs' is

an upright to rounded shrub 6–8' tall and wide, distinguished by its heavy fruiting. REDWING ('J.N. Select'), a Chicagoland Grows selection, has red-tinged new foliage and bright red to wine red fall color. It grows 8–10' tall and 6–8' wide. The bright red fruit persists into early winter. (Zones 2–7)

Problems & Pests

Aphids, borers, mealybugs, scale insects, treehoppers, weevils, dieback, downy mildew, gray mold, leaf spot, powdery mildew, *Verticillium* wilt and wood rot can affect viburnums.

Virginia Creeper

Boston Ivy
Parthenocissus

Features: summer and fall foliage, habit **Habit:** clinging, woody, deciduous climber **Height:** 30–70' **Spread:** 30–70' **Planting:** container; spring or fall **Zones:** 3–9

THESE VIGOROUS VINES ARE OFTEN MISTAKEN for ivy and indeed behave like many of the true ivies (*Hedera* species). They can cling to nearly any vertical surface or can be grown as groundcovers. And if you are a baseball fan, you might recognize *P. tricuspidata* as the 'ivy' that grows on the outfield walls at Chicago's Wrigley Field.

Growing

These vines grow well in any light from **full sun to full shade.** The soil should preferably be **fertile** and **well drained.** The plants will adapt to clay or sandy soils.

You may need to trim back these vigorous growers frequently to keep them where you want them.

Virginia creeper and Boston ivy can cover the sides of buildings and help keep them cool in summer heat. Cut plants back to keep windows and doors accessible.

Tips

Virginia creeper and Boston ivy can cover an entire building, given enough time. They do not require support because they have clinging rootlets that can adhere to just about any surface—even smooth wood, vinyl or metal. Give the plants lots of space and let them cover a wall, fence or arbor. Note that when a vine is pulled off, the sticky ends leave little marks that can be hard to remove or even paint over.

P. tricuspidata 'Lowii'

These vines can be used as groundcovers. In this form they spread 50' but grow up to only 12" tall.

These vines are useful for softening hard edges in any landscape.

The fruit is poisonous.

P. quinquefolia

Recommended

P. quinquefolia (Virginia creeper, woodbine) is native to Illinois. This climber can grow 30–50' tall. The dark green foliage turns flame red in fall. Each leaf is divided into five leaflets. '**Engelmanii**' (var. *engelmanii*) has rich, deep green leaves that turn crimson in fall. Its bluish black berries are relished by birds. This cultivar clings better and spreads less aggressively than the species. STAR SHOWERS ('Monham') has green foliage splashed with white and shades of pink in cooler weather. (Zones 3–9)

P. tricuspidata (Boston ivy, Japanese creeper) is a climber that grows 50–70' tall. The three-lobed leaves turn red in fall. '**Fenway Park**' has new yellow foliage that matures to green in summer then turns red in fall. '**Lowii**' has dainty leaves and brilliant red fall color. (Zones 4–8)

Problems & Pests

Aphids, grape-leaf beetle, leafhoppers, leaf skeletonizers, scale insects, bacterial leaf scorch, canker, dieback, downy mildew, leaf spot, powdery mildew and scab can cause trouble.

Weigela
Weigela

Features: flowers, foliage, habit **Habit:** upright or low, spreading, deciduous shrub **Height:** 1–9' **Spread:** 1–12' **Planting:** bare-root, container; spring or fall **Zones:** 3–8

WEIGELA EARNS ITS WAY INTO ILLINOIS GARDENS BECAUSE OF ITS striking, long-lasting bloom. The bright, trumpet-shaped flowers attract attention and hummingbirds. Newer cultivars feature dark foliage that offers a contrast in the shrub border or with perennials. 'Carnaval' has red, white and pink blooms all on the same plant, and the plant is floriferous enough to draw comparisons to azaleas.

This shrub's name honors German botanist Christian Weigel (1748–1831).

Growing

Weigela prefers **full sun** but tolerates partial shade. For the best leaf color, grow purple-leaved plants in full sun and yellow-leaved plants in partial shade. The soil should be **fertile** and **well drained**. Weigela will adapt to most well-drained soils.

Once flowering is finished, cut flowering shoots back to strong buds or branch junctions. One-third of the old growth can be cut back to the ground at the same time.

Tips

Weigela can be used in a shrub or mixed border, in an open woodland garden or as an informal barrier planting.

Recommended

W. florida is a spreading shrub with arching branches. It grows 6–9' tall and spreads 8–12'. Dark pink flower clusters appear in late spring and early summer. 'Carnaval' bears red, pink and white flowers on one plant.

W. florida cultivar (above), WINE AND ROSES (center)

MIDNIGHT WINE (below)

W. florida cultivar

Weigela is one of the longest-blooming shrubs—the main flush of blooms lasts six weeks, and sporadic flowers appear all summer.

FRENCH LACE ('Brigela') has lime green to yellow leaf margins. The flowers are dark reddish pink. MIDNIGHT WINE ('Elvera') is a dwarf plant that grows up to 12" tall and spreads 12–18". The foliage is purple and the flowers are pink. 'Minuet' is a compact, spreading shrub 24–36" tall and about 3–4' wide. The dark pink flowers have yellow throats. The foliage is a purplish green that matures to dark green over the summer. This cultivar is hardy in Zones 3–7. 'Pink Princess' is a spreading shrub with an open habit and lavender pink flowers. It grows 5–6' tall and 4–6' wide. 'Red Prince' is an upright shrub. It grows 5–6' tall, spreads about 5' and is hardy in Zones 4–7. Bright red flowers appear in early summer, with a second flush later in summer. 'Rumba' is a compact, spreading plant 3–3$^{1}/_{2}$' tall and wide. It has purple-edged, yellow-green foliage and produces abundant,

W. florida

yellow-throated, dark red flowers from early summer to early fall. 'Samba' has purple-edged, dark green leaves. It is a vigorous, spreading shrub 36" tall and wide, with yellow-throated red flowers. 'Tango' has dark purple-green foliage with some bronze tinges. This is a hardy selection that grows 24–30" tall and wide. It has deep red flowers with yellow throats. 'Rumba,' 'Samba' and 'Tango' are hardy in Zones 4–8. 'Variegata' is a compact plant about 5' tall, with an equal spread. The flowers are pale pink and the leaves have creamy white margins. This cultivar is hardy to Zone 5. WINE AND ROSES ('Alexandra') has dark purple foliage and vivid pink flowers.

Problems & Pests

Foliar nematodes, scale insects, twig dieback and *Verticillium* wilt are possible, but usually not serious, problems.

FRENCH LACE

Plant breeders have given us weigela cultivars with yellow, purple or variegated foliage and pink, red, purple or white flowers.

WINE AND ROSES

Willow

Salix

Features: form, foliage, young stem color **Habit:** deciduous; large tree with broad, open crown, or small to large, oval to rounded shrub **Height:** 3–100' **Spread:** 3–70' **Planting:** B & B, container; spring or fall **Zones:** 2–8

WILLOWS ARE LARGE, WISPY-LOOKING TREES AND shrubs, many of which have excellent landscape value. Just a couple of caveats. Weeping willows (typically *S. alba* 'Tristis') are problematic in home situations because of their weak branches and aggressive roots; they are better left to office building surrounds, campuses and shoreline areas. Pussy willow *(S. discolor)* is an unruly shrub that is prone to disease. It is best left to those who have fields to cultivate this species for its wonderful, decorative stems with the furry catkins. If you can't grow pussy willow, buy the stems from your florist.

These fast-growing shrubs or trees come in a wide range of growth habits and sizes, and some have colorful stems and foliage.

Growing

Willows will grow best in **full sun** with **deep, moist, well-drained** soil. *S. elaeagnos* and *S. purpurea* suit wet areas. Do not plant *S. alba* near water lines because the roots may invade the pipes and cause expensive blockages.

Prune willows in early spring before new growth begins. For all willows, remove dead, diseased and damaged branches and any branches that spoil the form.

S. alba needs only minimal pruning. It is best to establish the framework when the plant is young. Hire a professional tree service to remove large branches.

Stem coloring is best on the young growth, so shrubby forms grown for this feature need regular rejuvenation. *S. alba* 'Flame,' *S. elaeagnos* and *S. integra* 'Hakuro Nishiki' look best when cut to within 6" of the ground in early spring every couple of years. *S. purpurea* can be pruned lightly in

S. elaeagnos

Most willows grow easily from cuttings, an attribute that has allowed plants with desirable features to be cloned thousands of times over many years.

S. alba 'Tristis'

S. *integra* 'Hakuro Nishiki'
S. *alba* 'Tristis'

early spring if needed. It can also be cut back hard to two to three buds above the ground for rejuvenation.

Tips
Willows are grown for their attractive habits and sometimes colorful stems or foliage. *S. alba* makes a good specimen for large spaces. The smaller species look great as specimens or in a shrub border. Many willows are very effective next to water features.

Recommended
S. alba (white willow) is a large, fast-growing, low-branching, suckering tree that forms a broad, open crown. It grows 80' tall and 50–70' wide. It has silky-hairy, lance-shaped, dull green leaves and light yellow-green new stems. **'Britzensis'** (coralbark willow) has bright orange-red new shoots and pale yellow-green foliage. **'Flame'** is a large, densely branched shrub about 15' tall and wide, with an oval crown. The young stems are

dark red, and the fall color is golden yellow. 'Tristis' is the standard weeping willow. It can sometimes reach 75–100' in height but is usually about the same size as the species. (Zones 2–8)

S. elaeagnos (rosemary willow, hoary willow) is a delicate, arching shrub that grows about 10–12' tall and 12–15' wide. It shows off the white, woolly undersides of its long, shiny, narrow, green leaves in a breeze. Fall color is yellow. (Zones 5–7)

S. elaeagnos

Willow bark contains salicin, which is the original source of aspirin (acetylsalicylic acid).

S. alba

S. integra **'Hakuro Nishiki'** (dappled willow) is a somewhat weeping shrub 3–5' tall and wide. Its stems and flower buds are tinged orange-pink, and its light green foliage is mottled with white and pink. This shrub is often grafted on a stem to create a standard form. (Zones 5–8)

S. purpurea (purple willow, basket willow, purple osier willow) is a large, spreading shrub or small, upright tree with arching branches. It grows 10–15' tall and wide. The foliage is dark green to blue-green, and the young stems are purple. The silvery green catkins appear before the foliage. **'Nana'** is a compact shrub 3–5' tall and wide, with blue-green to gray-green foliage. (Zones 4–7)

Problems & Pests
Possible problems include aphids, borers, caterpillars, leaf beetles, nematodes, scale insects, canker, crown gall, heart and root rot, powdery mildew and rust. These problems aren't likely to trouble willows if these vigorous growers are grown in appropriate conditions.

Witchhazel

Hamamelis

Features: flowers, foliage, habit **Habit:** spreading, deciduous shrub or small tree
Height: 6–20' or more **Spread:** 6–20' or more **Planting:** B & B, container; spring
or fall **Zones:** 3–9

THE WITCHHAZELS ARE VALUED FOR THEIR FLOWERING CYCLES.
Some species and hybrids bloom incredibly early, often in February in years
when winter is not overly brutal. Others, such as the common witchhazel,
bloom in mid-fall when the accompanying foliage obscures the delicate yellow flowers. The fall bloomers work particularly well as understory plants in
shady conditions, where their naturalistic look works to full advantage.

Growing

Witchhazels grow well in **full sun** or **light shade**. The soil should be of **average fertility, neutral to acidic, moist** and **well drained**.

Pruning is rarely required. Remove awkward shoots once flowering is complete.

Tips

Witchhazels work well individually or in groups. They can be used as specimen plants, in shrub or mixed borders or in woodland gardens. As small trees, they are ideal for space-limited gardens.

The unique flowers have long, narrow, crinkled petals that give the plant a spidery appearance when in bloom. If the weather gets too cold, the petals roll up, protecting the flowers and extending the flowering season.

H. virginiana (above)

H. x intermedia 'Jelena'

The branches of H. vernalis *and* H. x intermedia *can be cut in winter and forced into bloom indoors.*

H. virginiana with *Hydrangea*

H. x *intermedia* 'Arnold Promise' (above)

H. virginiana (center & below)

Recommended

H. x *intermedia* is not reliably hardy in the Chicagoland area and is better used in the southern half of Illinois. It is a vase-shaped, spreading shrub growing 10–20' tall, with an equal spread. Clusters of fragrant yellow, orange or red flowers appear in late winter. The leaves turn attractive shades of orange, red and bronze in fall. **'Arnold Promise'** has large, fragrant, bright yellow or yellow-orange flowers. **'Diane'** ('Diana') bears dark red flowers, and its fall foliage is yellow, orange and red. **'Jelena'** ('Copper Beauty') has a horizontal branching habit. The fragrant flowers are coppery orange, and the fall color is orange-red. **'Pallida'** is a more compact plant, growing to 12' tall and wide. It bears very fragrant, bright yellow flowers. **'Ruby Glow'** is a vigorous, upright shrub with deep orange flowers. (Zones 5–9)

H. mollis 'Brevipetala' is an erect shrub with spreading branches. It generally grows 10–15' tall and wide but can reach 20' or more in ideal conditions. It has slightly fuzzy, gray-green to blue-green foliage and bright yellow fall color. In late winter it produces clusters of fragrant, golden yellow flowers with reddish centers and long, twisted petals. (Zones 5–9)

H. vernalis (vernal witchhazel) is a rounded, upright, often suckering shrub. It grows 6–15' tall, with an equal spread. Very fragrant yellow, orange or red flowers are borne in early spring. The foliage turns bright yellow in fall. **'Autumn Embers'** ('Klmnineteen') has fragrant yellow-orange flowers and burgundy red fall foliage. It has an upright to rounded habit and reaches 6' in height and spread. **'Sandra'** has purplish young foliage that turns to purple-tinged green in summer and to yellow, orange or red in fall. It has dark yellow flowers. (Zones 4–8)

H. virginiana (common witchhazel) is a large, rounded, spreading shrub or small tree 12–20' or more in height, with an equal spread. Yellow fall flowers are often hidden by the foliage that turns yellow at the same time, but this native Illinoisan species is attractive nonetheless. (Zones 3–8)

Problems & Pests
Aphids, leaf rollers, scale insects, leaf spot, powdery mildew and wood rot are possible, but rarely serious, problems.

H. vernalis

A witchhazel extract was used traditionally as a general remedy for burns and skin inflammations. Today it is often sold as a mild astringent for skin care.

H. mollis 'Brevipetala'

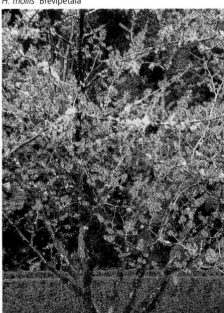

Yew

Taxus

Features: foliage, habit, red seed cups **Habit:** evergreen; conical or columnar tree or bushy or spreading shrub **Height:** 2–50' **Spread:** 1–30' **Planting:** B & B, container; spring or fall **Zones:** 4–7

YEWS ARE THE GREAT FORGIVERS OF THE EVERGREEN GARDEN. They can be shaped to whatever form the gardener desires—from formal hedges to whimsical topiary figures. Their uses are nearly limitless, their tolerance nearly inexhaustible. While upright species form a tree shape if left unpruned, annual shearing can keep these plants in bounds set by the gardener. The strong green color is maintained year-round and is much valued in the winter garden. And where else can an enterprising homeowner get such a fresh and fragrant holiday decoration? A few selective prunings from a yew shrub make a quick swag or the fixings for a wreath frame.

Growing

Yews grow well in any light conditions from **full sun to full shade**.
The soil should be **fertile, moist** and
well drained. Yews dislike very wet
soil and soil contaminated with
road salt. Do not plant them near
downspouts or other places where
water collects.

Hedges and topiary can be trimmed
back in summer and fall. Yews can
be cut back very hard to reduce
their size or to rejuvenate them.
New growth will sprout from old
wood after a hard pruning.

T. cuspidata (above), *T.* x *media* cultivar (center)

Tips

Yews can be used in borders or as
specimens, hedges, topiary and
groundcovers. There are separate
male and female plants, and both
must be present for the attractive
red arils (seed cups) to form.

*All parts of yews are poisonous, except
the pleasant-tasting, fleshy red cup
that surrounds the inedible hard seed.*

T. x *media* 'Densiformis'

T. cuspidata

T. x media cultivar

Recommended

T. cuspidata (Japanese yew) is a slow-growing, broad, columnar or conical tree. It grows 30–50' tall and spreads 20–30'. **'Capitata'** is a pyramidal form that can grow up to 30' tall and 20' wide if left unpruned. **'Green Wave'** is a spreading, mound-forming plant that grows 3–4' tall and spreads up to 5'. **'Nana'** is a dwarf cultivar that grows to 10' tall and twice as wide. With age and in ideal conditions, it may reach over 20' in height. It has dark green foliage.

T. x media (English Japanese yew, Anglo-Japanese yew), a cross between *T. baccata* (English yew) and *T. cuspidata,* has the vigor of English yew and the cold hardiness of Japanese yew. It forms a rounded, upright tree or shrub of variable height and spread, depending on the cultivar. **'Brownii'** is globe shaped and about 5' tall and wide. **'Densiformis'** is a wide, dense, rounded shrub 6–8' tall and wide. **'Everlow'** grows 24–36" tall and 4–5' wide. Its dark green needles resist wind burn. **'Hicksii'** is an open, columnar tree 15–25' tall and 5–10' in spread. This narrow, upright yew is a good choice in colder climates. **'Runyan'** grows in a rounded shape to 4' tall and 6' across. It has dark green foliage and will tolerate alkaline soils if they are well drained. **'Sentinalis'** is a narrow, upright form that grows about 10' tall, with a spread of 24–30". **'Tauntonii'** is a spreading cultivar that is both cold and heat hardy, suffering very little foliage browning in either temperature extreme. It grows 3–4' in height and spreads up to 6'. **'Viridis'** (greenleaf yew) is a columnar, narrow shrub that reaches 12' in height and only 12–24" in spread. Its twisted needles are yellow-green initially and mature to a darker green over their first season. **'Wardii'** is a dark green, wide-spreading, flat-topped shrub with a mature height of 8'. It can spread to 20'.

Problems & Pests

Black vine weevil, mealybugs, mites, scale insects, dieback, needle blight and root rot are possible, but not serious, problems. Deer browsing can be a concern in some areas.

These attractive evergreens are widely used because they grow well in deep shade, adapt to various soil conditions and tolerate any degree of pruning.

T. cuspidata 'Capitata' (above)

T. x *media* 'Tauntonii'

T. cuspidata 'Green Wave'

QUICK REFERENCE CHART

TREE HEIGHT LEGEND: Short: < 25' • Medium: 25–50' • Tall: > 50'

SPECIES by Common Name	FORM						FOLIAGE							
	Tall Tree	Medium Tree	Short Tree	Shrub	Groundcover	Climber	Evergreen	Deciduous	Variegated	Blue/White	Purple/Red	Yellow/Gold	Dark Green	Light Green
American Yellowwood		•						•						•
Arborvitae		•	•	•			•		•			•	•	•
Ash	•	•						•					•	•
Bald-Cypress	•							•					•	
Barberry				•				•			•	•	•	
Bearberry					•	•	•						•	
Beech	•	•						•			•		•	
Birch	•	•	•					•						•
Black Locust	•	•	•					•				•	•	
Black Tupelo	•	•						•					•	
Boxwood				•			•						•	
Butterfly Bush				•			•						•	
Cherry	•	•	•	•				•			•		•	
Chokeberry				•				•					•	
Cotoneaster					•	•	•	•					•	
Crabapple		•	•					•					•	
Daphne				•			•	•	•				•	
Dawn Redwood	•							•				•		•
Deutzia				•				•						•
Dogwood		•	•	•				•	•				•	•
Elderberry				•				•			•	•		•
Elm	•	•	•					•					•	
Euonymus				•			•	•	•				•	•
False Cypress	•	•		•			•					•	•	
Filbert			•	•				•			•		•	•
Fir	•	•	•	•			•			•			•	

Form	Flowers	Foliage	Bark	Fruit/Cones	Scent	Spines	Fall Color	Winter Interest	Spring	Summer	Fall	Zones	Page Number	SPECIES by Common Name
•	•	•	•		•		•		•	•		4–8	76	American Yellowwood
•		•	•		•			•				2–9	78	Arborvitae
							•		•	•		3–9	82	Ash
•		•		•	•							4-9	84	Bald-Cypress
	•	•		•		•			•			4–8	86	Barberry
	•	•		•					•			2–7	88	Bearberry
•		•	•				•		•			4–9	90	Beech
•	•	•	•				•	•	•			2–9	94	Birch
	•	•			•	•				•		3–8	98	Black Locust
•		•					•			•		4–9	100	Black Tupelo
•		•			•				•			4–8	102	Boxwood
•	•	•			•				•	•	•	4–9	106	Butterfly Bush
	•		•	•	•		•		•			2–9	110	Cherry
	•				•		•		•	•		3–8	116	Chokeberry
•	•	•		•					•	•		4–8	118	Cotoneaster
•	•		•	•	•		•		•			4–8	122	Crabapple
	•	•			•				•			4–7	128	Daphne
		•	•				•					5–8	132	Dawn Redwood
	•								•	•		4–9	134	Deutzia
•	•			•			•		•	•		2–9	136	Dogwood
	•	•		•					•	•		3–9	142	Elderberry
•			•				•		•			2–9	146	Elm
		•	•				•	•	•	•		3–9	150	Euonymus
•		•	•									4–8	154	False Cypress
•		•		•			•		•			3–9	158	Filbert
•		•		•	•							3–7	162	Fir

TREE HEIGHT LEGEND: Short: < 25' • Medium: 25–50' • Tall: > 50'

SPECIES by Common Name	Tall Tree	Medium Tree	Short Tree	Shrub	Groundcover	Climber	Evergreen	Deciduous	Variegated	Blue/White	Purple/Red	Yellow/Gold	Dark Green	Light Green
Forsythia				•				•	•				•	•
Fothergilla				•				•					•	
Fringe Tree			•	•				•					•	•
Ginkgo	•	•						•						•
Golden Rain Tree		•						•						•
Hawthorn		•	•					•					•	•
Hemlock	•	•	•	•			•							•
Holly		•		•			•						•	•
Honeylocust	•	•	•	•				•				•	•	•
Honeysuckle				•		•		•		•			•	
Hornbeam	•	•	•					•					•	•
Horsechestnut	•	•	•	•				•					•	•
Hydrangea		•	•			•		•					•	•
Juniper	•	•	•				•			•		•	•	•
Katsura-Tree	•	•	•					•		•	•			•
Kentucky Coffee Tree	•	•						•		•			•	
Kerria				•				•	•				•	
Larch	•	•						•		•				•
Lilac			•	•				•					•	
Linden	•	•						•					•	
Magnolia		•	•	•				•					•	•
Maple	•	•	•	•				•	•		•		•	
Mountain-Ash		•	•					•					•	
Ninebark				•				•			•	•	•	•
Oak	•	•						•				•	•	
Pear		•						•					•	

Form	Flowers	Foliage	Bark	Fruit/Cones	Scent	Spines	Fall Color	Winter Interest	Spring	Summer	Fall	Zones	Page Number	by Common Name
	•								•			4–9	166	Forsythia
	•				•		•		•			4–9	170	Fothergilla
•	•		•	•	•						•	4–9	172	Fringe Tree
•		•	•	•	•		•		•			3–9	174	Ginkgo
•	•	•								•	•	6–8	176	Golden Rain Tree
	•	•		•		•			•	•		3–8	178	Hawthorn
•		•		•								3–8	182	Hemlock
•		•		•				•	•	•		3–9	184	Holly
•		•					•		•			4–8	190	Honeylocust
•	•			•	•				•	•		4–8	192	Honeysuckle
•							•		•			3–9	196	Hornbeam
	•	•		•			•		•	•		3–9	198	Horsechestnut
•	•						•			•	•	3–9	202	Hydrangea
•		•			•							2–9	208	Juniper
		•			•		•		•			4–8	214	Katsura-Tree
•		•	•	•			•		•	•		3–8	216	Kentucky Coffee Tree
•	•								•			4–9	218	Kerria
•		•		•			•					1–7	220	Larch
•	•				•				•	•		2–8	222	Lilac
•		•			•					•		2–8	228	Linden
•	•	•	•	•	•				•			3–9	232	Magnolia
•	•	•	•	•			•		•			2–9	236	Maple
•	•	•		•			•		•			2–8	244	Mountain-Ash
	•	•	•	•					•	•		2–8	246	Ninebark
•		•	•	•			•		•			2–9	248	Oak
•	•			•			•		•			5–8	252	Pear

TREE HEIGHT LEGEND: Short: < 25' • Medium: 25–50' • Tall: > 50'

SPECIES by Common Name	Tall Tree	Medium Tree	Short Tree	Shrub	Groundcover	Climber	Evergreen	Deciduous	Variegated	Blue/White	Purple/Red	Yellow/Gold	Dark Green	Light Green
Pine	•	•	•	•	•	•	•			•			•	
Potentilla				•				•					•	
Privet				•				•					•	
Redbud			•	•				•	•		•		•	
Rhododendron				•			•	•					•	•
Rose-of-Sharon				•				•	•				•	
Sassafras	•	•						•						•
Serviceberry			•	•				•			•		•	•
Smokebush				•				•			•	•		•
Spirea				•				•	•		•	•		•
Spruce	•	•	•	•	•	•	•			•			•	
Stewartia		•	•					•					•	
St. Johnswort				•			•	•		•			•	
Sumac			•	•				•			•		•	•
Summersweet Clethra				•				•					•	•
Sweetgum	•							•	•				•	
Sweetspire				•				•					•	•
Tulip Tree	•							•	•					•
Viburnum				•				•			•		•	•
Virginia Creeper						•		•						
Weigela				•				•	•		•	•	•	•
Willow	•		•	•				•		•		•		
Witchhazel		•	•					•				•	•	•
Yew		•	•	•			•						•	

| | FEATURES | | | | | | | | BLOOMING | | | | | SPECIES by Common Name |
Form	Flowers	Foliage	Bark	Fruit/Cones	Scent	Spines	Fall Color	Winter Interest	Spring	Summer	Fall	Zones	Page Number	
•		•	•	•	•							2–8	254	Pine
•	•	•							•	•		2–8	260	Potentilla
•					•					•		3–7	264	Privet
	•						•		•			4–9	266	Redbud
•	•	•							•	•		3–8	268	Rhododendron
	•									•	•	5–9	272	Rose-of-Sharon
•		•	•		•		•		•			4–8	276	Sassafras
•	•		•	•			•		•	•		3–9	278	Serviceberry
	•	•					•			•		4–8	282	Smokebush
•	•									•		3–9	284	Spirea
•		•		•								2–8	288	Spruce
	•	•	•				•			•		5–7	292	Stewartia
•	•	•								•	•	4–8	294	St. Johnswort
•	•	•		•	•		•			•		2–9	296	Sumac
•	•	•			•		•			•		3–9	300	Summersweet Clethra
•			•	•			•		•			5–9	302	Sweetgum
•					•		•		•	•		5–9	304	Sweetspire
•	•	•		•			•			•		4–9	306	Tulip Tree
•	•	•		•	•		•		•	•		2–9	308	Viburnum
•		•					•		•	•		3–9	316	Virginia Creeper
•	•	•							•	•		3–8	318	Weigela
•		•	•						•			2–8	322	Willow
•	•	•							•		•	3–9	326	Witchhazel
•		•		•					•			4–7	330	Yew

GLOSSARY

B & B: abbreviation for balled-and-burlapped stock, i.e., plants that have been dug out of the ground and have had their rootballs wrapped in burlap

Bonsai: the art of training plants into miniature trees and landscapes

Bract: a modified leaf at the base of a flower or flower cluster; bracts can be showy, as in flowering dogwood blossoms

Candles: the new, soft spring growth of needle-leaved evergreens such as pine, spruce and fir

Crown: the part of a plant at or just below the soil where the stems meet the roots; also, the top of a tree, including the branches and leaves

Cultivar: a *culti*vated plant *vari*ety with one or more distinct differences from the species; e.g., *Thuja plicata* is a botanical species, of which 'Zebrina' is a cultivar distinguished by leaf variegation

Deadhead: to remove spent flowers in order to maintain a neat appearance, encourage a longer bloom and prevent the plant from expending energy on fruit production

Dieback: death of a branch from the tip inwards; usually used to describe winter damage

Double flower: a flower with an unusually large number of petals, often caused by mutation of the stamens into petals

Dripline: the area around the bottom of a tree, directly under the tips of the farthest-extending branches

Dwarf: a plant that is small compared to the normal growth of the species; dwarf growth is often cultivated by plant breeders

Espalier: the training of a tree or shrub to grow in two dimensions

Forma (*abbrev.* f.): a naturally occurring variant of a species; below the level of subspecies in biological classification and similar to variety

Gall: an abnormal outgrowth or swelling produced as a reaction to sucking insects, other pests or diseases

Genus: a category of biological classification between the species and family levels; the first word in a scientific name indicates the genus, e.g., *Pinus* in *Pinus mugo*

Girdling: a restricted flow of water and nutrients in a plant caused by something tied tightly around a trunk, branch or root, or by an encircling cut

Heartwood: the wood in the center of a stem or branch consisting of old, dense, nonfunctional conducting tissue

Hybrid: a plant resulting from natural or artificial cross-breeding between varieties, species or genera; hybrids are often sterile but more vigorous than either parent and have attributes of both. Hybrids are indicated in scientific names by an *x*, e.g., *Forsythia* x *intermedia*

Inflorescence: a flower cluster

Leader: the dominant upward growth at the top of a tree; may be erect or drooping

Nodes: the places on the stem from where leaves grow; when cuttings are planted, new roots grow from the nodes under the soil

pH: a measure of acidity or alkalinity (the lower the pH below 7, the greater the acidity; the higher the pH between 7 and 14, the greater the alkalinity); soil pH influences nutrient availability for plants

Pollarding: a severe form of pruning in which young branches of a tree are cut back virtually to the trunk to encourage bushy new growth

Procumbent, prostrate: terms used to describe plants that grow along the ground

Rhizome: a modified stem that grows horizontally underground

Rootball: the root mass and surrounding soil of a container-grown or dug-out plant

Semi-evergreen: describes evergreen plants that in cold climates lose some or all of their leaves over winter

Single flower: a flower with a single ring of typically four or five petals

Species: the original plant from which cultivars are derived; the fundamental unit of biological classification, indicated by a two-part scientific name, e.g., *Pinus mugo* (*mugo* is the specific epithet)

Standard: a shrub or small tree grown with an erect main stem; accomplished either through pruning and training or by grafting the plant onto a tall, straight stock

Subshrub: a somewhat shrubby plant with a woody basal stem; the upper parts are herbaceous and die back each year

Subspecies (*abbrev.* subsp.): a naturally occurring, regional form of a species, often geographically isolated from other subspecies but still potentially able to interbreed with them

Sucker: a shoot that comes up from a root, often some distance from the plant; it can be separated to form a new plant once it develops its own roots

Topiary: the training of plants into geometric, animal or other unique shapes

Variegation: describes foliage that has more than one color, often patched or striped or bearing differently colored leaf margins

Variety (*abbrev.* var.): a naturally occurring variant of a species; below the level of subspecies in biological classification

RESOURCES

Dirr, M.A. 1997. *Dirr's Hardy Trees and Shrubs: An Illustrated Encyclopedia.* Timber Press, Portland, Oregon.

Dirr, M.A. 1998. *Manual of Woody Landscape Plants.* 5th ed. Stipes Publishing, Champaign, Illinois.

Dirr, M.A. and C.W. Heuser, Jr. 1987. *The Reference Manual of Woody Plant Propagation.* Varsity Press, Athens, Georgia.

Ellis, B.W. and F.M. Bradley, eds. 1996. *The Organic Gardener's Handbook of Natural Insect and Disease Control.* Rodale Press, Emmaus, Pennsylvania.

Fiala, J.L. 1988. *Lilacs: The Genus* Syringa. Timber Press, Portland, Oregon.

Flint, H.L. 1997. *Landscape Plants for Eastern North America.* 2nd ed. John Wiley and Sons, New York.

Galle, F.C. 1997. *Hollies: The Genus* Ilex. Timber Press, Portland, Oregon.

Kelly, J. and J. Hillier, eds. 1997. *The Hillier Gardener's Guide to Trees and Shrubs.* Reader's Digest Association, Pleasantville, New York.

Phillips, R. and M. Rix. 1989. *The Random House Book of Shrubs.* Random House, New York.

Thompson, P. 1992. *Creative Propagation: A Grower's Guide.* Timber Press, Portland, Oregon.

Tripp, K.E. and J.C. Raulston. 1995. *The Year in Trees: Superb Woody Plants for Four-Season Gardens.* Timber Press, Portland, Oregon.

• International Society of Arboriculture
http://www.isa-arbor.com/

• University of Illinois Extension
http://www.extension.uiuc.edu/

• Chicagoland Grows
http://www.chicagolandgrows.org/

• Chicago Botanic Garden
http://www.chicago-botanic.org/

• Morton Arboretum
http://www.mortonarb.org/index.html

• National list of arboretums
www.colorchoiceplants.com/gardens.htm

INDEX OF PLANT NAMES